the CSIRO total wellbeing diet
recipe book

The Commonwealth Scientific and Industrial Research Organisation (CSIRO), Australia's national science agency, has been dedicated to the practical application of knowledge and science for society and industry since 1928. Today the CSIRO ranks in the top one per cent of world scientific institutions in twelve out of twenty-two research fields. CSIRO Food and Nutritional Sciences conducts research into human health, including disease prevention, diagnosis and innovative treatment.

Associate Professor Manny Noakes is the stream leader for the Diet and Lifestyle program at CSIRO Food and Nutritional Sciences. With her team, she manages clinical trials that provide scientific evidence for the efficacy of diet and exercise programs on health. Manny has published over 100 scientific papers, with a major emphasis on diet composition, weight-loss and cardiovascular health.

www.csiro.com.au

the CSIRO total wellbeing diet recipe book

introduction by
Associate Professor Manny Noakes

photography by Alan Benson

PENGUIN BOOKS

Published by the Penguin Group
Penguin Group (Australia)
250 Camberwell Road, Camberwell, Victoria 3124, Australia
(a division of Pearson Australia Group Pty Ltd)
Penguin Group (USA) Inc.
375 Hudson Street, New York, New York 10014, USA
Penguin Group (Canada)
90 Eglinton Avenue East, Suite 700, Toronto, Canada ON M4P 2Y3
(a division of Pearson Penguin Canada Inc.)
Penguin Books Ltd
80 Strand, London WC2R 0RL, England
Penguin Ireland
25 St Stephen's Green, Dublin 2, Ireland
(a division of Penguin Books Ltd)
Penguin Books India Pvt Ltd
11 Community Centre, Panchsheel Park, New Delhi – 110 017, India
Penguin Group (NZ)
67 Apollo Drive, Rosedale, North Shore 0632, New Zealand
(a division of Pearson New Zealand Ltd)
Penguin Books (South Africa) (Pty) Ltd
24 Sturdee Avenue, Rosebank, Johannesburg 2196, South Africa

Penguin Books Ltd, Registered Offices: 80 Strand, London, WC2R 0RL, England

First published by Penguin Group (Australia), 2010

10 9 8 7 6 5 4 3 2 1

Text copyright © CSIRO 2010
Photographs copyright © Alan Benson 2010

The moral right of the author has been asserted

All rights reserved. Without limiting the rights under copyright reserved above, no part of this publication may be reproduced, stored in or introduced into a retrieval system, or transmitted, in any form or by any means (electronic, mechanical, photocopying, recording or otherwise), without the prior written permission of both the copyright owner and the above publisher of this book.

Design by Elissa Webb © Penguin Group (Australia)
Photography by Alan Benson
Styling by Jann Hann and Sarah O'Brien
Typeset in Meta and Berkeley Oldstyle by Post Pre-press Group, Brisbane, Queensland
Colour reproduction by Splitting Image, Clayton, Victoria
Printed and bound in China by 1010 Printing International Ltd

National Library of Australia
Cataloguing-in-Publication data:

   The CSIRO total wellbeing diet recipe book / CSIRO
   9780143203452 (pbk.)
   Includes index.
   Reducing diets--Recipes.
   Other Authors/Contributors:
        CSIRO.

613.25

penguin.com.au

acknowledgements

The CSIRO acknowledges Associate Professor Manny Noakes, Professor Peter Clifton, Professor Richard Head, Doctor Grant Brinkworth and Belinda Wyld for their ongoing research into the development of the CSIRO Total Wellbeing Diet and Exercise Program. The organisation also acknowledges and thanks all those who have funded the research involved in developing the program: CSIRO Food and Nutritional Sciences; CSIRO Preventative Health Flagship; Dairy Australia; Goodman Fielder; Meat and Livestock Australia; The National Heart Foundation; The National Centre of Excellence for Functional Foods; and The National Health and Medical Research Council.

    Thanks to the team at Penguin involved in producing this book: Julie Gibbs, Ingrid Ohlsson, Rachel Carter, Bethan Waterhouse, Elissa Webb, Tracey Jarrett and Megan Pigott; recipe writer and home economist Grace Campbell; and the photographic team, Alan Benson (photography) and Sarah O'Brien and Jane Hann (styling).

contents

- 1 introduction by Associate Professor Manny Noakes
- 4 the CSIRO total wellbeing diet basic plan
- 6 sample eating styles
- 8 stocking your kitchen

11 breakfasts
Start the day well with these healthy recipes

17 simple lunches and salads
Easy meals to take to work or have at home

43 family lunch get-together
A simple and satisfying spread for loved-ones

49 weeknight dinners
Easy-to-follow recipes for when you're hungry but pressed for time

77 weekend barbecue get-together
Enjoy entertaining friends with this delicious selection of nutritious dishes

83 on a shoestring
These recipes are big on flavour yet ideal for a small budget

113 watching sport get-together
Settle down to watch the big game and cure the munchies with these nutritious nibbles

119 comfort classics
All your favourite traditional meals lightened up so they won't weigh you down

145 dinner party get-together
Impress your guests and stick to a healthy eating plan at the same time

151 stock and store
Save time and prepare these meals on the weekend, then reheat and serve when you're ready for them

177 something sweet
Guilt-free desserts are back on the menu

- 198 index

introduction

by Associate Professor Manny Noakes

The CSIRO Total Wellbeing Diet (or TWD, as we like to call it) continues to be one of Australia's most popular approaches to weight loss and achieving a healthy lifestyle. Over one million CSIRO Total Wellbeing Diet books have been sold in Australia. The books have been translated into 17 different languages and are also available in audio format.

Here at the CSIRO, we continue to respond to readers' queries and comments and have been overwhelmed with positive feedback regarding our previous books. If we had to describe the reason for the TWD's popularity, most would say simply, 'It's because it works'. But that would not adequately acknowledge the combination of scientific and consumer research that forms the basis of the diet.

So what is it about the TWD that makes it 'work'? In a nutshell, the science supports the value of:

- an eating pattern higher in protein for improved control of hunger and to prevent excess muscle loss while losing weight

- portion control and balanced nutrition through a representation of all food groups in an eating pattern

- structure in an eating pattern, involving regular meals and planned snacks, the use of meal plans, shopping lists and recipes that all assist in achieving controlled eating

- 'self monitoring' – that is, keeping track of what we eat and drink and how much exercise we do.

But even with all of these scientific ingredients in a weight-loss program, if the food and meals didn't fit with what we are familiar with and what we enjoy, it's unlikely that Australians would have been so enthusiastic about the TWD.

Just prior to the launch of *The CSIRO Total Wellbeing Diet Book 2*, we commissioned a survey of a nationally representative sample of over 5000 Australians to understand more about what impact the TWD had in our community. The results were reassuring and enlightening.

Based on the population figures for Australians aged between 15 and 64 years,[1] *The CSIRO Total Wellbeing Diet Book 1* has been used by 889,200 Australians since its release.

According to the survey, the four most highly regarded features of the TWD were: the recipes (86%); the flexibility with food and lifestyle (78%); the CSIRO brand (73%); and information about weight maintenance (76%). Interestingly, only 13% commented that they disliked the cost of the food.

There were surprisingly few differences in the types of people that used the TWD, although women and couples with no children were more likely to have used it.

Here are some other interesting facts gleaned from the survey:

- The TWD is being used in a number of different ways, with the majority of users gaining recipes and meal ideas, or adapting the basic principles to their lifestyle.

- The average amount of weight lost when following the TWD is 6.1 kg per user.

- 65% of Australians (or 8.9 million aged 15–65 years) have heard about the TWD, predominately through traditional media channels.

- 10% of Australians (approximately 1.3 million aged 15–65 years) live in a household that has used the TWD in some way.

- Since following the TWD, users have noticed improvements in the following areas of their lives:
  - attitude to health and wellbeing (71%)
  - weight (64%)
  - overall health (63%)
  - energy levels (61%)
  - level of concern they have about their health (57%)
  - overall fitness (57%)
  - personal body image (50%)
  - overall mood (46%).

- Approximately 547,200 Australians have lost weight on the TWD to date.

- The majority of Australians who have lost weight on the TWD were overweight or obese prior to starting the TWD.

- Younger age groups (18–24 year olds) are more likely to be looking for general information and advice about nutrition, while older age groups (60+ year olds) are more likely to be concerned about overall health issues. The TWD appealed to both of these categories and is a flexible, easy and convenient long-term eating plan.

- The main barrier to the uptake of the TWD for those Australians who have bought or seen the book but have not used it seems to be procrastination – they have the intention to use it but have not yet taken the action to do so.

Despite the popularity of the TWD it has not been without its critics. The most vocal of complaints have related to the amount of red meat in the eating plan and concerns that this may increase risks of colorectal cancer. The CSIRO response has consistently been that the diet as a whole is designed to reduce overall risk of many diseases, including cancer, diabetes and heart disease. The CSIRO continues to contribute research on nutrition in health and disease and monitor the scientific literature relevant to this area.

Since the release of the TWD series, a major report from the World Cancer Research Fund (WCRF) has been released. The report recommends that for those people who eat red meat, red meat intake should be limited to 700–750 g (raw weight) per week as very high intakes of red meat, particularly processed meats, were ruled to be convincing or probable causes of colorectal cancer. The evidence appears stronger for processed meats and so the recommendation is that very little of our meat intake should be processed meat. The WCRF report emphasises that red meat is a valuable source of nutrients, particularly iron and zinc, which are two of the most prevalent nutrient deficiencies, and that it is not advocating avoiding meat or animal based foods. The report also emphasises the importance of weight control, being physically active, limiting alcohol, 'fast foods' and sugary drinks, and eating a variety of non-starchy vegetables each day – all important features of the TWD.

The TWD recommends protein from red meat four times per week. If this is eaten as one lunch meal (up to 100 g) and at three evening meals (200 g per meal) per week, this will be within the WCRF recommendations.

Although much of the TWD criticism has been about red meat, the eating plan is in fact highest in vegetables, fruit and dairy foods. It is a balanced lifestyle program that recommends all the necessary nutrition and exercise to achieve a healthy weight.

Our consumer survey showed that impressions of the diet book were that it was mostly about an eating plan for overall wellbeing (85%), a healthy way of eating (86%), and a long-term lifestyle pattern (80%). Only 36% of the sample reported that they felt the TWD was a meat-based diet, with 29% stating the contrary – that is, that TWD was not a meat-based diet.

Everyone has different preferences and styles of eating and there are many ways to achieve healthy eating. The CSIRO has developed healthy-eating advice to suit many of these differences. *The CSIRO Healthy Heart Program* includes flexibility for people who prefer more starchy foods like pasta and rice as well as vegetarian eating styles. *The CSIRO Wellbeing Plan for Kids* provides more general healthy-eating and lifestyle advice aimed at families with children. Finally, *The CSIRO Home Energy Saving Handbook* embraces a healthy and sustainable approach to growing and choosing our food.

This recipe book has been developed in response to high demand for more recipes that follow the TWD guidelines. We hope that it will help to inspire people to take up or maintain a healthy lifestyle.

---

[1] An independently conducted survey sampling 5026 Australian men and women between 18 and 64 years of age, *Inside Story*, 'THE CSIRO TOTAL WELLBEING DIET IMPACT STUDY', December 2006.

The sample used for this study was representative of the general Australian population aged 15–64 years, as determined by comparison to 2005 ABS statistics. Where the sample differed from the population at large, weighting was used so that the sample accurately reflected the population and socio-demographic breakdown. As such, the results obtained from the present impact study can be extrapolated to the general Australian community.

the CSIRO total wellbeing diet basic plan

Your daily food allowance

LEAN PROTEIN FOODS
– 2 units a day for dinner

1 unit is equal to 100 g raw weight of protein food, including red meat, chicken or fish. Eat red meat 3 times a week for dinner. Eat fish at least twice a week for dinner.

– up to 1 unit a day for lunch

Eat up to 100 g (raw weight) of any lean protein source (tinned or fresh fish or seafood, chicken, turkey, red meat or 2 eggs) each day for lunch. Eat red meat once a week for lunch.

WHOLEGRAIN BREAD
– 2 units a day

1 unit is equal to one 35 g slice. You can replace 1 unit each day with any of the following:
- 1 slice fruit loaf
- 2 crispbread, such as Ryvita
- 1 medium potato (about 150 g)
- 4 tablespoons cooked rice or noodles
- ½ cup (about 50 g) cooked pasta
- 4 tablespoons baked beans, or cooked lentils, kidney beans or other legumes

HIGH-FIBRE CEREAL
– 1 unit a day

1 unit is equal to:
- 40 g any high-fibre breakfast cereal (e.g. Sultana Bran, Fibre Plus)
- 1 Weet-Bix plus ½ cup (35 g) All-Bran
- 40 g rolled oats
- 1 slice wholegrain toast

DAIRY
– 3 units a day

1 unit is equal to:
- 250 ml reduced-fat milk
- 200 g reduced-fat or diet yoghurt
- 200 g reduced-fat custard or dairy dessert
- 25 g cheddar cheese or other full-fat cheese
- 50 g reduced-fat cheese (less than 10 per cent fat)

FRUIT
– 2 units a day

1 unit is equal to 150 g fresh or tinned, unsweetened fruit, 150 ml unsweetened fruit juice, or 30 g dried fruit.

VEGETABLES
– at least 2½ units a day from free list

1 unit is equal to 1 cup (80–150 g) cooked vegetables. See free list (right) for vegetables you can eat. We recommend ½ unit salad and 2 cups (160–300 g) cooked vegetables each day.

FATS AND OILS
– 3 units added oils or fats a day

1 unit is equal to 1 teaspoon any liquid oil such as canola, olive or sunflower oil. 3 units oil is equal to:
- 3 teaspoons soft (trans-fat-free) margarine
- 6 teaspoons light margarine
- 3 teaspoons curry paste in canola oil
- 60 g avocado
- 20 g nuts or seeds

INDULGENCE FOODS
– up to 2 units a week

This depends on the level of plan best for you (see *The CSIRO Total Wellbeing Diet Books 1 and 2*). As a general rule, 1 unit is equal to any food or drink providing approximately 450 kJ, such as 150 ml wine or 20 g chocolate.

THE FREE LIST: ANYTIME FOODS

The vegetables below contain minimal kilojoules, so eat them freely with your meals.

Artichokes, asparagus, bean sprouts, beetroot, bok choy, broccoli, brussels sprouts, cabbage, capsicum (pepper), carrots, cauliflower, celery, chilli, chives, choko, corn, cucumber, eggplant (aubergine), fennel, fresh herbs, green beans, lettuce, marrow, mushrooms, onion, parsnips, peas, pumpkin (squash), radishes, rhubarb, silverbeet, spinach, swedes, tomatoes, turnip, zucchini (courgette).

READING THE RECIPES IN THIS BOOK

The nutritional units contained in each recipe are displayed to the left of the ingredients list. You will find many of the recipes will suggest serving the meal with a side of vegetables or salad. The additional units for these serving suggestions are indicated by an asterisk, but do not appear in the ingredients list.

FOR MORE INFORMATION

Please refer to *The CSIRO Total Wellbeing Diet Books* for more extensive diet and lifestyle information.

sample eating styles

BREAKFAST	**1 unit cereal, 1 unit dairy, 1 unit fruit, 1 unit fats** 1 slice wholegrain toast with 1 teaspoon margarine 1 cup (250 ml) reduced-fat milk 1 banana	**1 unit cereal, 1½ units dairy, 1 unit fruit** Cinnamon and sultana porridge (see page 13) 1 cup (250 ml) reduced-fat milk	**1 unit cereal, 2 units dairy, 2 units fat** 1 slice wholegrain toast spread with 40 g avocado and sprinkled with 25 g grated cheddar 1 cup (250 ml) reduced-fat milk
LUNCH & SNACKS	**1 unit protein, 1 unit bread, 1 unit dairy, 1½ units vegetables, 1 unit fats** 100 g tinned tuna or salmon 1 cup (40 g) mixed salad leaves 1 piece wholemeal pita bread with 1 teaspoon margarine ½ carrot, cut into sticks 200 g reduced-fat or diet yoghurt	**1 unit protein, 1 unit bread, 1 unit dairy, 1½ units vegetables, 1 unit fats** Chicken cakes (see page 25) 1 piece wholemeal pita bread 1 cup (40 g) mixed salad leaves dressed with 1 teaspoon olive oil and 1 teaspoon white wine vinegar 200 g reduced-fat or diet yoghurt	**1 unit protein, 1 unit bread, 1 unit dairy, 1 unit fruit, 1½ units vegetables** Spicy chicken noodle salad (see page 38) 200 g reduced-fat or diet yoghurt with 1 piece fresh fruit, chopped
DINNER	**2 units protein, 1 unit bread, 1 unit dairy, 1 unit fruit, 1 unit vegetables, 1 unit fats** Chicken gumbo (see page 136) 4 tablespoons cooked rice 1 piece fresh fruit 200 g reduced-fat dairy dessert	**2 units protein, 1 unit bread, ½ unit dairy, 1 unit fruit, 1 unit vegetables, 2 units fat** Beef goulash (see page 152) 4 tablespoons cooked noodles or 150 g mashed potato 1 cup (80–150 g) steamed vegetables Cinnamon oranges with spiced yoghurt (see page 182)	**2 units protein, 1 unit bread, 1 unit fruit, 1 unit vegetables, 1 unit fats** Thai-style beef and bean stir-fry (see page 53) 4 tablespoons cooked rice Watermelon sorbet (see page 179)
DAY'S TOTAL UNITS	3 units protein 2 units bread 1 unit cereal 3 units dairy 2 units fruit 2½ units vegetables 3 units fats	3 units protein 2 units bread 1 unit cereal 3 units dairy 2 units fruit 2½ units vegetables 3 units fats	3 units protein 2 units bread 1 unit cereal 3 units dairy 2 units fruit 2½ units vegetables 3 units fats

1 unit protein, 1 unit cereal, 1½ units dairy Tomato and cheese mini frittatas (see page 14) 1 slice wholegrain toast with Vegemite 1 cup (250 ml) reduced-fat milk	**1 unit cereal, 1 unit dairy, 1 unit fruit** 40 g high-fibre cereal served with 30 g dried fruit 1 cup (250 ml) reduced-fat milk	**1 unit cereal, 1½ units dairy, 1 unit fruit, 1 unit vegetables, 1 unit fats** Warm mushroom salad on toast (see page 15) 1 piece fresh fruit 1 cup (250 ml) reduced-fat milk	**1 unit cereal, 1 unit dairy, 1 unit fruit** 40 g high-fibre cereal 1 cup (250 ml) reduced-fat milk 150 g mixed berries or 1 sliced banana
1 unit protein, 1½ units bread, ¼ unit dairy, 1 unit fruit, 1½ units vegetables, 3 units fat Warm lamb salad with yoghurt dressing (see page 41) 1 large piece wholemeal flatbread 1 piece fresh fruit 20 g nuts or seeds	**1 unit protein, 1 unit bread, 1 unit dairy, 1 unit fruit, 1 unit vegetables, 1 unit fats** Rocket, sweet potato and chickpea salad (see page 35) 1 hard-boiled egg, sliced 50 g reduced-fat feta 1 piece fresh fruit	**1 unit protein, 2 units bread, 1½ units dairy, ½ unit vegetables, 1 unit fats** wholegrain bread roll, filled with 1 serve Tuna, ricotta and red onion spread (see page 23), 20 g avocado and ½ cup (20 g) salad leaves 200 g reduced-fat or diet yoghurt	**1 unit protein, 1 unit bread, 1 unit dairy, ½ unit fruit, 1 unit vegetables, 2 units fats** Chicken and mango salad (see page 41) 20 g avocado, sliced and tossed through the salad 1 slice wholegrain bread 200 g reduced-fat or diet yoghurt
1 unit protein, ½ unit bread, 1¼ units dairy, 1 unit fruit, 1 unit vegetables Salmon fishcakes with lemon yoghurt sauce and salad (see page 108) 1 piece fresh fruit 200 g reduced-fat dairy dessert	**2 units protein, 1 unit bread, 1 unit dairy, 1½ units vegetables, 1 unit fats** Pan-fried lamb steaks with minted pea puree (see page 92) 1 medium potato, boiled or steamed 1 cup (80–150 g) cooked vegetables 200 g reduced-fat dairy dessert	**2 units protein, 1 unit fruit, 1 unit vegetables, 1 unit fats** Honey-mustard pork with warm cabbage salad (see page 63) Berry banana freeze (see page 180)	**2 units protein, 1 unit bread, 1 unit dairy, ½ unit fruit, 1½ units vegetables, 1 unit fats** Spanish-style fish stew (see page 170) 1 medium potato, diced and added to the stew 200 g reduced-fat custard or dairy dessert with 75 g fresh or tinned fruit
3 units protein 2 units bread 1 unit cereal 3 units dairy 2 units fruit 2½ units vegetables 3 units fats	3 units protein 2 units bread 1 unit cereal 3 units dairy 2 units fruit 2½ units vegetables 2 units fats	3 units protein 2 units bread 1 unit cereal 3 units dairy 2 units fruit 2½ units vegetables 3 units fats	3 units protein 2 units bread 1 unit cereal 3 units dairy 2 units fruit 2½ units vegetables 3 units fats

stocking your kitchen

IN THE FRIDGE AND FREEZER

- cheeses, such as reduced-fat ricotta, reduced-fat cheddar, reduced-fat feta, bocconcini and pecorino
- eggs
- filo pastry
- fresh fruit and vegetables, particularly those in season
- fresh herbs (or grow your own)
- frozen fruit, such as mixed berries and raspberries
- frozen vegetables, such as corn kernels and peas
- lean meat and poultry
- light margarine
- reduced-fat custard
- reduced-fat milk
- reduced-fat sour cream
- reduced-fat vanilla, natural or Greek-style yoghurt
- seafood, such as prawns, smoked salmon, white fish fillets and mussels

IN THE PANTRY

- baking powder
- breads, such as wholemeal flatbreads, mountain bread and flour tortillas
- capers
- Chinese cooking wine (shaohsing rice wine) and rice wine
- cornflour
- dried fruit, such as apples, apricots, cranberries and sultanas
- dried herbs and ground spices
- dried pasta, such as penne, spaghetti and lasagne sheets; try wholegrain varieties
- dried yeast
- flour, such as wholemeal and white plain flours
- grains, such as polenta, couscous and pearl barley
- honey
- noodles, such as egg noodles and rice vermicelli
- nuts, such as flaked and slivered almonds, pine nuts and walnuts
- oils, such as extra virgin olive oil, olive oil spray, sesame oil and vegetable oil
- olives
- peppercorns
- reduced-fat coconut-flavoured evaporated milk or reduced-fat coconut milk
- rice, preferably basmati and brown rice
- rolled oats
- salt-reduced beef, chicken and/or vegetable stock
- salt-reduced tomato passata

- seeds, such as sesame, poppy, caraway and sunflower seeds
- semi-dried tomatoes
- sugar or powdered sweetener
- tahini
- tinned or dried beans, chickpeas, lentils and other legumes
- tinned tuna and salmon
- tinned unsweetened fruit
- tinned vegetables, such as baby beetroot, tomatoes and corn kernels
- tomato paste (puree)
- vanilla bean paste or extract
- vegetable staples, such as onions, garlic, sweet potato and pumpkin
- vinegar, such as balsamic, verjuice, rice vinegar, white wine and red wine vinegar

CONDIMENTS

- curry paste
- fish sauce
- horseradish cream
- laksa paste or red curry paste
- lemon juice
- lime juice
- mirin
- mustard: English, Dijon and/or seeded
- nori sheets
- olive tapenade
- oyster sauce
- reduced-fat hummus
- reduced-fat mayonnaise
- reduced-fat tartare sauce
- salt-reduced soy sauce
- salt-reduced tomato salsa
- sweet chilli sauce
- Tabasco sauce
- teriyaki sauce
- tomato ketchup
- Vegemite
- wasabi
- white miso
- Worcestershire sauce

breakfasts

It's a good idea to start most days with a high-fibre cereal, reduced-fat milk and perhaps a piece of fruit; however, here are some recipes for those special occasions, like a weekend brunch with friends, where you have more time to enjoy something a bit different.

Mixed berry smoothie

This fresh, fruity smoothie is a great option for busy mornings when you don't have time for a sit-down breakfast.

Serves 4

Prep time
5 minutes

1 serve =
½ unit cereal
1 unit dairy
½ unit fruit

2 cups (500 ml) reduced-fat milk,
400 g reduced-fat vanilla yoghurt
2 cups (300 g) frozen mixed berries
2 tablespoons unprocessed bran

1. Process all the ingredients in a blender until smooth. Pour into four glasses and serve.

Muesli

Muesli is a really good way to fuel up in the morning and this homemade version will keep you going until lunch time.

Serves 8

Prep time
10 minutes

Cooking time
20 minutes

1 serve =
1 unit cereal
1 unit fruit
3 units fats

4 cups (360 g) rolled oats
100 g slivered almonds
60 g sunflower seeds
100 g dried apricots, chopped
80 g dried cranberries (craisins)
60 g dried apple, chopped

1. Preheat the oven to 180°C and line a baking tray with baking paper.
2. Spread the oats and almonds on the tray and bake for 15–20 minutes, tossing occasionally until toasted and lightly golden. Cool, then mix with sunflower seeds, apricots, cranberries and apple. Store in an airtight container.

> You can vary this muesli by incorporating different dried fruit, such as figs, prunes or pears, and nuts, such as hazelnuts, pecans or macadamias.

12 breakfasts

Cinnamon and sultana porridge

Warm yourself up on a cool morning with this breakfast favourite. The cinnamon and dried fruit add a flavour burst to every mouthful.

Serves 4

Prep time
5 minutes

Cooking time
5 minutes

1 serve =
1 unit cereal
½ unit dairy
1 unit fruit

- 2 cups (180 g) rolled oats
- 2 cups (500 ml) reduced-fat milk
- 1 teaspoon ground cinnamon
- 120 g sultanas or chopped dried apricots
- 1 tablespoon honey (optional)

1. Place all the ingredients in a saucepan with 2 cups (500 ml) water and bring to the boil. Reduce the heat and simmer for 3–4 minutes or until cooked. Alternatively, follow the microwave instructions on the packet of oats.

> The milk can be replaced with additional water, if desired.

Dried fruit compote

Put this compote together the night before and bring something special to your morning. It also makes a great addition to a weekend brunch with friends, or a fabulous dessert with 1½ tablespoons brandy or Grand Marnier added to the marinade.

Serves 4

Prep time
10 minutes, plus overnight soaking

1 serve =
½ unit dairy
2 units fruit

- 120 g dried apricots
- 100 g prunes, pitted
- 20 g sultanas
- 1 tablespoon honey
- 1 cinnamon stick
- 400 g reduced-fat vanilla yoghurt
- 1 tablespoon finely grated orange zest (optional)

1. Combine the apricots, prunes, sultanas, honey and cinnamon stick in a large bowl and pour over just enough boiling water to cover. Stir and refrigerate overnight.

2. Combine the yoghurt and zest (if using) and serve with the fruit. The fruit can be served warm or cold.

Ricotta hotcakes

These light and fluffy hotcakes may be served with a variety of toppings. They are sure to be popular with kids and adults alike.

Serves 4

Prep time
10 minutes

Cooking time
15 minutes

1 serve =
1 unit bread
1½ units dairy

250 g reduced-fat ricotta
¾ cup (185 ml) reduced-fat milk
2 egg yolks
½ cup (80 g) wholemeal plain flour
½ cup (75 g) plain flour
2 teaspoons baking powder
2 tablespoons sugar or powdered sweetener
2 egg whites
olive oil spray

1. Combine the ricotta, milk and egg yolks in a large bowl and mix until smooth. Sift the flours, baking powder and sugar or sweetener (tipping the bran back in) into the ricotta mixture and stir until smooth.

2. Whisk the egg whites to form soft peaks. Gently fold half the egg white into the ricotta mixture, then fold in the remaining egg white.

3. Heat a non-stick frying pan over medium heat and spray with olive oil. For each hotcake, spoon about 3 tablespoons of the mixture into the pan and spread to form a 10 cm round. Cook until bubbles appear on the surface, then turn and cook the other side until golden. Remove and keep warm while you make the remaining hotcakes. Serve with your choice of toppings (see left).

- Drizzle with a teaspoon of maple syrup or honey.
- Top with mixed berries and reduced-fat yoghurt.
- Spoon over stewed fruit of your choice, such as apple, apricot, pear, or the rhubarb and strawberry filling from page 191.

Tomato and cheese mini frittatas

These frittatas offer a lovely savoury start to your day, and also make a great light lunch or afternoon snack.

Serves 4

Prep time
10 minutes

Cooking time
20 minutes

1 serve =
1 unit protein
½ unit dairy
¼ unit vegetables

olive oil spray
8 eggs
2 tomatoes, diced
2 tablespoons chopped flat-leaf parsley
100 g grated reduced-fat cheddar

1. Preheat the oven to 180°C. Spray eight ½ cup (125 ml) muffin holes with olive oil.

2. In a large bowl, whisk the eggs until well combined. Mix through the tomato, parsley, half the cheddar and a pinch of pepper.

3. Divide the mixture among the muffin holes and top with the remaining cheddar. Bake for 20 minutes or until puffed and golden.

Mexican eggs

For those days when you need a bit of a kickstart to get you going, these Mexican eggs are a feisty option.

Serves 4
Prep time 10 minutes
Cooking time 25 minutes
1 serve =
½ unit protein
1 unit vegetables
1 unit fats

1 tablespoon extra virgin olive oil
1 onion, finely chopped
3 cloves garlic, crushed
½–1 teaspoon chilli flakes
1 teaspoon ground cumin
2 × 400 g tins chopped tomatoes
½ cup (15 g) chopped flat-leaf parsley or coriander, plus extra to serve
4 eggs

1. Heat the olive oil in a large frying pan over medium heat. Add the onion and cook, stirring, for 5 minutes or until softened. Add the garlic, chilli and cumin and cook for 1 minute or until fragrant. Add the tomato and simmer for 10 minutes or until the mixture thickens. Season to taste, then stir in the parsley or coriander.

2. Make four hollows in the tomato mixture, then break an egg into each hollow. Cover and simmer gently for 5–10 minutes or until the eggs are cooked to your liking. Serve topped with extra parsley or coriander.

* These are great served on wholegrain toast.
* Make the sauce the night before for a quick breakfast the next day. If you like, add some finely sliced capsicum with the tomatoes for extra flavour.

Warm mushroom salad on toast

The nutty flavours of this dish are great for those who enjoy a savoury start to the morning.

Serves 4
Prep time 10 minutes
Cooking time 10 minutes
1 serve =
1 unit cereal
½ unit dairy
1 unit vegetables
1 unit fats

2 teaspoons extra virgin olive oil
350 g mixed mushrooms (such as Swiss brown, oyster and field), sliced
1 clove garlic, crushed
2 spring onions, finely chopped
1 tablespoon red wine vinegar
15 g pine nuts, toasted and chopped
50 g rocket
4 slices wholegrain bread
100 g reduced-fat ricotta

1. Heat the olive oil in a large frying pan over high heat. Add the mushrooms and cook, stirring, for 5 minutes or until they are coloured. Add the garlic and spring onion and stir for 1 minute. Remove from the heat and stir in the vinegar and a pinch of pepper. Combine the mushrooms with pine nuts and rocket.

2. Meanwhile, toast the bread. Spread with the ricotta and top with the mushroom mixture.

simple lunches and salads

Whether you're at work, home or school during the day, you still want to be able to eat healthy and varied meals for lunch. Here is a collection of new recipes filled with delicious flavours and helpful suggestions to adapt them to your liking. Some dishes are best eaten as soon as they are prepared, such as bruschetta; others, such as Thai fish cakes and frittata, travel well in a lunchbox.

Bruschetta

This recipe for bruschetta is simple to prepare, and with three flavoursome topping options it is bound to appeal to a variety of tastes.

Serves 4

Prep time
5 minutes

Cooking time
5 minutes

1 serve =
2 units bread

8 slices good-quality crusty bread
1 clove garlic

1. Toast the bread in a toaster, under the grill or on a chargrill. Cut the garlic clove in half, then rub the cut side over the toast while it is still warm.

2. Add your choice of topping (see below) and eat straight away. Or, if you are packing the toast for a lunchbox, allow it to cool before wrapping. Seal the topping in an airtight container and add it when you are ready to eat.

Tomato and basil

1 serve =
1 unit dairy
½ unit vegetables
1 unit fats

Combine 6 diced tomatoes, 1 tablespoon balsamic vinegar, 1 tablespoon extra virgin olive oil and some shredded basil and season with salt and pepper. Spoon onto the bread and top with 100 g sliced bocconcini (optional). Garnish with small basil leaves, if liked.

Artichoke and rocket

1 serve =
½ unit vegetables

Combine 8 marinated artichokes, drained well and sliced, 1 crushed clove garlic, 1 teaspoon capers, rinsed and drained, 8 olives, pitted and chopped, 1 tablespoon chopped flat-leaf parsley, 1 tablespoon lemon juice and 40 g rocket leaves. Spoon onto the bread.

Tuna and olive

1 serve =
1 unit protein
½ unit vegetables

Drain a 425 g tin tuna in spring water and break the tuna into large flakes. Place in a bowl with 3 tablespoons reduced-fat mayonnaise, 8 large black olives, pitted and chopped, 1 diced tomato, 2 teaspoons lemon juice, 1 tablespoon roughly torn flat-leaf parsley and a dash of Tabasco sauce (optional). Gently combine the ingredients so as not to break up the tuna too much, then season to taste. Spoon onto the bread and top with lettuce or rocket leaves.

Pancetta and semi-dried tomato tarts

These delicious tarts take their inspiration from the flavours of the Mediterranean. Serve them for lunch, brunch or as a lunchbox snack.

Serves 4

Prep time
15 minutes

Cooking time
30 minutes

1 serve =
1 unit protein
2 units bread
1 unit dairy

* 1 unit vegetables with serving suggestion

olive oil spray
8 slices wholegrain bread
5 eggs, beaten
½ cup (125 ml) reduced-fat milk
85 g grated pecorino or parmesan
150 g thin slices pancetta, trimmed of fat and finely diced
100 g semi-dried tomatoes, drained of any oil, roughly chopped
basil leaves, to serve (optional)

1. Preheat the oven to 180°C. Spray eight ½ cup (125 ml) muffin holes with olive oil. Trim the crusts off the bread and, using a rolling pin, roll the slices to a thickness of 3 mm. Place a slice of bread in each muffin hole and press it in firmly. Bake for 10 minutes or until lightly golden. Allow to cool slightly. Reduce the oven temperature to 160°C.

2. Combine the eggs, milk and 40 g of the pecorino or parmesan in a bowl. Divide the pancetta amongst the bread cases and top with the semi-dried tomatoes. Pour the egg mixture evenly into the holes, taking care not to overfill them, and sprinkle with the remaining pecorino or parmesan.

3. Bake for 20 minutes or until set. Allow to cool in the tin for 10 minutes, then place two tarts on each plate, sprinkle with basil leaves (if using) and serve warm or cold with salad.

> You can use lean bacon instead of pancetta, but you will need to cook it first. Semi-dried tomatoes can be replaced with roasted capsicum (drained of any oil) or diced fresh tomato. You can buy jars of low-fat sun-dried tomatoes from the long-life deli section of the supermarket.

Some sliced loaves are smaller than others — these tarts require the larger slices or you may have a little filling left over.

Pinwheel sandwiches

These attractive sandwiches make a nice change from the traditional version.
We've suggested a few fillings below, but try experimenting with your own combinations.

Serves 4

Prep time
15 minutes

1 serve =
1 unit bread

4 slices wholemeal mountain bread

1. Spread your choice of filling (see below) over the bread and roll up tightly. Cut into 2 cm thick slices and serve.

Salmon and ricotta

1 serve =
½ unit protein
1 unit dairy
½ unit vegetables

Combine 200 g reduced-fat ricotta, 2 teaspoons horseradish cream, 2 teaspoons lemon juice and 2 tablespoons finely chopped dill or mint in a bowl. Spread over 4 slices mountain bread, top with 200 g smoked salmon and 2 handfuls of baby rocket leaves, and roll up tightly.

Ham and cheese

1 serve =
½ unit protein
1 unit dairy

Spread 2 tablespoons Dijon mustard over 4 slices mountain bread and top with 200 g thinly sliced reduced-fat ham and 200 g grated reduced-fat cheddar. Roll up tightly.

Chargrilled vegetable

1 serve =
½ unit protein
(if using hummus or bean dip)
1 unit vegetables

Spread 1 cup (250 g) grilled eggplant dip (see page 114), hummus (see page 115) or other vegetable dip over 4 slices mountain bread. Top with 4 slices chargrilled eggplant (aubergine), roughly torn, 8 slices chargrilled zucchini (courgette), 1 chargrilled capsicum (pepper), cut into strips, and a scattering of flat-leaf parsley. Roll up tightly.

Layered sushi

Even if you aren't a fan of raw fish, this sushi recipe is still worth trying. There is plenty of scope for designing healthy fillings to suit individual tastes.

Serves 4

Prep time
15 minutes

Cooking time
20 minutes

1 serve =
2 units bread

1⅓ cups (265 g) short-grain rice
4 tablespoons rice vinegar
3 teaspoons sugar
4 sheets nori
light soy sauce, to serve
wasabi, to serve

1. Steam the rice according to the packet instructions and spread out on a tray while still hot. Combine the vinegar and sugar and pour over the rice, stirring to mix through. Set aside to cool.

2. Lay two sheets of nori on a tray and top each with a quarter of the rice mixture. Layer your choice of filling (see left) over the rice, then top with the remaining rice and another sheet of nori. Press firmly to flatten, then cut into squares with a serrated knife. Cover with plastic wrap and store in the fridge until ready to eat. Serve with soy sauce and wasabi.

Any combination of grated carrot, sliced cucumber, strips of capsicum (pepper), raw or smoked salmon, raw, cooked or tinned tuna, and pickled ginger would make an excellent filling.

Tuna, ricotta and red onion spread

This versatile spread can be served simply with wholemeal bread, or offered as a dip with sliced vegetables and grilled pita bread.

Serves 4

Prep time
10 minutes

1 serve =
1 unit protein
½ unit dairy

* 1 unit vegetables with serving suggestion

1 × 425 g tin tuna, drained
100 g reduced-fat ricotta
1 clove garlic, crushed
½ small red (Spanish) onion, finely chopped
1 tablespoon lemon juice
1 teaspoon Worcestershire sauce

1. Combine all the ingredients in a food processor and process until smooth. Season to taste.

2. Serve with crispbread or bread from your daily allowance, as a dip with vegetable sticks, or use as a sandwich filling with salad.

simple lunches and salads

Chicken cakes

Kids love these chicken cakes and they're delicious hot or cold. Wrap any leftovers in plastic film and pack them into a lunchbox for a tasty treat the next day.

Serves 4

Prep time
15 minutes

Cooking time
25 minutes

1 serve =
1 unit protein
½ unit vegetables*

* or 1½ units with serving suggestion

olive oil spray
400 g lean minced chicken
½ small onion, chopped
2 cloves garlic, crushed
¼ red capsicum (pepper), diced
1 small zucchini (courgette), diced
1 tablespoon soy sauce
1 egg
2 tablespoons roughly chopped coriander
sweet chilli sauce, to serve (optional)

1. Preheat the oven to 180°C. Spray eight ½ cup (125 ml) muffin holes with olive oil.

2. Place all the ingredients (except the chilli sauce) in a food processor and process until smooth. Spoon into the prepared muffin holes.

3. Bake for 20–25 minutes or until golden and firm. Serve two per person with mixed baby salad leaves and sweet chilli sauce, if liked.

These cakes also work well with minced pork or turkey.

Baked ricotta with chilli and olives

Enjoy this creamy ricotta spread on grilled wholemeal pita bread or toasted wholegrain bread, sprinkled with your favourite fresh herbs.

Serves 4

Prep time
15 minutes, plus standing time

Cooking time
30 minutes

1 serve =
2 units dairy

450 g fresh reduced-fat ricotta
olive oil spray
3 tablespoons chopped mixed herbs (such as parsley, basil or oregano)
2 cloves garlic, crushed
1 teaspoon dried chilli flakes
12 black olives, pitted

1. Place the ricotta in a sieve over a bowl and set aside in the refrigerator for at least a couple of hours to drain any excess liquid.

2. Preheat the oven to 180°C. Spray four ¾ cup (185 ml) baking dishes or Texas muffin tins with olive oil and line the base with baking paper.

3. Combine the ricotta, chopped herbs, garlic and chilli flakes in a bowl and season with salt and pepper. Spoon the ricotta mixture into the baking dishes and smooth the surface. Divide the olives among the dishes and gently press into the mixture. Spray lightly with olive oil, then bake for 30 minutes or until risen and firm. Serve hot or cold with wholegrain bread from your daily bread allowance.

Smoked salmon and asparagus frittata

A slice of this lovely frittata makes a great packed lunch, or serve it with baby salad leaves as a starter at your next dinner party.

Serves 4

Prep time
15 minutes

Cooking time
30 minutes

1 serve =
1½ units protein
½ unit dairy
½ unit vegetables*

* or 1½ units with serving suggestion

- 12 spears asparagus (preferably thin stemmed), trimmed
- 8 eggs
- 3 tablespoons chopped dill
- 200 g smoked salmon, cut into strips
- 50 g grated parmesan

1. Preheat the oven to 150°C. Line a 20 cm square cake tin with baking paper.

2. Bring a large saucepan of water to the boil, add the asparagus and cook until just tender. Drain and rinse under cold water, then cut into 1 cm lengths.

3. Whisk together the eggs and dill in a bowl. Season, then stir in the asparagus and smoked salmon. Pour into the prepared tin and sprinkle with grated parmesan. Bake for 25 minutes or until just set. Remove from the oven and allow to cool. Cut into pieces and serve with a green salad.

✱ Try replacing the smoked salmon with smoked trout, or well-drained tinned salmon or tuna could be used for a budget option.

✱ Once opened, smoked salmon can be kept in the fridge for up to a week as long as it is tightly wrapped in plastic film. Or freeze it for up to 3 months.

Thai fishcakes with lime and chilli sauce

Everybody's favourite, these spicy fishcakes make an impressive weekend lunch to share with family or friends.

Serves 4

Prep time
20 minutes

Cooking time
10 minutes

1 serve =
1 unit protein
¼ unit vegetables*
2 units fats

* or 1¼ units with serving suggestion

400 g white fish fillets, skin and bones removed
1–2 tablespoons red curry paste
1 egg white
1 tablespoon chopped coriander
2 teaspoons fish sauce
1 red chilli, chopped (optional)
2 spring onions, thinly sliced
50 g green beans, thinly sliced
1 tablespoon vegetable oil
lime wedges, to serve

Lime and chilli sauce
4 tablespoons light soy sauce
1½ tablespoons lime juice
2 teaspoons grated ginger
1 small red chilli, seeded and finely chopped
1 tablespoon finely chopped coriander

1 To make the lime and chilli sauce, combine all the ingredients in a bowl.

2 Place the fish fillets, curry paste, egg white, chopped coriander, fish sauce and chilli (if using) in a food processor and process until smooth. Place in a bowl with the spring onion and beans and mix well. Form the mixture into 12 patties.

3 Heat the oil in a non-stick frying pan over medium heat. Cook the patties for 3–4 minutes on each side until golden. Serve with the sauce and a salad, with lime wedges to the side.

> If you're running short of time, use a shop-bought sweet chilli sauce instead of making your own.

simple lunches and salads

> These can be made into bite-sized balls and served as finger food with the sauce as a dipping sauce. The cooking time will be reduced to 2–3 minutes.

Chicken and vegetable pasta salad

The dressing for this colourful salad provides a tangy kick that complements the tender chicken and crisp vegetables.

Serves 4

Prep time
15 minutes

Cooking time
20 minutes

1 serve =
1 unit protein
1 unit bread
1 unit vegetables
1 unit fats

180 g penne (or other short pasta)
1 cup (160 g) frozen corn kernels
200 g green beans, sliced
3 tomatoes, chopped
1 red capsicum (pepper), diced
300 g cooked chicken, diced
2 handfuls of baby spinach leaves

Dressing
1 teaspoon Dijon mustard
1 clove garlic, crushed
1 tablespoon lemon juice
1 tablespoon balsamic vinegar
1 tablespoon extra virgin olive oil

1. Cook the pasta according to the packet instructions. Drain and rinse under cold water to cool.

2. Bring a large saucepan of water to the boil. Add the corn and beans and cook for 1 minute. Drain and refresh under cold water.

3. In a large bowl combine the pasta, corn mix, tomato, capsicum, chicken and spinach leaves.

4. To make the dressing, combine the ingredients in a jar with a screw-top lid. Toss through the salad and serve.

✻ This salad is a great way to use up leftover chicken from a roast, but if you don't have any chicken, use shredded turkey or tinned tuna. It is a natural home for leftover pasta too, or try it with rice.

✻ Play around with the flavours and use whatever fresh vegetables you have on hand – peas, asparagus or broccoli are all delicious.

Salad Niçoise

This is a simple take on the classic salad originating from the sunny South of France.

Serves 4

Prep time
15 minutes

Cooking time
15 minutes

1 serve =
1½ units protein
½ unit bread
1½ units vegetables
1 unit fats

300 g potatoes
100 g green beans, trimmed
1 clove garlic, cut in half
1 tablespoon extra virgin olive oil
2 teaspoons white wine vinegar or lemon juice
1 teaspoon Dijon mustard
100 g salad leaves
4 tomatoes, cut into wedges
1 × 425 g tin tuna in spring water, drained
4 hard-boiled eggs, shelled and quartered
50 g chargrilled capsicum (pepper), rinsed if in oil
4 tablespoons black olives

1. Boil the potatoes in a saucepan of boiling water for 15 minutes or until tender. Drain, cool then slice.

2. Meanwhile, steam the beans for 2–3 minutes or until tender but still bright green.

3. To prepare a dressing, rub the inside of a glass jar with the cut sides of the garlic clove. Add the olive oil, vinegar or lemon juice and mustard, season with salt and pepper and shake to combine.

4. Divide the salad leaves among four plates. Arrange the potato slices, beans, tomato, tuna, eggs, capsicum and black olives over the top. Drizzle with the dressing and serve immediately.

> ✻ This is also delicious with seared or poached tuna or salmon.
>
> ✻ If you have used your bread quota for the day, leave out the potatoes.

Fennel and red onion salad

Fennel has a sweet fragrance and distinctive aniseed or licorice flavour. It is a good idea to remove the tough outer layers of the fennel bulbs and slice 1 cm off the base before preparing it for the salad.

Serves 4

Prep time
10 minutes

1 serve =
1 unit vegetables
½ unit fats

3 baby fennel bulbs, thinly sliced (preferably with a mandolin)
½ red (Spanish) onion, thinly sliced
handful of flat-leaf parsley, shredded
2 teaspoons extra virgin olive oil
2 teaspoons lemon juice
2 teaspoons Dijon mustard

1. Combine the fennel, onion and parsley in a large bowl.
2. Whisk together the remaining ingredients and pour over the vegetables. Season, then gently toss together.

Shaved cabbage and brussels sprout salad

This crisp, refreshing salad makes a wonderful counterpoint to simply grilled chicken or barbecued meats.

Serves 4

Prep time
20 minutes

1 serve =
½ unit dairy
2 units vegetables
1 unit fats

200 g savoy cabbage, core and outer leaves removed
125 g brussels sprouts, trimmed
50 g finely shredded cos lettuce
½ red (Spanish) onion, thinly sliced
1½ tablespoons lemon juice
1½ tablespoons white wine vinegar
1 tablespoon extra virgin olive oil
50 g parmesan, finely grated
1 tablespoon balsamic vinegar

1. Finely shred the cabbage and brussels sprouts with a mandolin or sharp knife. Combine in a large bowl with the cos lettuce and onion.
2. Whisk together the lemon juice, white wine vinegar and olive oil. Pour the dressing over the vegetables and gently toss. Sprinkle with parmesan and drizzle with balsamic vinegar just before serving.

simple lunches and salads

This makes a delicious accompaniment to barbecued lamb or grilled chicken.

Rocket, sweet potato and chickpea salad

This salad can be a fresh and satisfying lunch, and also makes an excellent accompaniment to a summer barbecue.

Serves 4

Prep time
15 minutes

Cooking time
25 minutes

1 serve =
½ unit protein
1 unit bread
1 unit vegetables
1 unit fats

500 g sweet potato, peeled and cut into cubes
olive oil spray
1 tablespoon extra virgin olive oil
2 tablespoons orange juice
1 teaspoon grated orange zest
2 teaspoons white wine vinegar
1 teaspoon balsamic vinegar
1 × 400 g tin chickpeas, rinsed and drained
1 red capsicum (pepper), seeded and thinly sliced
100 g rocket leaves

1. Preheat the oven to 180°C and line a baking tray with baking paper. Spray the sweet potato with olive oil, place on the tray and roast for 20–25 minutes or until golden and tender.

2. Meanwhile, whisk together the olive oil, orange juice, orange zest and both vinegars.

3. Combine the sweet potato, chickpeas, capsicum and rocket in a large bowl. Add the dressing and mix to combine. Season and serve.

> The sweet potato can be replaced with pumpkin, and if you don't have any rocket in the crisper, any type of salad leaves would work here.

Antipasto salad

This innovative recipe brings together a variety of antipasto favourites, ready for a lunchbox or a comforting meal in a bowl.

Serves 4

Prep time
15 minutes

Cooking time
25 minutes

1 serve =
1 unit dairy
1½ units vegetables
1 unit fats

- 200 g pumpkin (squash), peeled and diced
- olive oil spray
- 150 g baby roma (plum) tomatoes on the vine
- 2 tablespoons lemon juice
- 1 tablespoon extra virgin olive oil
- ½ teaspoon Dijon mustard
- 1 clove garlic, crushed
- 150 g spinach leaves
- 100 g marinated artichoke hearts, drained of all oil
- 4 tablespoons black olives
- 100 g goat's cheese, crumbled

1. Preheat the oven to 180°C and line a baking tray with baking paper. Place the pumpkin on the prepared tray and spray with olive oil. Roast for 25 minutes or until golden and cooked through. Add the tomatoes for the last 15 minutes of cooking.

2. Whisk together the lemon juice, olive oil, Dijon mustard and garlic.

3. Arrange the spinach leaves on a serving platter and top with the pumpkin, tomatoes, artichoke hearts, olives and goat's cheese. Pour the dressing over the salad and serve immediately.

The roasted vegetables may be added to the salad when hot or cold.

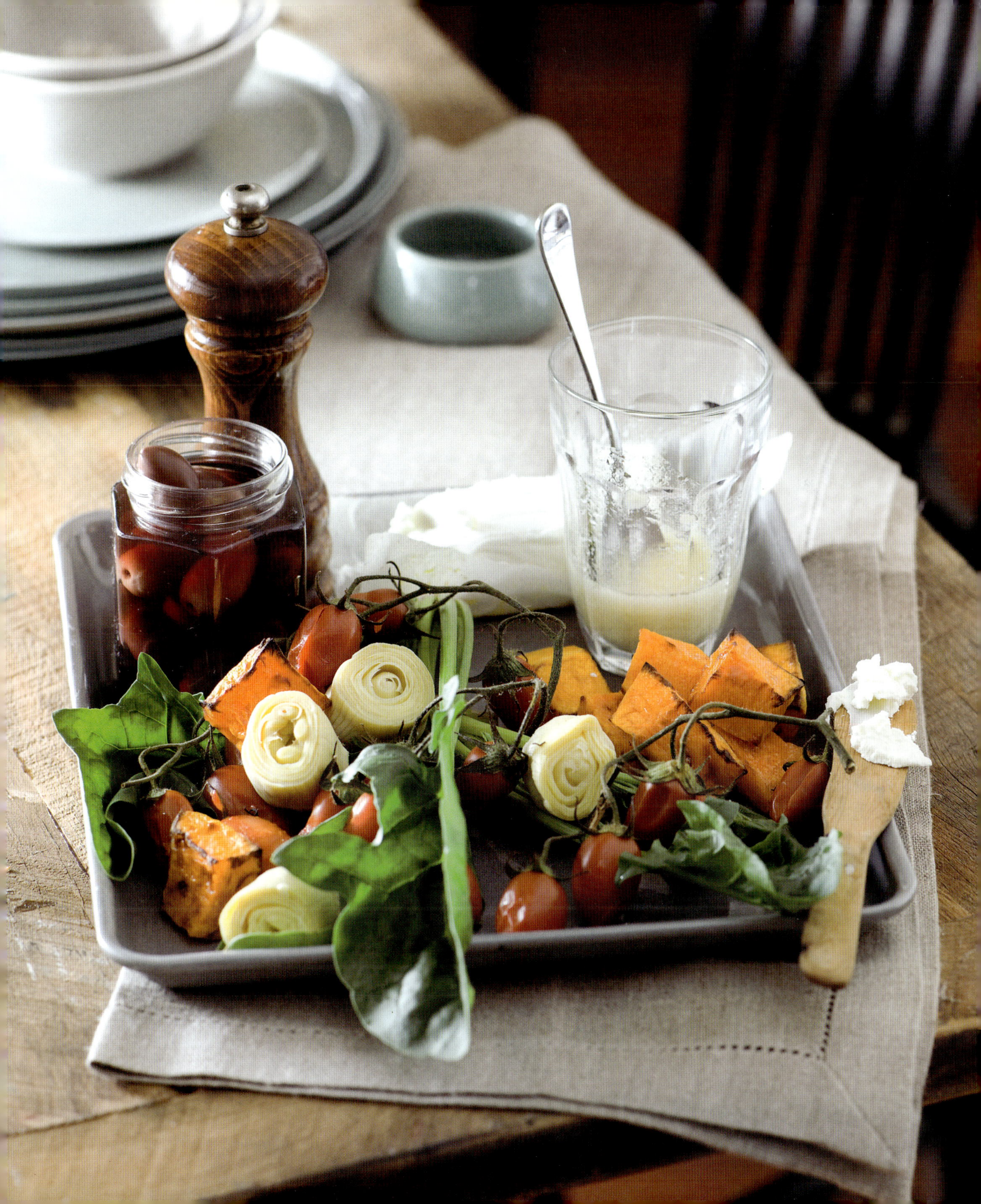

Spicy chicken noodle salad

Spice up the middle of your day with this Asian-inspired concoction. The crisp vegetables add a pleasing crunch, while the herbs bring a freshness to every mouthful.

Serves 4

Prep time
20 minutes

Cooking time
15 minutes

1 serve =
1 unit protein
1 unit bread
1½ units vegetables

- 400 g chicken breast fillet
- 100 g rice vermicelli noodles
- 2 tablespoons lime juice
- 1 teaspoon brown sugar
- 1 tablespoon fish sauce
- 1 small red chilli, finely chopped (optional)
- ¼ Chinese cabbage, finely shredded
- 1 carrot, cut into matchsticks
- 1 red capsicum (pepper), cut into thin strips
- 1 cup (80 g) bean sprouts
- ½ cup (25 g) shredded mint
- ½ cup (25 g) shredded coriander
- lime wedges, to serve

1. Place the chicken in a small saucepan and cover with water. Bring to the boil over medium heat, then reduce the heat to low and simmer for 10 minutes. Remove the pan from the heat and set aside to cool.

2. Meanwhile, prepare the noodles according to the packet instructions. Drain well.

3. Make a quick dressing by combining the lime juice, sugar, fish sauce and chilli (if using) in a bowl, stirring until the sugar has dissolved.

4. Finely shred the cooled chicken and combine in a large bowl with the noodles, Chinese cabbage, carrot, capsicum, bean sprouts, mint and coriander. Pour the dressing over the top and serve with lime wedges.

> If you are taking the salad to school or work for lunch, pack the dressing separately and add it just before eating.

This is another great way to use up leftover cooked chicken, or try it with pork.

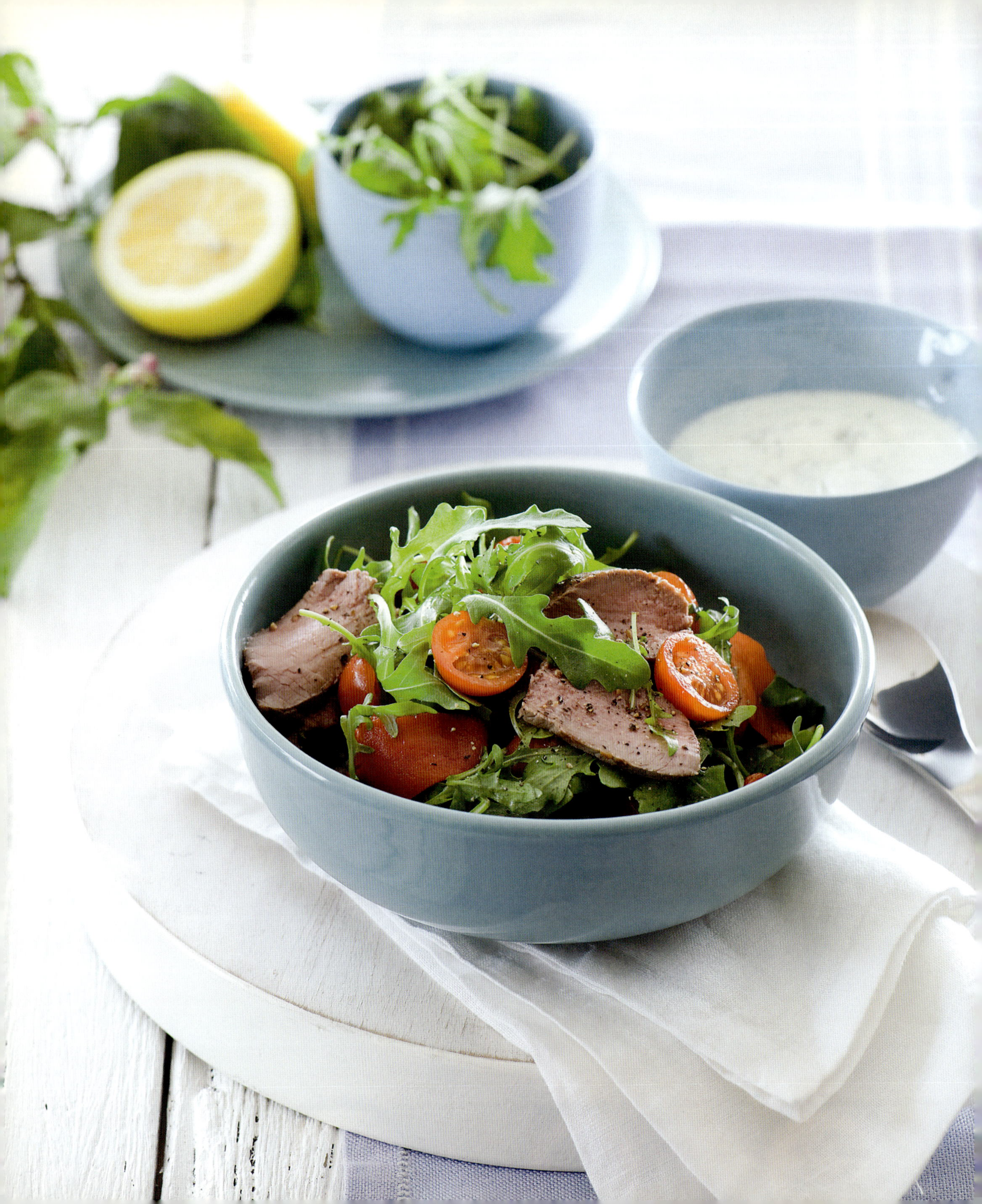

Chicken and mango salad

The Asian flavours in the dressing bring to life the gently poached chicken and sweet slices of mango.

Serves 4
Prep time 15 minutes
Cooking time 10 minutes

1 serve =
1 unit protein
½ unit fruit
1 unit vegetables
1 unit fats

400 g chicken breast fillet
100 g salad leaves
1 mango, peeled and sliced
1 Lebanese (small) cucumber, halved and sliced
½ red (Spanish) onion, thinly sliced
1 tablespoon extra virgin olive oil
2 tablespoons lime juice
½ teaspoon grated ginger
1 teaspoon soy sauce
chopped chilli, to taste (optional)
3 tablespoons roughly chopped coriander

1. Place the chicken in a small saucepan and cover with water. Bring to the boil over medium heat, then reduce the heat to low and simmer gently for 10 minutes. Remove the pan from the heat and set aside to cool, then shred the meat.

2. Arrange the salad leaves on a serving platter or indivdual plates and top with the chicken, mango, cucumber and onion.

3. Whisk together the olive oil, lime juice, grated ginger, soy sauce and chilli (if using). Pour the dressing over the salad and sprinkle with coriander.

Warm lamb salad with yoghurt dressing

Enjoy all the flavours of traditional Greek cuisine in one easy-to-prepare salad.

Serves 4
Prep time 15 minutes
Cooking time 6 minutes

1 serve =
1 unit protein
¼ unit dairy
1½ units vegetables

400 g lamb backstraps, trimmed
olive oil spray
200 g reduced-fat Greek-style yoghurt
grated zest and juice of ½ lemon
1 clove garlic, crushed
1 tablespoon finely chopped mint
250 g grape or cherry tomatoes, halved
100 g rocket leaves
1 roasted red capsicum (pepper), sliced

1. Heat a chargrill or frying pan over high heat. Season the lamb backstraps and spray with olive oil. Cook for 3 minutes each side or until cooked to your liking, then set aside to rest.

2. Whisk together the yoghurt, lemon zest and juice, garlic and mint until smooth. Season to taste.

3. Combine the tomatoes, rocket and capsicum on a large serving platter. Slice the lamb and toss through the salad. Serve with the yoghurt dressing.

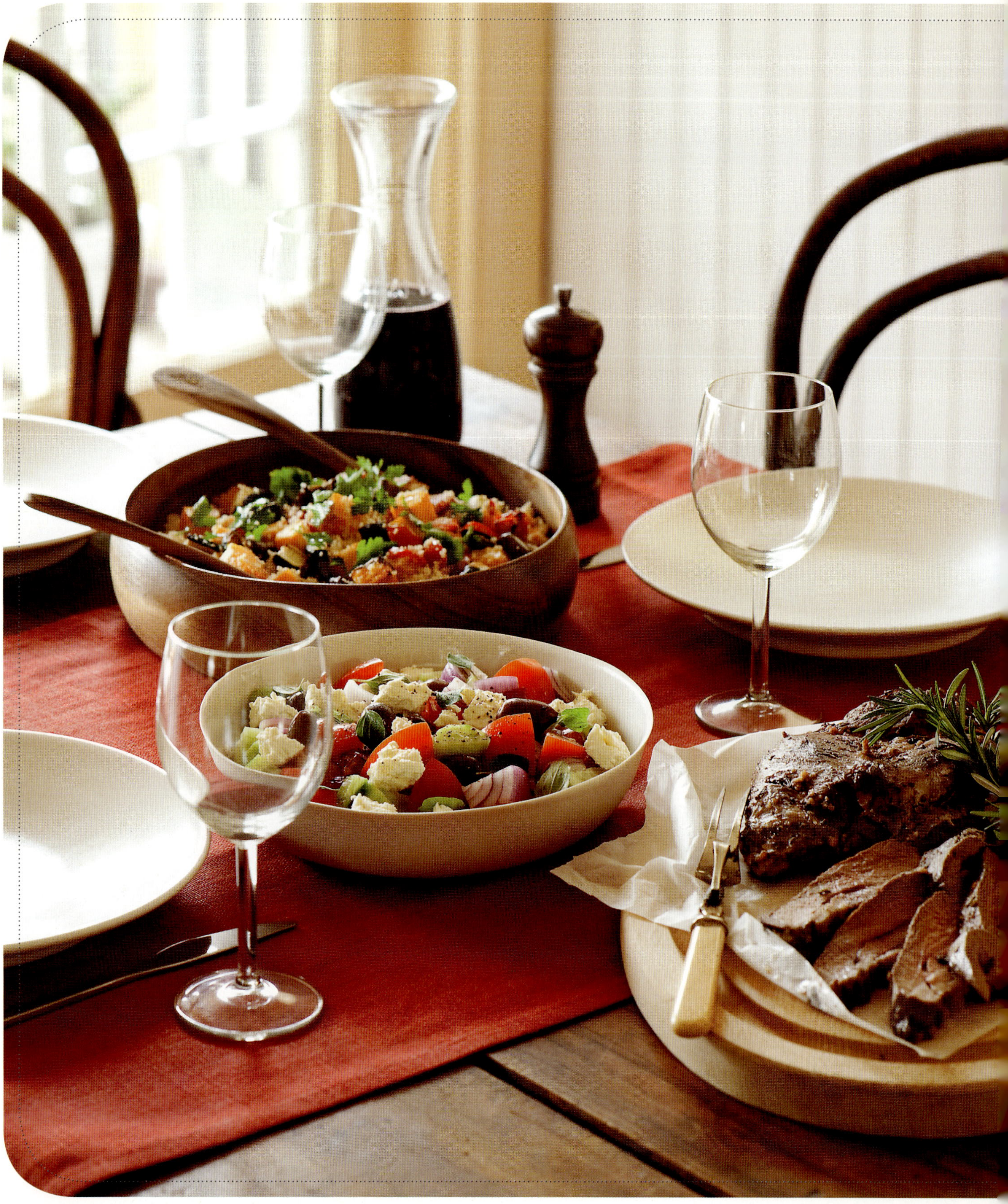

family lunch get-together

This is an easy menu for a casual Sunday lunch with the family.

Prawn and avocado salad

Garlic and herb butterflied leg of lamb

Greek salad

Roast vegetable and couscous salad

Apple crumble

Prawn and avocado salad

The luscious combination of prawns and avocado sets the tone perfectly for a long weekend lunch. The quantities can easily be doubled if you are feeding a crowd.

Serves 4 as a starter or side dish

Prep time 20 minutes

1 serve =
1 unit protein
1 unit vegetables
2 units fats

75 g mixed lettuce leaves
8 cherry tomatoes, quartered
80 g avocado, halved, seeded and sliced
400 g cooked medium prawns, peeled and deveined, tails intact

Mustard dressing
1 tablespoon extra virgin olive oil
2 tablespoons red wine vinegar
1 tablespoon seeded mustard

1. To make the dressing, combine all the ingredients in a screw-top jar and shake well to combine. Season with a pinch of salt and pepper.

2. Place the lettuce and tomato on serving plates and arrange the avocado slices and prawns on top. Drizzle with the dressing and serve.

Other types of cooked seafood or chicken can be used in place of the prawns, if preferred.

Garlic and herb butterflied leg of lamb

Start this the night before, then let the oven do its magic while you enjoy the company of your guests.

Serves 4

Prep time
10 minutes, plus marinating time

Cooking time
35 minutes

1 serve =
2 units protein
1 unit fats

1 tablespoon olive oil
3 cloves garlic, crushed
juice of 2 lemons
2 tablespoons chopped rosemary
2 tablespoons chopped oregano
1 × 800 g leg of lamb, boned and butterflied (ask your butcher to do this)

1. Combine the olive oil, garlic, lemon juice, herbs, salt and pepper in a large shallow dish. Add the lamb and turn to coat well. Cover with plastic wrap and marinate in the refrigerator for up to 24 hours.

2. Preheat the oven to 200°C or the barbecue to medium–high.

3. If using the oven, heat a large frying pan over high heat. Add the lamb and cook each side for 5 minutes or until browned. Transfer to a roasting tin, then place in the oven and roast for 20–25 minutes or until cooked to your liking. If using the barbecue, grill the lamb for about 15 minutes each side or until cooked to your liking.

4. Regardless of which cooking method you choose, rest the lamb for 15–20 minutes. Serve drizzled with the pan juices, alongside the Greek and couscous salads (see pages 46 and 47).

> If you find yourself with leftover lamb, it makes a perfect addition to lunch the next day. Either serve it in a wholegrain sandwich with salad leaves and some seeded mustard, or shredded and tossed through a salad (see, for example, the warm lamb salad on page 41).

Greek salad

The freshness of the tomatoes and cucumber, the creaminess of the feta and the natural saltiness of the olives offset each other perfectly in this traditional salad.

Serves 4

Prep time
10 minutes

1 serve =
1 unit dairy
1 unit vegetables
1 unit fats

4 tomatoes, diced
2 Lebanese (small) cucumbers, diced
1 red (Spanish) onion, diced
200 g reduced-fat feta
1 tablespoon roughly chopped oregano
12 black olives

Dressing
1 tablespoon extra virgin olive oil
2 tablespoons lemon juice

1 To make the dressing, combine the olive oil and lemon juice in a screw-top jar and shake well to combine. Season with a little pepper.

2 Place the salad ingredients in a large bowl, pour on the dressing and toss to coat.

> This salad can be prepared 30 minutes before serving, and stored in the refrigerator, covered with plastic wrap. Dress before refrigerating to give the flavours time to infuse.

family lunch get-together

Roast vegetable and couscous salad

A North African staple, couscous is quick and easy to prepare. Store any leftovers in an airtight container in the fridge and enjoy them for lunch the next day.

Serves 4

Prep time
20 minutes

Cooking time
20 minutes

1 serve =
1 unit bread
1 unit vegetables
1 unit fats

- 1 cup (150 g) diced pumpkin (squash)
- 1 red capsicum (pepper), diced
- 1 zucchini (courgette), diced
- 1 small eggplant (aubergine), diced
- 1 tablespoon olive oil
- 1 cup (250 ml) salt-reduced chicken stock
- 1 cup (200 g) couscous
- 1 tablespoon lemon juice
- 3 tablespoons chopped flat-leaf parsley

1. Preheat the oven to 200°C and line a baking tray with baking paper.

2. Combine the pumpkin, capsicum, zucchini and eggplant in a bowl, drizzle with the olive oil and toss to coat. Spread the vegetables in a single layer on the prepared tray and bake for 20 minutes or until tender.

3. Meanwhile, bring the stock to the boil in a medium saucepan over medium heat. Place the couscous in a heatproof bowl and pour on the hot stock, then cover and set aside for 10 minutes. Fluff up the couscous with a fork and transfer to a large salad bowl.

4. Add the roast vegetables, lemon juice and parsley to the bowl and toss through the couscous. Serve warm.

> You can easily vary the flavour with different herbs or spices. For instance, add a teaspoon ground cumin to the hot stock, and stir in 3 tablespoons chopped coriander just before serving.

*

for the **Apple crumble** recipe, see page 189

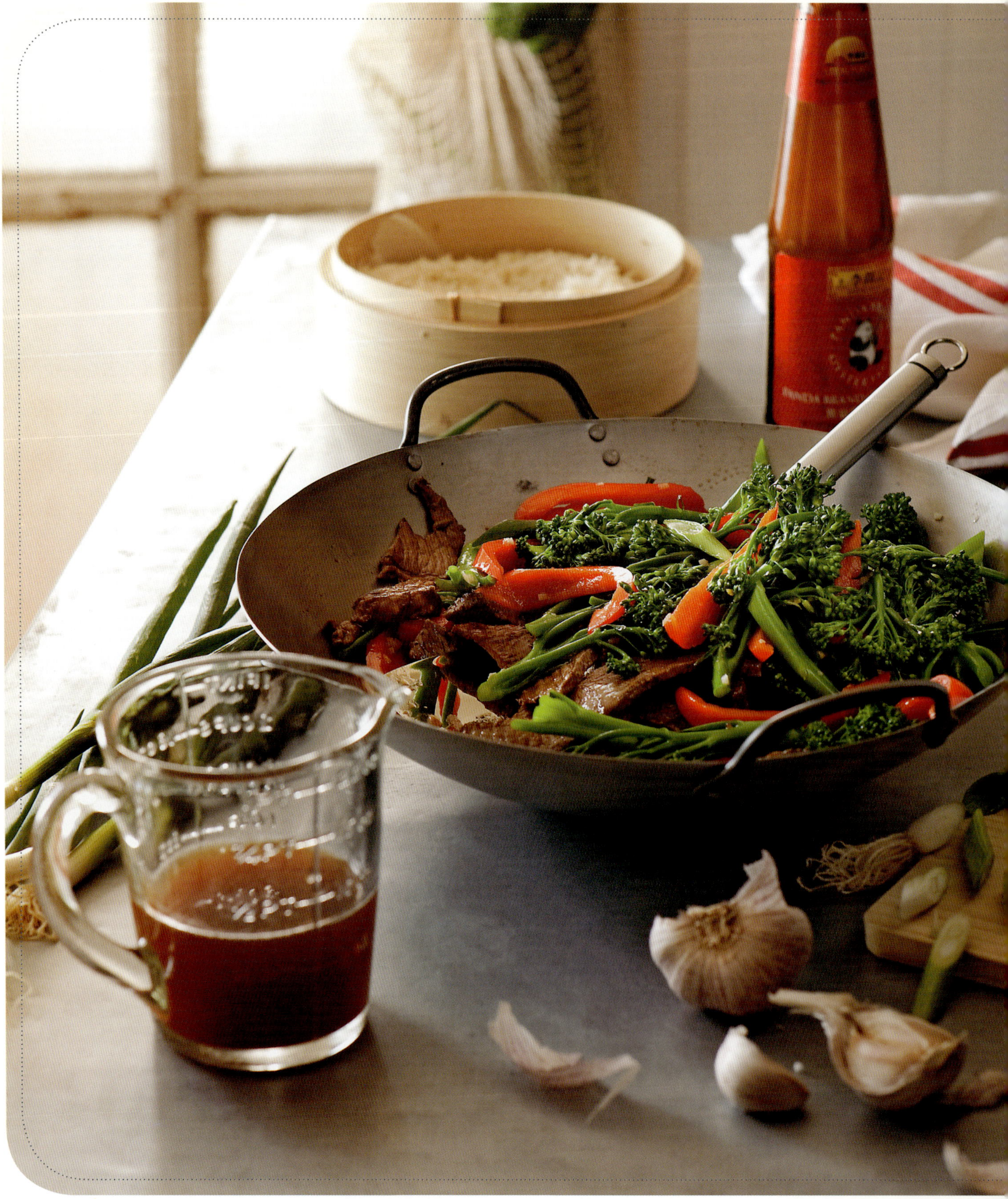

weeknight dinners

After a busy day, the last thing you want is to be slaving away in the kitchen for hours or lost for ideas on what to eat. These recipes are simple and easy to follow. Whether you're after a burger or a stir-fry, chops or kebabs, you're sure to find some new favourites on the following pages.

Beef burgers with salsa

Sink your teeth into this satisfying meal and enjoy the freshness of the tomato salsa, which is made in a flash.

Serves 4

Prep time
20 minutes, plus chilling time

Cooking time
10 minutes

1 serve =
2 units protein
2 units bread
½ unit vegetables*
1 unit fats

* or 1½ units with serving suggestion

700 g lean minced beef
1 tablespoon finely chopped thyme
1 onion, grated
3 cloves garlic, crushed
1 tablespoon tomato paste (puree)
1 tablespoon Worcestershire sauce
2 eggs, lightly beaten
1 tablespoon olive oil
4 wholemeal bread rolls, to serve (optional)

Salsa
1 × 400 g tin chopped tomatoes, drained
1 red capsicum (pepper), seeded and finely diced
1 small red (Spanish) onion, finely diced
½–1 teaspoon Tabasco sauce (to taste)
2 tablespoons finely chopped basil
1 tablespoon lemon juice, or to taste

1. Combine the beef, thyme, onion, garlic, tomato paste, Worcestershire sauce and egg in a large bowl. Form into four patties, then cover with plastic wrap and refrigerate for 30 minutes.

2. To make salsa, mix together all the ingredients.

3. Heat the olive oil in a heavy-based non-stick frying pan over medium heat. Add the burgers and cook for 5 minutes each side, flattening regularly.

4. Serve the burgers in the bread rolls (if using) with a dollop of salsa and a green salad.

> The salsa also makes a great dip, served with sliced vegetables or grilled flatbread. If you prefer a smoother texture, pulse all the ingredients in a food processor until the desired consistency is reached.

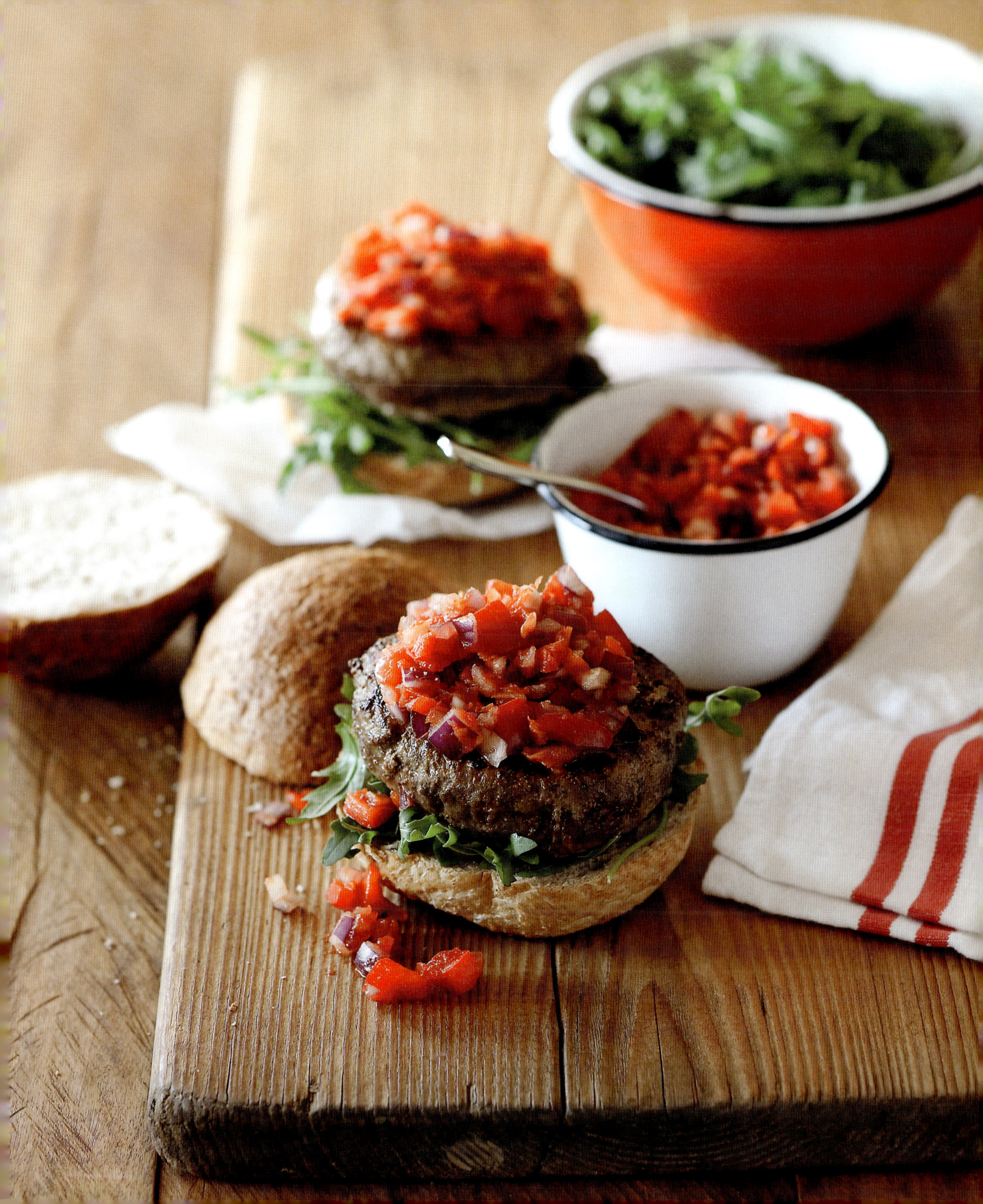

Try using oyster, shiitake or button mushrooms, or a combination of all three.

Thai-style beef and bean stir-fry

Give your local Thai takeaway a miss and whip up this homemade version instead. It's simple to prepare and much healthier than a bought version.

Serves 4

Prep time
15 minutes

Cooking time
5 minutes

1 serve =
2 units protein
1 unit vegetables
2 unit fats

3 cloves garlic, roughly chopped
1–2 long red chillies, seeded and thinly sliced
1 tablespoons chopped coriander roots and stems
2 tablespoon vegetable oil
800 g beef fillet, trimmed of fat and thinly sliced
200 g green beans, trimmed and cut into short lengths
100 g mixed mushrooms
1 tablespoon light soy sauce
1 tablespoon oyster sauce
3 tablespoons salt-reduced chicken stock
coriander leaves, to serve (optional)
1 red chilli, extra, thinly sliced (optional)

1. Combine the garlic, chilli and coriander roots and stems in a small food processor to make a paste.

2. Heat the oil in a wok or large frying pan over high heat. Add the garlic paste and beef slices and stir-fry for 2 minutes or until golden brown. Add the beans, mushrooms, sauces and stock and cook for 2 minutes or until the beans are just tender.

3. Garnish the stir-fry with coriander leaves and extra chilli (if using) and serve with steamed rice from your daily bread allowance.

> Coriander roots and stems are often discarded; however, they are full of flavour and can add a powerful boost to the taste of a meal.

Veal saltimbocca with tomatoes and zucchini

This attractive recipe is a great one to prepare when entertaining friends at short notice, or to make you feel a little special midweek.

Serves 4

Prep time
15 minutes

Cooking time
15 minutes

1 serve =
2 units protein
1 unit vegetables
2 units fats

600 g veal escalopes
200 g lean ham slices
8 sage leaves
2 tablespoons olive oil
100 ml white wine
400 g zucchini (courgettes), sliced
2 cloves garlic, crushed
2 tomatoes, diced
3 tablespoons shredded basil
1 teaspoon balsamic vinegar
small basil leaves, extra, to garnish

> ✱ Did you know saltimbocca means 'jump in your mouth' in Italian?
>
> ✱ You can replace the lean ham slices with slices of pancetta or prosciutto for a more authentic Italian flavour.

1. Spread a large piece of plastic wrap on your work surface. Place the veal escalopes on top and cover with second piece of plastic wrap. Using a rolling pin, flatten the escalopes to a thickness of about 5 mm. Season with salt and pepper.

2. Lay a slice of ham over each escalope, and place a sage leaf on top. Fold the overlapping edges of ham under and secure with a cocktail stick.

3. Heat 1 tablespoon of the olive oil in a non-stick frying pan over high heat. Add the veal, ham-side down, and cook for 2 minutes each side until browned. Reduce the heat and add the wine. Cook for about 2 minutes or until the liquid has evaporated. Transfer the escalopes to serving plates and remove the cocktail sticks.

4. Meanwhile, heat the remaining oil in a saucepan over medium heat. Add the zucchini and cook for about 2–3 minutes or until coloured and just tender. Add the garlic and cook for 1 minute. Stir in the tomato and basil and cook until heated through. Remove the pan from the heat and stir in the balsamic vinegar. Season to taste. Garnish with the extra basil leaves and serve with the veal saltimbocca.

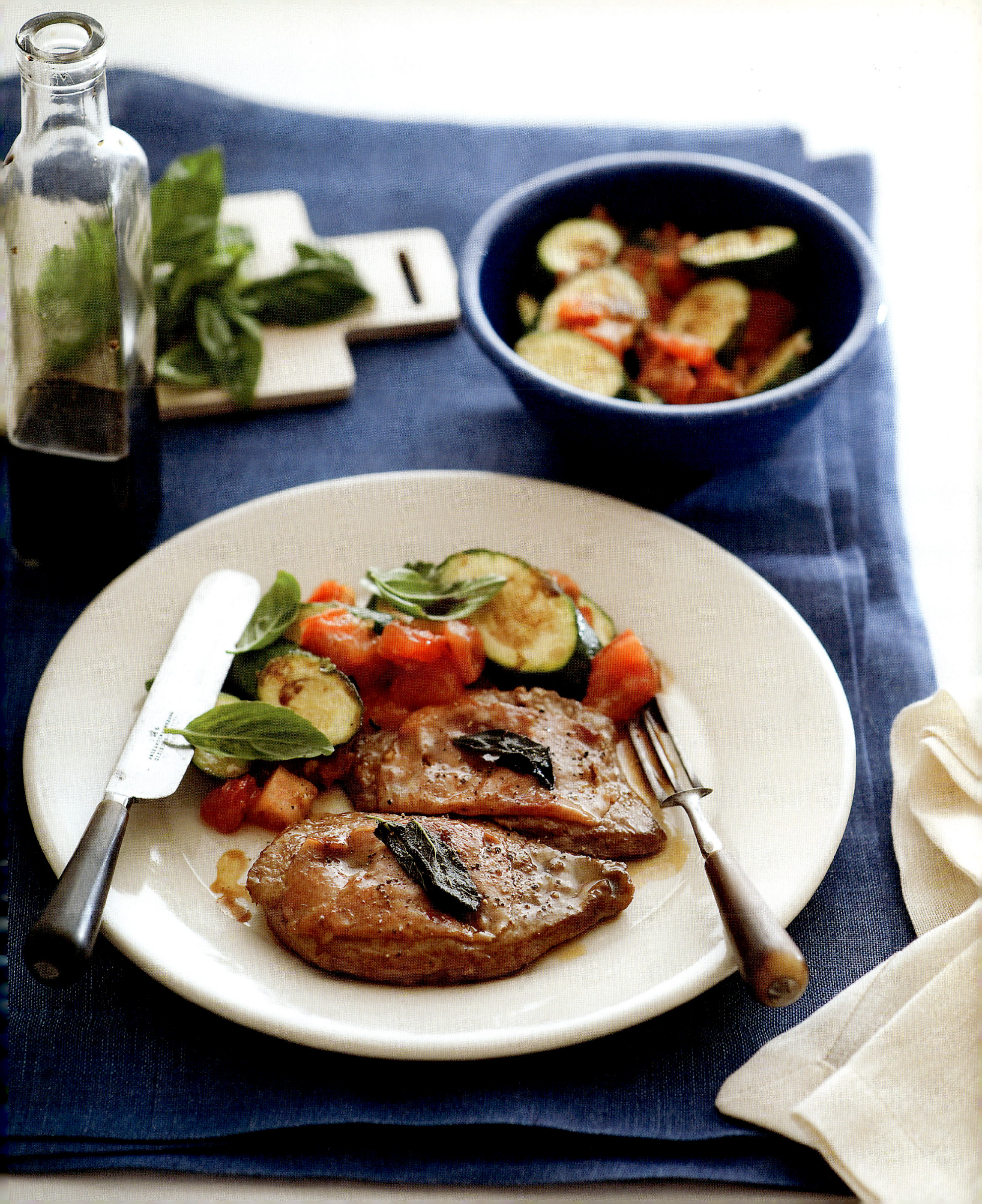

Teriyaki beef with egg noodles

Ready in 30 minutes, this is a terrific meal to throw together at the end of a busy day.

Serves 4

Prep time
15 minutes

Cooking time
15 minutes

1 serve =
2 units protein
1 unit bread
½ unit vegetables*
1 unit fats

* or 1½ units with serving suggestion

2 teaspoons sesame oil
2 teaspoons vegetable oil
4 × 200 g beef steaks, trimmed of fat and thinly sliced
2 small onions, sliced
3 cloves garlic, crushed
1 × 3 cm piece ginger, grated
150 g mushrooms, sliced
3 tablespoons teriyaki sauce
coriander leaves, to serve (optional)

Noodles

1⅓ cups (160 g) cooked egg noodles, still hot
1 red capsicum (pepper), cut into thin strips
6 spring onions, sliced
1 teaspoon sesame oil

1. Heat the oils in a wok or large non-stick frying pan over high heat. Stir-fry the beef in batches, then remove from the wok and drain on paper towel.

2. Add the onion, garlic and mushrooms to the wok or pan and stir-fry for 2–3 minutes. Return the beef to the wok, add the teriyaki sauce and mix until heated through. If the mixture is too dry, add a little water.

3. To prepare the noodles, combine all the ingredients. Divide among four noodle bowls and top with the teriyaki beef and coriander leaves (if using). Serve with steamed Asian greens.

> ✷ To make chicken teriyaki, simply replace the beef with the same quantity of chicken breasts.

Stir-fried beef and broccolini in oyster sauce

A hybrid blend of broccoli and Chinese kale, broccolini is a delicious, tender vegetable with thinner stalks than regular broccoli. If you can't find it, regular broccoli works just as well in this dish.

Serves 4

Prep time
15 minutes

Cooking time
15 minutes

1 serve =
2 units protein
1 unit vegetables
1 unit fats

1–1½ tablespoons vegetable oil
800 g lean beef, thinly sliced
3 cloves garlic, crushed
350 g broccolini, trimmed
1 red capsicum (pepper), sliced
6 spring onions, cut into 3 cm pieces
½ cup (125 ml) salt-reduced chicken stock
2 tablespoons oyster sauce

1. Heat a tablespoon of the oil in a wok or large frying pan over high heat. Stir-fry the beef in batches, adding more oil if necessary. Drain on paper towel.

2. Add the garlic and vegetables to the wok and stir-fry until just starting to soften. Add the stock, oyster sauce and beef and toss until heated through. Serve with steamed rice from your daily bread allowance.

Teriyaki sauce is a blend of soy sauce and sweet rice wine, and is great for marinating meat and vegetables. It is available in supermarkets and Asian grocers.

Veal cutlets with tomato risotto

The tomato risotto is baked in the oven, making it fuss-free and easy to do. It's a good match for the juicy veal cutlets – perfect with the piquant capers and a squeeze of lemon.

Serves 4

Prep time
10 minutes

Cooking time
45 minutes

1 serve =
2 units protein
1½ units bread
½ unit vegetables*
1 unit fats

* or 1½ units with serving suggestion

olive oil spray
4 × 200 g veal cutlets
2 teaspoons capers, rinsed and drained
lemon wedges, to serve (optional)

Tomato risotto
1 tablespoon olive oil
1 onion, finely diced
2 cloves garlic, crushed
1 cup (200 g) short-grain rice
1 zucchini (courgette), finely diced
1½ cups (375 ml) salt-reduced chicken stock
1 × 400 g tin chopped tomatoes
50 g parmesan, shaved or grated

1. Preheat the oven to 200°C.

2. To make the risotto, heat the olive oil in a 1.5 litre flameproof casserole dish and cook the onion for about 5 minutes or until soft. Add the garlic, rice and zucchini and stir until the rice is well coated with oil. Add the stock and tomatoes and bring to a simmer, then cover and bake in the oven for 35 minutes.

3. About 10 minutes before serving time, spray a large frying pan with olive oil and heat over high heat. Season the veal cutlets with salt and pepper, then add them to the pan and cook for 3–4 minutes each side, or until cooked to your liking.

4. Sprinkle the parmesan over the risotto and serve with the veal cutlets, capers and lemon wedges (if using), and your choice of salad and vegetables to the side.

> ✳ Lamb or veal steaks also work wonderfully here, if you are looking for a cheaper option.
>
> ✳ The risotto can be simmered on the stovetop, if preferred.

To boost the vegetable content, add a cup or so of finely diced vegetables with the rice and zucchini.

Chimichurri steak with cos salad

Chimichurri sauce is a popular accompaniment to grilled meats in Argentina. Simple to make, yet richly flavoured, it is sure to become a regular weeknight hit.

Serves 4
Prep time 20 minutes
Cooking time 5 minutes

1 serve =
2 units protein
1½ units vegetables
1½ units fats

4 × 200 g beef steaks, trimmed of fat
olive oil spray

Chimichurri sauce
1 cup (20 g) flat-leaf parsley leaves
4 cloves garlic, roughly chopped
1 red (Spanish) onion, diced
2 teaspoons dried oregano
1 teaspoon sweet paprika
2 tablespoons olive oil
3 tablespoons red wine vinegar
¼ teaspoon chilli flakes (optional)

Salad
1 cos lettuce, quartered and cut into 5 mm slices
4 roma (plum) tomatoes, cut into wedges
1 red (Spanish) onion, thinly sliced
1 red capsicum (pepper), cut into thin strips
2 tablespoons red wine vinegar
½ teaspoon Dijon mustard
2 teaspoons olive oil

1. To prepare the chimichurri sauce, combine all the ingredients and a generous pinch of salt and pepper in a food processor. Pulse to form a coarse paste. Coat the steaks with half the sauce (save the rest for later) and leave the meat to marinate while you make the salad.

2. To prepare the salad, combine all the vegetables in a bowl. Mix together the vinegar, mustard and olive oil in a screw-top jar and shake well. Pour over the salad and toss to combine.

3. Heat a chargrill or heavy-based frying pan over high heat. Spray with olive oil and cook the steaks for 2–3 minutes each side or until cooked to your liking.

4. Top the steaks with the remaining chimichurri sauce and serve with the salad.

> * The chimichurri sauce flavours become richer and more intense over time, so if you can, prepare it the night before you plan to use it.
>
> * Be careful not to cross-contaminate the portion of chimichurri sauce reserved as a sauce to serve. The raw meat should not make contact with it as the sauce will not be cooked.

Mongolian lamb

You can still enjoy this popular takeaway dish by making this lighter homemade version.

Serves 4

Prep time
10 minutes, plus marinating time

Cooking time
15 minutes

1 serve =
2 units protein
1 unit vegetables*
1 unit fats

* or 2 units with serving suggestion

2 tablespoons soy sauce
1½ tablespoons Chinese cooking wine or sherry
4 × 200 g lamb steaks, trimmed of fat and thinly sliced
½ cup (125 ml) salt-reduced chicken stock, at room temperature
1 teaspoon cornflour
1 tablespoon vegetable oil
1 teaspoon sesame oil
2 onions, cut into wedges
1 green capsicum (pepper), cut into strips
4 cloves garlic, crushed
1 teaspoon grated ginger
1–2 red chillies, seeded and chopped
1 tablespoon oyster sauce
roughly chopped coriander, to serve

1 Combine the soy sauce and Chinese cooking wine or sherry in a large bowl, add the lamb and turn to coat. Cover and marinate in the refrigerator for 30 minutes.

2 Slowly stir the stock into the cornflour, mixing well to smooth out any lumps (it's important that the stock is cool when added to the cornflour so that it doesn't thicken and turn lumpy). Set aside.

3 Remove the lamb from the bowl, reserving the marinade. Heat the oils in a wok or large frying pan over medium heat and stir-fry the lamb in batches until golden brown. Remove and set aside.

4 Add the onion and capsicum to the wok and stir-fry for 2 minutes. Add the garlic, ginger and chilli and cook for 1 minute. Return the lamb to the wok and add the cornflour mixture and oyster sauce. Stir gently until the sauce has thickened. Sprinkle with coriander and serve with steamed rice from your daily bread allowance and steamed vegetables.

> A little bit of sesame oil goes a long way so take care not to use too much.

weeknight dinners

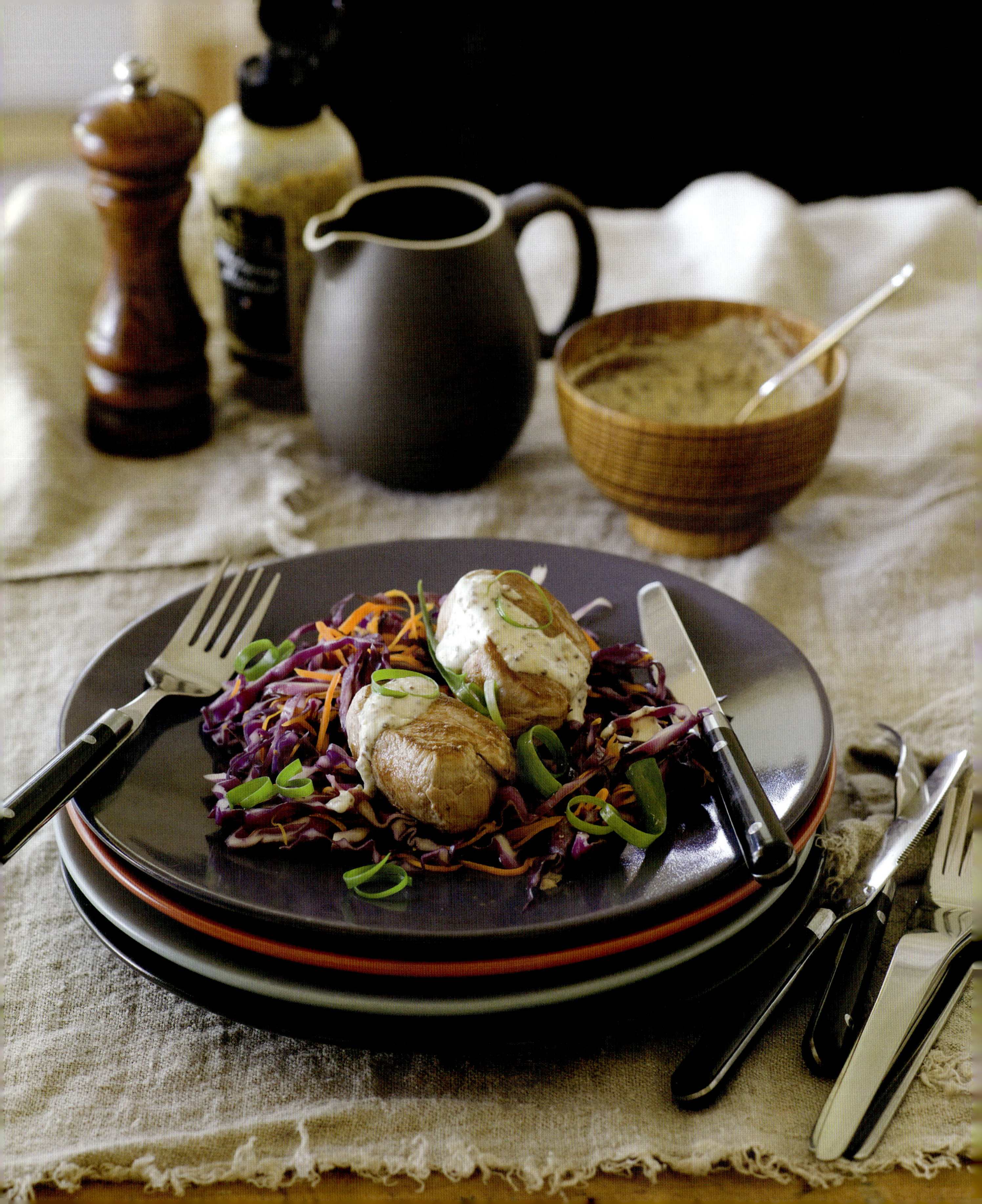

Honey-mustard pork with warm cabbage salad

The sweetness of the honey and the tanginess of the mustard create a wonderful contrast in this dish.

Serves 4

Prep time
15 minutes

Cooking time
15 minutes

1 serve =
2 units protein
1 unit vegetables
1 unit fats

✱ Experiment with different mustards – Dijon would make a nice change.

800 g pork fillet, trimmed of fat and cut into 4 cm slices
olive oil spray
3 tablespoons salt-reduced chicken stock
3 tablespoons honey or seeded mustard
3 tablespoons reduced-fat sour cream

Warm cabbage salad
1 tablespoon olive oil
2 cups (160 g) shredded cabbage (red, white or a combination of both)
2 carrots, grated
3 spring onions, sliced
½ cup (125 ml) white wine vinegar

1. Heat a large heavy-based frying pan over medium heat. Season the pork, then spray with olive oil and cook for 3–4 minutes each side or until cooked to your liking. Remove from the pan, cover with foil and keep warm.

2. Add the stock to the pan and stir to remove any caramelised bits of pork stuck on the base. Add the mustard and sour cream and stir until well combined and heated through.

3. Meanwhile, to make the salad, heat the olive oil in a large saucepan over medium heat. Add the cabbage, carrot and spring onion and cook, stirring, until the vegetables are just softened. Stir in the vinegar.

4. Divide the pork among four plates and drizzle with the honey-mustard sauce. Serve with the cabbage salad.

> Pork fillet is very lean and tender – cut it into thick slices and gently flatten with your fingers (on the cut side). The fillet can be replaced with pork schnitzel slices, but make sure you halve the cooking time.

weeknight dinners **63**

Chicken tikka with cherry tomato and cucumber salad

A tikka masala curry paste works very well in this recipe. It is deliciously aromatic, with a rich, slightly smoky flavour.

Serves 4

Prep time
15 minutes

Cooking time
10 minutes

1 serve =
2 units protein
1 unit bread
½ unit dairy
1 unit vegetables

2 tablespoons curry paste (use whatever you have to hand)
400 g reduced-fat natural yoghurt
800 g chicken breast fillets, trimmed of fat and cut into strips
4 wholemeal flatbreads
lime wedges, to serve

Cherry tomato and cucumber salad

250 g cherry tomatoes, quartered
2 Lebanese (small) cucumbers, peeled and diced
1 red (Spanish) onion, finely diced
3 tablespoons coriander leaves
2 tablespoons lemon juice

1. Combine the curry paste and half the yoghurt in a large bowl. Add the chicken and mix to coat.

2. Preheat a chargrill or barbecue to medium. Grill the chicken, turning, for about 5–10 minutes or until browned and cooked through.

3. Meanwhile, combine all the salad ingredients in a medium bowl and toss gently to combine.

4. Place a quarter of the chicken strips on each flatbread and serve with the cherry tomato and cucumber salad, an extra dollop of yoghurt and lime wedges.

> For greater depth of flavour, coat the chicken in the yoghurt mixture the night before and leave it to marinate in the fridge overnight.

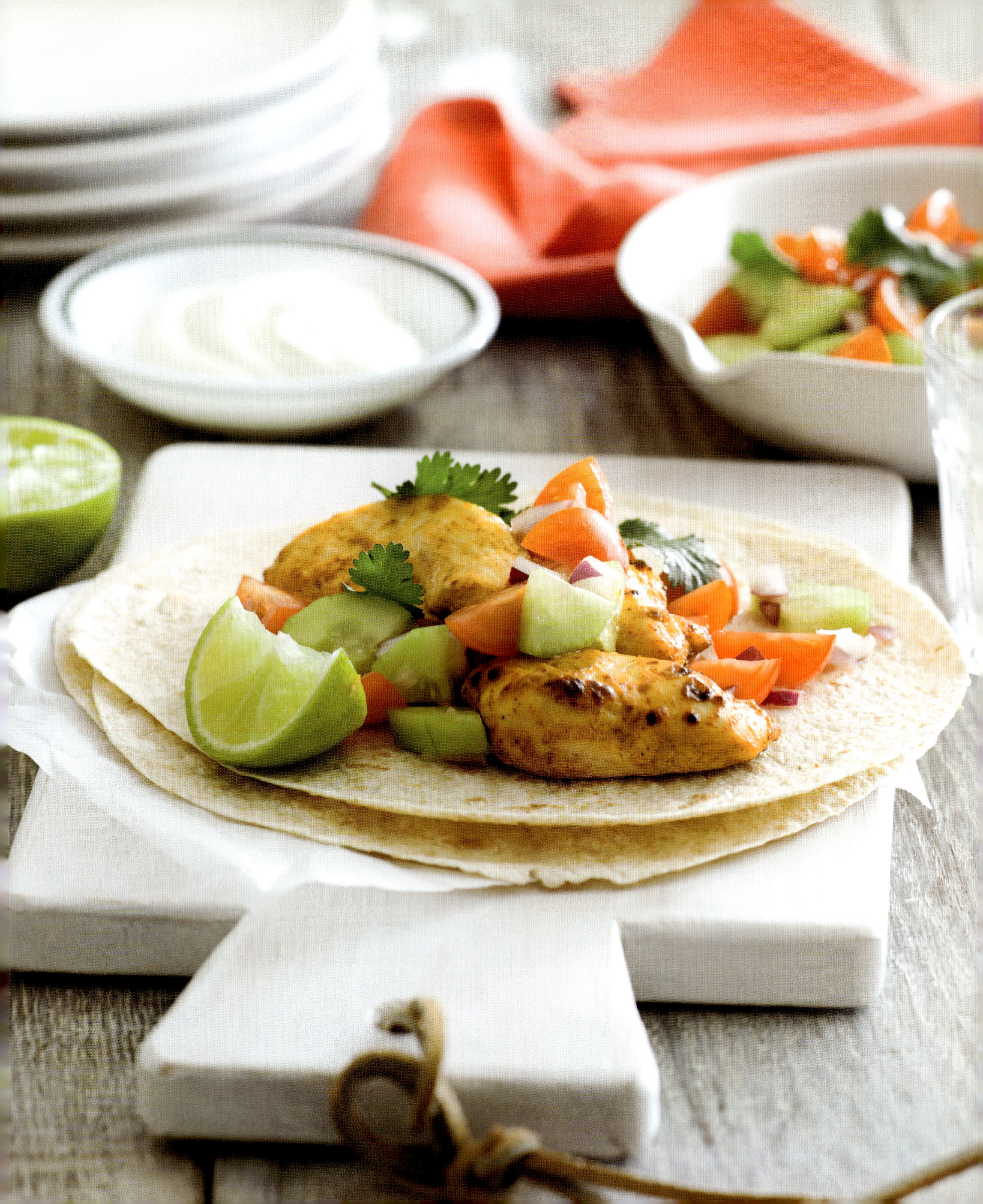

Variation — use sweet potato instead of the potato and flavour with a little Cajun spice mix before baking.

Chicken nuggets with potato wedges

This is bound to be a favourite with the kids. They'll enjoy helping you prepare them too, particularly smashing the cornflakes!

Serves 4

Prep time
20 minutes

Cooking time
35 minutes

1 serve =
2 units protein
1½ units bread
1 unit fats

* 1 unit vegetables with serving suggestion

4 medium potatoes, cut into wedges
olive oil spray
lemon wedges, to serve

Nuggets
600 g chicken breast fillets, trimmed of fat and cut into bite-sized pieces
2 eggs, lightly beaten
½ cup (75 g) cornflake crumbs
olive oil spray

1. Preheat the oven to 200°C.
2. Spray the potato wedges with olive oil and place in a single layer on a baking tray. Bake for 30–35 minutes or until crisp and golden, turning from time to time.
3. Meanwhile, line a baking tray with baking paper and prepare the chicken. Dip the chicken pieces into the egg and then into the cornflake crumbs to coat. Place in a single layer on the baking tray, spray with olive oil and bake for 15–20 minutes or until golden and crisp.
4. Serve the wedges and nuggets with lemon wedges and your favourite salad or steamed vegetables.

> If you prefer, the cornflake crumbs may be replaced with breadcrumbs. Make your own breadcrumbs by pulsing day-old slices of wholemeal bread in a food processor until fine crumbs are formed.

Mediterranean-style chicken with olives and capers

The classic combination of tomatoes, capers and olives has always been a winner. Here it works beautifully with pan-fried chicken and steamed greens.

Serves 4

Prep time
15 minutes

Cooking time
35 minutes

1 serve =
2 units protein
1 unit vegetables
1 unit fats

1 tablespoon olive oil
800 g chicken thigh fillets, trimmed of fat and halved
1 cup (250 ml) red wine vinegar
1 cup (250 ml) salt-reduced chicken stock
1 × 400 g tin chopped tomatoes
½ cup (15 g) chopped flat-leaf parsley
12 black olives, pitted and chopped
2 teaspoons capers, rinsed and drained
175 g broccolini
100 g green beans, trimmed

1. Heat the olive oil in a large saucepan over medium heat. Add the chicken in batches and cook until browned.

2. Return all the chicken to the pan and add the vinegar. Bring to the boil and cook for about 5 minutes until the vinegar has reduced by half. Add the stock and tomatoes and simmer for 15 minutes or until the chicken is cooked through. Stir in the parsley, olives and capers.

3. Meanwhile, steam the broccolini and beans for 10 minutes or until tender. Serve with the chicken.

Cajun turkey skewers with orange and red onion salad

These spicy skewers would also work well with chicken or pork. If you are using wooden skewers, soak them in water for about 20 minutes before use to prevent scorching during cooking.

Serves 4

Prep time
20 minutes

Cooking time
6 minutes

1 serve =
2 units protein
½ unit fruit
1 unit vegetables
1 unit fats

800 g turkey tenderloins, trimmed of fat and cut into strips
1 tablespoon olive oil
2 tablespoons Cajun spice mix

Orange and red onion salad
100 g mixed salad leaves
2 oranges, peeled and sliced
2 tomatoes, sliced
1 red (Spanish) onion, sliced
2 teaspoons olive oil
2 teaspoons sherry or red wine vinegar

1. In a large bowl, combine the turkey, olive oil and spice mix until the meat is well coated. Divide the meat into eight portions, then thread each portion onto a skewer to make eight kebabs.

2. To make the salad, combine the salad leaves, orange, tomato and onion in a large bowl. Sprinkle the olive oil and vinegar over the top and gently toss to coat.

3. Heat a chargrill or large frying pan over medium heat and cook the turkey skewers for 2–3 minutes each side or until cooked through. Serve with the salad.

Fish kebabs with spiced corn and tomato

This is a great summer meal. The spiced corn and tomato would also make a lovely accompaniment to barbecued meats or chicken.

Serves 4

Prep time
20 minutes, plus marinating time

Cooking time
25 minutes

1 serve =
2 units protein
¼ unit dairy
1 unit vegetables
1 unit fats

200 g reduced-fat natural yoghurt
2 teaspoons curry powder
4 cloves garlic, crushed
3 teaspoons finely grated ginger
800 g thick white fish fillets, skin and bones removed, cut into large cubes
3 tablespoons coriander leaves
lemon wedges, to serve

Spiced corn and tomato
1 tablespoon olive oil
1 teaspoon cumin seeds
1 teaspoon ground turmeric
¼ teaspoon chilli powder
3 tomatoes, diced
1 × 350 g tin corn kernels, drained

1. In a large bowl, combine the yoghurt, curry powder, garlic and ginger. Add the fish and toss gently to coat with spice mixture. Cover and marinate for 15 minutes.

2. To prepare the spiced corn and tomato, heat the olive oil in a medium saucepan over medium heat and cook the spices for 1 minute or until fragrant. Add the tomato and cook for 3–4 minutes or until softened. Add the corn and ½ cup (125 ml) water and bring to the boil, then reduce the heat and simmer for 5 minutes or until thickened.

3. Preheat the oven grill to medium–high. Thread the fish onto eight skewers. Place on an oiled tray or grill plate and grill for 5 minutes each side, or until cooked through (the cooking time will depend on the thickness of the fish).

4. Sprinkle the kebabs with coriander leaves and serve with the spiced corn and tomato, lemon wedges and steamed rice from your daily bread allowance.

> ✻ If you are using wooden skewers, soak them in water for about 20 minutes so they don't scorch during cooking.
>
> ✻ You could also make the kebabs with chicken.

weeknight dinners

Mediterranean baked salmon with rocket salad

These salmon parcels are so simple to prepare. For a rustic presentation, serve the salmon still in the foil and let everyone open their own parcels.

Serves 4

Prep time
15 minutes

Cooking time
15 minutes

1 serve =
2 units protein
1 unit vegetables
1 unit fats

2 tomatoes, seeded and chopped
2 teaspoons capers, rinsed and drained
1 red (Spanish) onion, finely chopped
2 cloves garlic, crushed
1 teaspoon grated lemon zest
olive oil spray
4 × 200 g salmon fillets, skin and bones removed
truss cherry tomatoes, to serve
lemon wedges, to serve

Rocket salad
150 g baby rocket leaves
1 tablespoon lemon juice
1 tablespoon olive oil
3 tablespoons finely shredded basil

1. Preheat the oven to 200°C.

2. In a medium bowl, combine the tomato, capers, onion, garlic and lemon zest.

3. Spray four 30 cm square sheets of foil with olive oil and place a salmon fillet on each. Top with the tomato mixture, then bring the edges of the foil together and fold to enclose the fish securely. Place the fish parcels on a baking tray and bake for 10–15 minutes or until the fish is cooked through.

4. Meanwhile, to make the rocket salad, toss together all the ingredients in a bowl and divide among four serving plates.

5. Remove the cooked fish from the foil parcels and serve with the salad, cherry tomatoes and lemon wedges.

> You can also make this dish with white fish fillets.

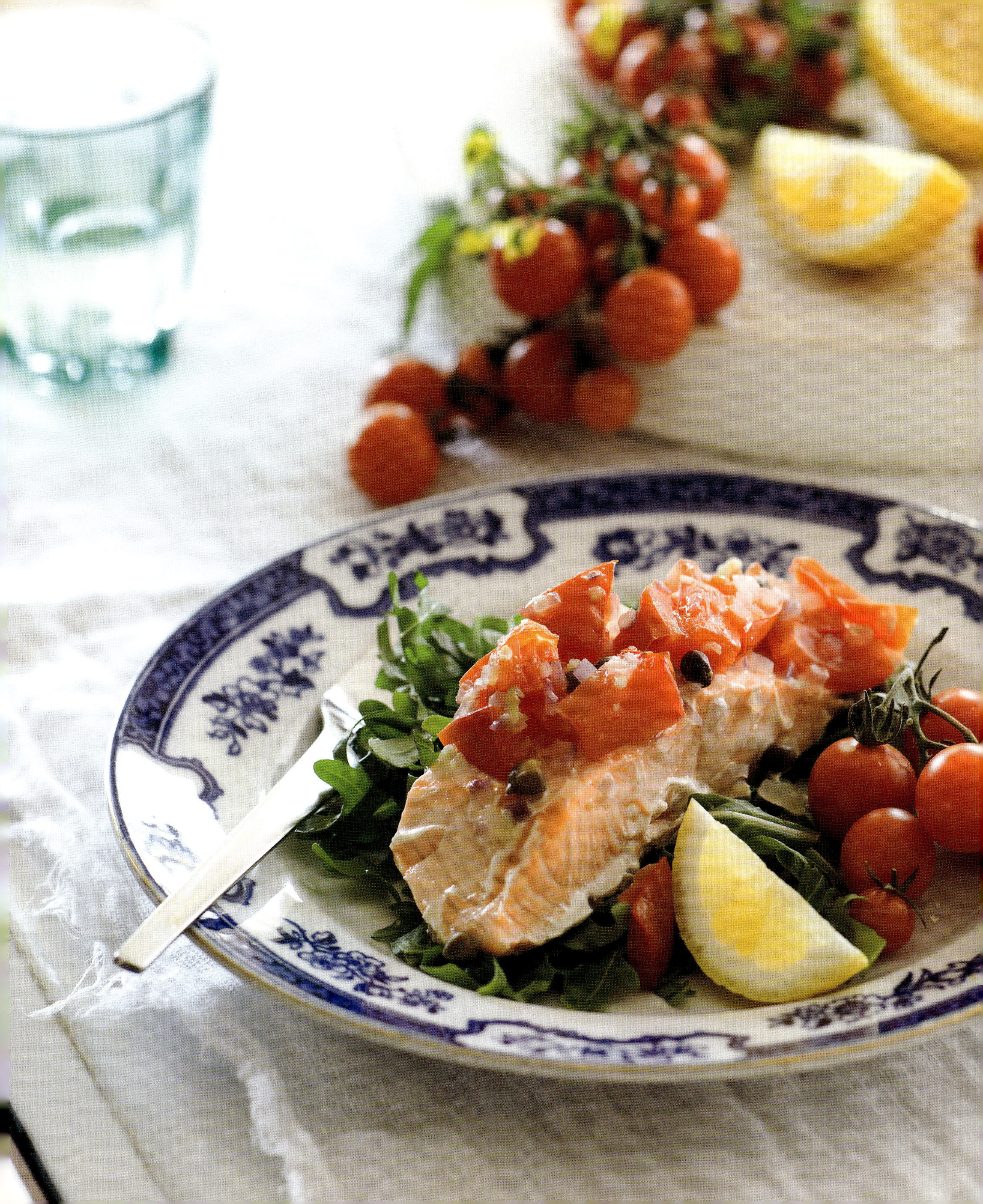

This is lovely with all types of white fish — try whiting, gemfish, snapper or flathead.

Japanese-style grilled fish with Asian greens

Lovely and light, this dish is based on the unique flavours of miso and mirin. The method is simplicity itself, but the results are spectacular.

Serves 4

Prep time
15 minutes

Cooking time
10 minutes

1 serve =
2 units protein
½ unit vegetables
½ unit fats

- 2 tablespoons white miso
- 2 tablespoons mirin, plus extra to serve
- 2 teaspoons olive oil
- 800 g white fish fillets, skin and bones removed
- 400 g Asian greens, such as pak choy or choy sum
- 4 spring onions, sliced
- light soy sauce, to serve

1. Combine the miso, mirin and olive oil in a small bowl. Rub the miso mixture over the fish fillets.

2. Preheat the oven grill to high. Place the fillets on a baking tray, then cook under the grill for 5–7 minutes or until just cooked through.

3. Meanwhile, steam the Asian greens until tender.

4. Sprinkle the fish with spring onion and drizzle with a little light soy sauce and extra mirin. Serve with the steamed Asian greens.

✳ Miso is a Japanese condiment made from fermented soy beans. It is sold in tubs or sachets and is available from the Asian section of your local supermarket.

✳ Mirin is a sweet Japanese rice wine only used in cooking. It's often used as a glaze or as part of a dipping sauce and can be added to stir-fries and marinades. Look for it in the Asian section of your local supermarket, or at an Asian grocery store.

Salt and pepper calamari with mango and watercress salad

This dish is popular in restaurants and cafes, and now you can make it at home whenever the mood takes you. It's perfect for enjoying on a sunny day by the water.

Serves 4
Prep time 20 minutes
Cooking time 5 minutes
1 serve = 2 units protein
1½ units vegetables
1½ units fat

800 g squid hoods, cleaned
1 teaspoon salt flakes
1 teaspoon coarsely ground black peppercorns
1 tablespoon vegetable oil
2 spring onions, sliced
1 red chilli, sliced (optional)

Mango and watercress salad
1 mango, peeled, seed removed and sliced
1 cucumber, peeled, halved lengthways and sliced
1 bunch (350 g) watercress, stalks discarded
½ red (Spanish) onion, peeled, halved and thinly sliced
1 tablespoon lime juice
2 teaspoons soy sauce
1 teaspoon sesame oil
1 teaspoon vegetable oil
pinch of sugar

1. To prepare the salad, combine the mango, cucumber, watercress and onion in a large bowl. Mix together the remaining ingredients to make a dressing and pour over the salad. Gently toss to combine.

2. Cut the squid hoods into 5 cm squares then, using a sharp knife, score the inside in a criss-cross pattern.

3. Combine the salt and pepper in a bowl. Add the calamari and stir to coat.

4. Heat the oil in a wok or large frying pan over high heat. Add the squid in two batches and stir-fry for about 2 minutes or until just cooked and coloured. Add the spring onion and chilli (if using) for the last 30 seconds of cooking. Serve immediately with the mango and watercress salad.

> Watercress is a delicious alternative to rocket or other salad leaves. It has a peppery, mustardy flavour that works well in salads, sandwiches and soups. Look for dark green leaves with no yellowing.

Chinese mushroom omelette

This scrumptious dish looks and tastes a treat. It's simple and quick to whip up at short notice.

Serves 4
Prep time
15 minutes
Cooking time
15 minutes

1 serve =
2 units protein
1 unit vegetables*
1½ units fats

* or 2 units with serving suggestion

8 eggs, lightly beaten
3 spring onions, finely sliced
1 tablespoon vegetable oil
coriander leaves, to serve
2 spring onions, finely sliced, extra, to serve

Filling

2 teaspoons vegetable oil
1 × 1 cm piece ginger, grated
1 clove garlic, crushed
400 g mixed mushrooms
1 cup (80 g) bean sprouts

Sauce

2 teaspoons rice vinegar
1 tablespoon oyster sauce
¼ teaspoon sesame oil

1. To prepare the sauce, combine all the ingredients in a small bowl and set aside.

2. To prepare the filling, heat the oil in a wok or large frying pan over high heat. Add the ginger, garlic and mushrooms and stir-fry for 3–4 minutes or until the mushrooms are just cooked. Remove the mixture to a plate and wipe the wok clean.

3. Combine the eggs and spring onion in a large bowl. Reheat the wok or frying pan over medium–high heat and add 1 teaspoon of the oil. When the oil is hot, add a quarter of the egg mix and swirl it around the wok.

4. When the base of the omelette is cooked and the top is still slightly soft, spread a quarter of the mushroom mix over half the omelette. Top with a quarter of the bean sprouts and fold the other half of the omelette over the top. Remove from the wok and keep warm while you make the remaining three omelettes.

5. Drizzle the sauce over the omelettes and garnish with the coriander leaves and extra spring onion. Serve with a green salad.

> Try using a mix of shiitake, oyster, enoki and/or button mushrooms for this recipe.

weeknight dinners

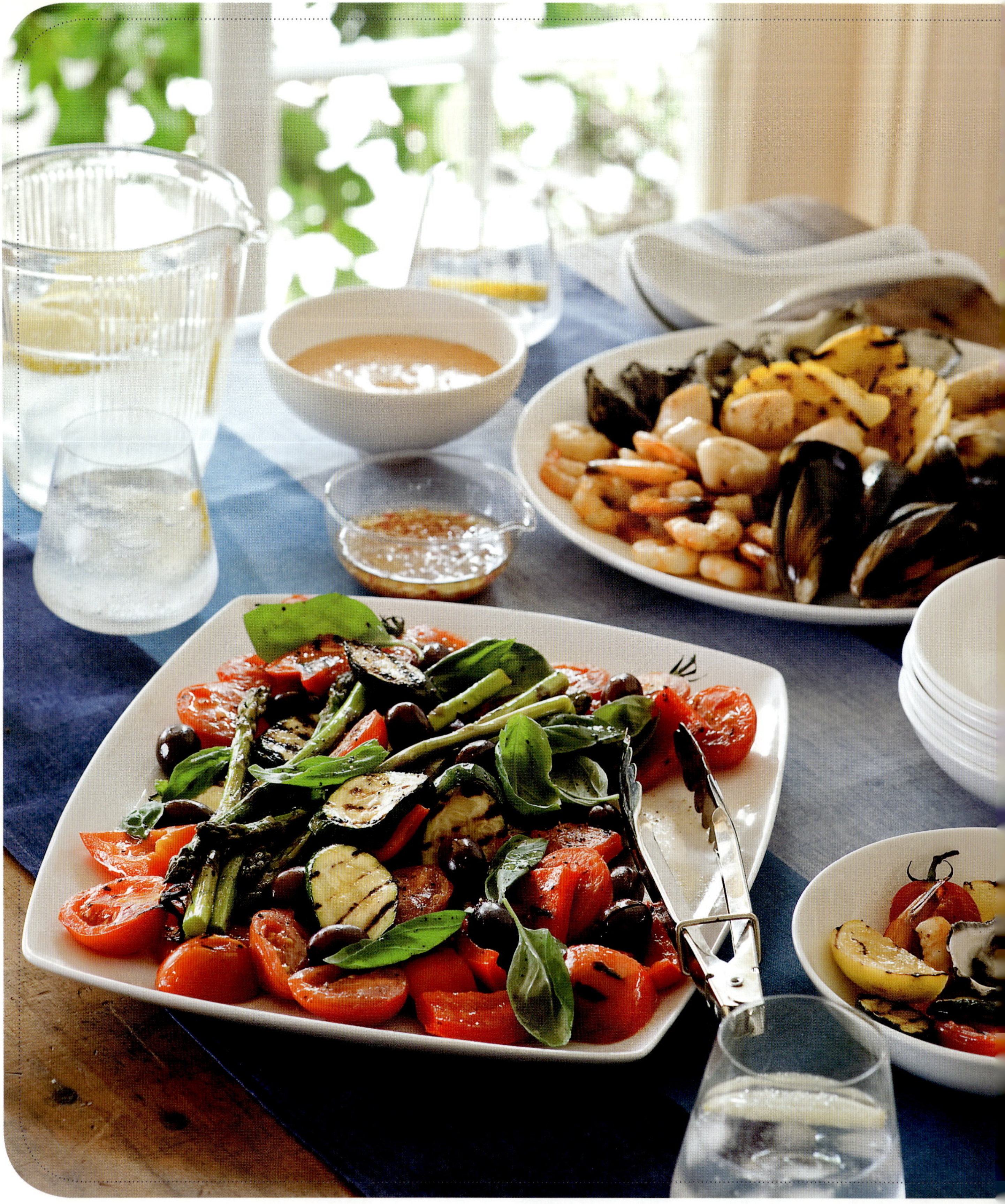

weekend barbecue get-together

This menu provides a good balance of protein and vegetable dishes.

Seafood platter

Barbecued lamb cutlets with minty yoghurt sauce

Chargrilled balsamic chicken

Grilled vegetable salad with basil and black olives

Warm eggplant salad

Spiced strawberries with ricotta cream

Seafood platter

What better way to enjoy the company of friends than over a platter of freshly grilled seafood? The dipping sauces enhance the wonderful flavours.

Serves 8
as a starter

Prep time
25 minutes, plus marinating time

Cooking time
3 minutes

1 serve =
1 unit protein
2 units fats
1 unit fats

1 tablespoon olive oil
2 tablespoons lemon juice
2 cloves garlic, crushed
2 tablespoons chopped flat-leaf parsley
250 g uncooked prawns, peeled and deveined, or 200 g squid hoods, cut into rings or pieces
8 scallops
300 g clams or mussels, scrubbed and debearded
150 g white fish fillets, skin and bones removed, cut into strips
12 oysters

Creamy tomato sauce
3 tablespoons reduced-fat mayonnaise
1 tablespoon tomato ketchup
1 teaspoon Worcestershire sauce
2 teaspoons lemon juice

Vinaigrette
2 golden shallots, finely chopped
2 tablespoons extra virgin olive oil
1 tablespoon white wine vinegar
1 tablespoon lemon or lime juice
1 teaspoon brown sugar

1. Combine the olive oil, lemon juice, garlic and parsley and brush over the prawns or squid, scallops, clams or mussels and fish. Cover and marinate in the refrigerator for 30 minutes.

2. To make the tomato sauce, combine all the ingredients in a small bowl, then transfer to a dipping bowl and set aside until ready to serve.

3. To make the vinaigrette, combine all the ingredients in a small bowl, then transfer to a dipping bowl and set aside until ready to serve.

4. Heat a chargrill or barbecue to medium. Add the marinated seafood and grill, turning, for 2–3 minutes or until just cooked. Arrange on a platter with the oysters and serve with the sauce and vinaigrette to the side.

> To save time on the day of the barbecue, you can make the marinade, sauce and vinaigrette in advance and store them in the refrigerator until ready to use.

Barbecued lamb cutlets with minty yoghurt sauce

This impressive dish is super quick to throw together. Marinate the cutlets overnight if you like, for a more powerful flavour kick.

Serves 8
as a part of the barbecue (or 4 as a main)

Prep time
15 minutes, plus marinating time

Cooking time
5 minutes

1 serve =
1 unit protein
½ unit fats

1 tablespoon olive oil
1 tablespoon Dijon mustard
3 tablespoons red wine vinegar
2 cloves garlic, crushed
1 teaspoon dried oregano
800 g lamb cutlets, trimmed of fat

Minty yoghurt sauce
100 g reduced-fat yoghurt
80 g reduced-fat hummus
2 spring onions, finely sliced
2 tablespoons chopped mint

1. Combine the olive oil, mustard, vinegar, garlic and oregano in a large bowl. Toss the cutlets in the marinade, then cover and marinate in the refrigerator for 2 hours or overnight.

2. Heat a chargrill or barbecue to medium. Add the cutlets and cook for 2 minutes each side or until cooked to your liking.

3. Meanwhile, to make the yoghurt sauce, combine all the ingredients in a medium bowl.

4. Serve the cutlets with a dollop of sauce and a fresh green salad.

For a budget alternative, try lamb or beef steaks in place of the lamb cutlets. They'll still taste great.

Chargrilled balsamic chicken

This recipe is a great example of how effective a few well-chosen ingredients can be – in this case, a clever combination of balsamic vinegar, garlic, olive oil and chicken.

Serves 8
as a part of the barbecue (or 4 as a main)

Prep time
10 minutes, plus marinating time

Cooking time
6 minutes

1 serve =
1 unit protein
½ unit fats

4 tablespoons balsamic vinegar
3 cloves garlic, crushed
1 tablespoon olive oil
800 g chicken thigh fillets, trimmed of fat and halved
lime wedges, to serve

1. Combine the vinegar, garlic and olive oil in a bowl. Add the chicken and toss to coat, then cover and marinate in the refrigerator for at least 30 minutes or overnight.

2. Heat a chargrill or barbecue to medium. Add the chicken pieces and cook for 3 minutes each side or until cooked through. Serve with lime wedges and a salad.

Grilled vegetable salad with basil and black olives

Grilling vegetables seems to enhance and condense their flavour, adding a smokiness that makes them hard to resist. The olives add a salty contrast.

Serves 8
as a part of the barbecue

Prep time
20 minutes

Cooking time
10 minutes

1 serve =
1½ units vegetables
1 unit fats

16 baby roma (plum) tomatoes, halved
2 zucchini (courgettes), thinly sliced
2 red capsicums (peppers), seeded and cut into strips
16 spears asparagus, trimmed
olive oil spray
200 g baby salad leaves
16 black olives, pitted
1 cup (50 g) shredded basil

Vinaigrette
2 cloves garlic, crushed
2 tablespoons extra virgin olive oil
4 tablespoons verjuice or white wine vinegar

1. Combine the vinaigrette ingredients in a screw-top jar and shake well to combine.

2. Heat a barbecue or chargrill to hot. Spray the tomato, zucchini, capsicum and asparagus with olive oil, then grill for 2–3 minutes each side, or until cooked through.

3. Place the salad leaves on a platter and top with the grilled vegetables, olives and basil. Pour the dressing over the top and serve.

> Try introducing other vegetables into this salad, such as diced eggplant, sliced fennel, sliced onion, or mushrooms.

Warm eggplant salad

Silky roast eggplant is combined with fragrant spices to create an extremely moreish side dish. This is particularly good with the lamb cutlets (see page 79).

Serves 8 as a part of the barbecue

Prep time 20 minutes

Cooking time 25 minutes

1 serve =
1 unit vegetables
1 unit fats

- 4 medium eggplants (aubergines), peeled and diced
- olive oil spray
- 2 tablespoons olive oil
- 2 red (Spanish) onions, chopped
- 2 teaspoons ground coriander
- 2 teaspoons ground cumin
- 2 teaspoons ground cinnamon
- 2 teaspoons sweet paprika
- 1–2 teaspoons chilli flakes
- 6 cloves garlic, crushed
- 2 × 400 g tins chopped tomatoes
- 1 teaspoon sugar
- ½ cup (25 g) chopped mint
- ½ cup (25 g) chopped coriander

1. Preheat the oven to 200°C and line a baking tray with baking paper.

2. Place the eggplants on the prepared tray and spray with olive oil. Roast for 25 minutes until tender.

3. Meanwhile, heat the olive oil in a pan over medium heat and cook the onion for 3–4 minutes or until it begins to soften. Add the ground spices and chilli flakes and stir until fragrant, then stir in the garlic, tomatoes and sugar and simmer for 5 minutes or until thickened.

4. Remove the pan from the heat. Stir in the eggplant, mint and coriander and serve.

> If you prefer, the eggplants can be cooked whole on a chargrill or barbecue. Turn them frequently until the skins are blackened, then remove them from the heat and allow to cool. Peel, discarding the skins, then chop the flesh into cubes.

---

* for the **Spiced strawberries with ricotta cream** recipe, see page 184

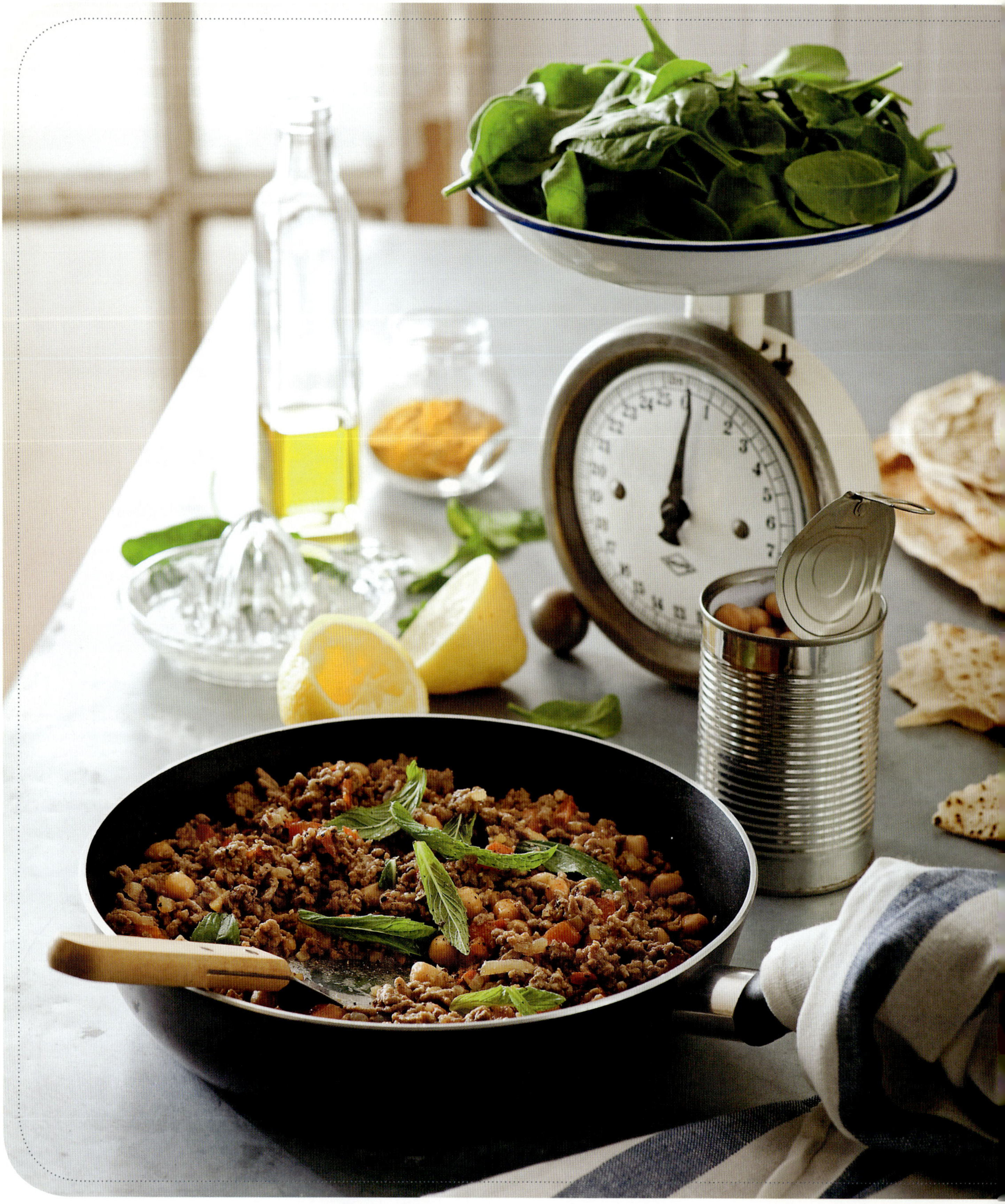

on a shoestring

Sometimes food costs can really add up, but here's your opportunity to make a little go a long way. These recipes, including aromatic curries and hearty roasts and soups, are big on flavour without blowing the budget.

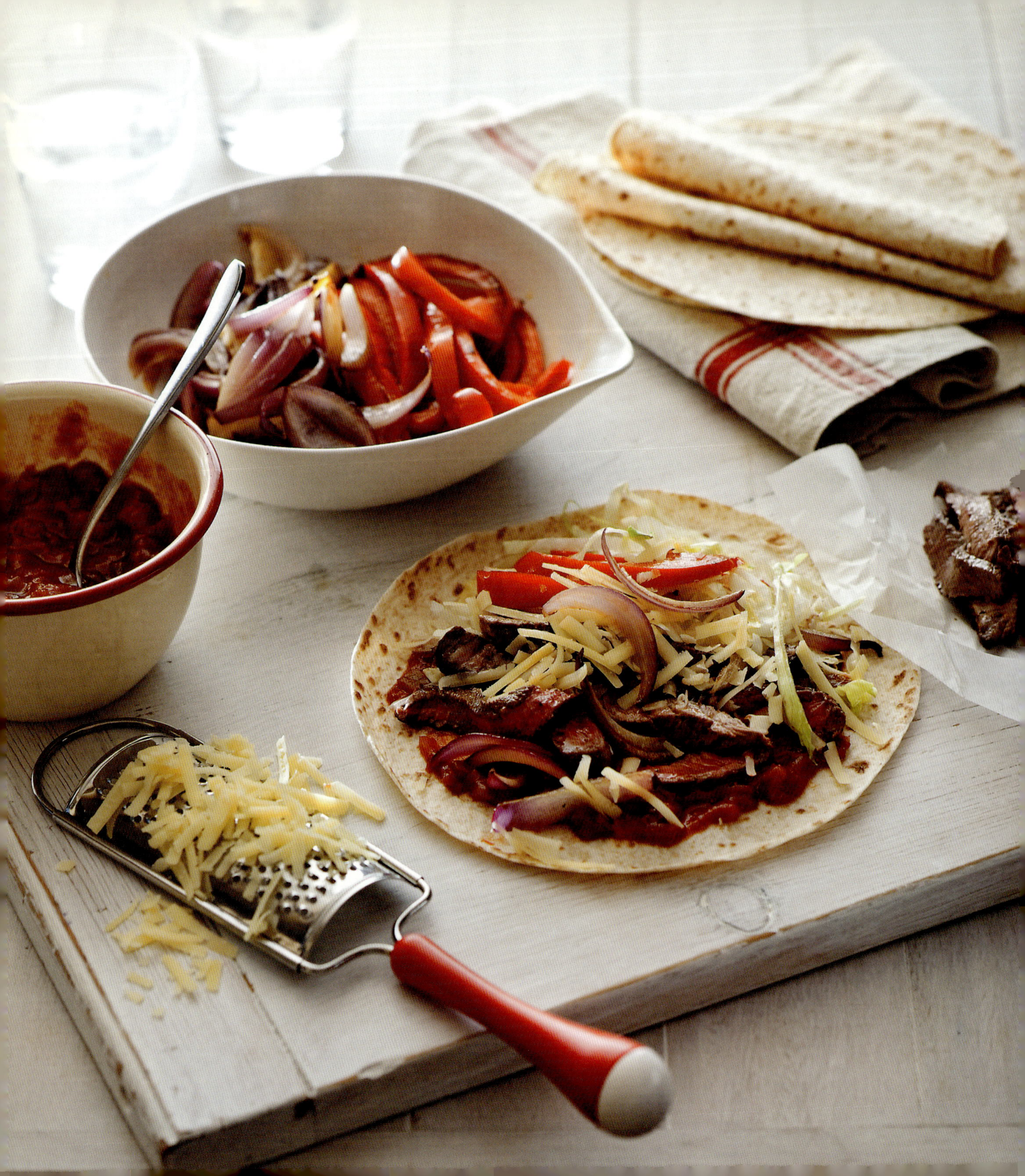

Beef fajitas

Kids love a hands-on approach to eating, so these sizzling fajitas are sure to be popular. Best of all, everyone can choose their own filling ingredients.

Serves 4

Prep time
20 minutes, plus marinating time

Cooking time
10 minutes

1 serve =
2 units protein
2 units bread
½ unit dairy
1 unit vegetables
1 unit fats

800 g rump or skirt steak
2 red capsicums (peppers), seeded and sliced
1 red (Spanish) onion, sliced
8 wholemeal wraps
shredded iceberg lettuce, to serve
ready-made tomato salsa, to serve
100 g grated reduced-fat cheddar

Marinade
1 tablespoon olive oil
3 tablespoons lime juice
2 teaspoons ground cumin
1 teaspoon dried oregano
2 teaspoons brown sugar

1. Combine the marinade ingredients in a bowl, add the steak and rub the marinade all over. Cover and marinate in the refrigerator for 2 hours or overnight.

2. Drain the steak. Heat a frying pan over medium heat and cook the steak for about 2 minutes each side. Remove and set aside to rest. Add the capsicum and onion to the pan and cook, stirring, until they start to colour and soften. Cut the steak into thin slices.

3. Warm the wraps in the microwave and top with the lettuce, steak, vegetables, salsa and grated cheese. Roll up and serve immediately.

* You can also make chicken fajitas based on this recipe – just substitute trimmed chicken or thigh breast fillet for the beef steak.

* For a quick homemade salsa, combine 4 diced tomatoes, ½ finely chopped onion and the juice of 1 lemon. Add a little finely sliced chilli to taste.

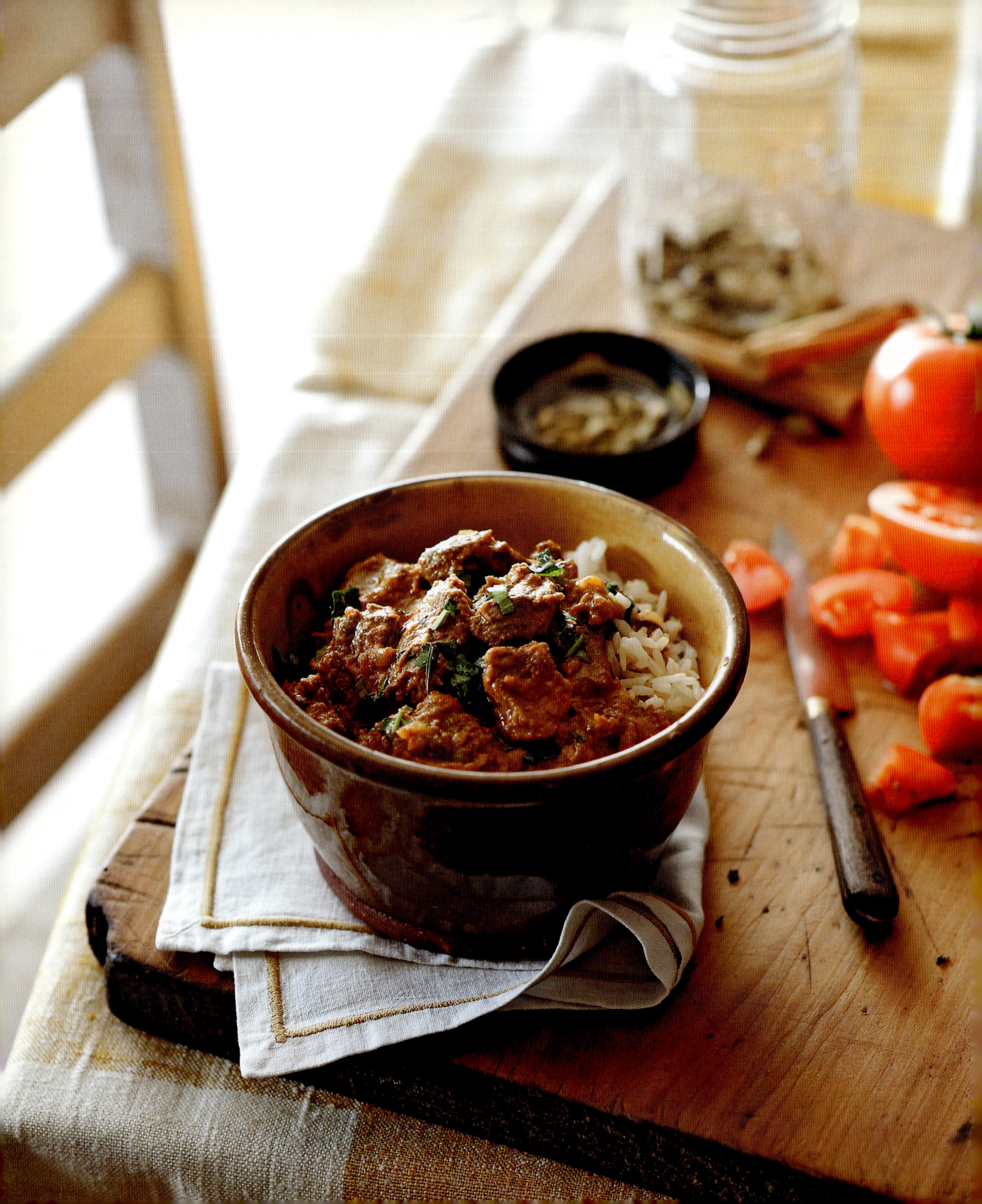

Beef rogan josh

Rogan josh is an aromatic North Indian curry. Not only is it much healthier to make your own (rather than having takeaway), you can also tailor the heat to suit your own taste. This curry is also delicious with lamb.

Serves 4

Prep time
15 minutes, plus marinating time

Cooking time
1 hour

1 serve =
2 units protein
¼ unit dairy
1 unit fats

* 1 unit vegetables with serving suggestion

- 800 g diced stewing beef, trimmed of fat
- 200 g reduced-fat natural yoghurt
- 1 tablespoon vegetable oil
- 1 onion, chopped
- 1 cinnamon stick
- 5 cardamom pods, bruised
- 1 teaspoon chilli powder, or to taste
- 1 teaspoon ground turmeric
- 3 cloves garlic, crushed
- 1 × 5 cm piece ginger, grated
- 3 tomatoes, diced
- 2 tablespoons tomato paste (puree)
- 4 tablespoons chopped coriander, plus extra to garnish
- 2 teaspoons garam masala

1. Combine the beef and yoghurt in a bowl and set aside for 30 minutes.

2. Heat the oil in a frying pan or medium saucepan with a tight-fitting lid over medium heat. Add the onion and cook, stirring, for about 10 minutes until golden. Add the spices, garlic and ginger and stir until fragrant. Stir in the beef and marinade, tomato and tomato paste.

3. Cover and cook over low heat for 40 minutes, checking from time to time and adding a little water if it starts to stick. When the beef is tender, add the coriander and garam masala. Garnish with extra coriander and serve with steamed rice from your daily bread allowance and steamed vegetables to the side.

> Although this is a mild curry, you can remove the chilli so it's absolutely kid-friendly. Likewise, you can increase the chilli according to taste.

on a shoestring

Vietnamese beef broth

Also known as beef pho, this broth packs in a lot of flavour. The stock is hot enough to cook the thinly sliced beef in the serving bowls, so there is no need to cook it separately.

Serves 4

Prep time
15 minutes

Cooking time
20 minutes

1 serve =
1 unit protein
1 unit bread
½ unit vegetables

✷ You can replace the rice noodles with any other type of thin noodles; for example, egg noodles.

1 litre salt-reduced beef stock
2 slices ginger
1 clove garlic, sliced
1 stalk lemongrass, lightly crushed with a knife
4 star anise
1 cinnamon stick
1 tablespoon fish sauce, plus extra to serve
1 tablespoon lime juice
1 teaspoon sugar
1 onion, thinly sliced
1⅓ cups (200 g) cooked rice noodles
400 g rump steak, trimmed of fat and thinly sliced
4 spring onions, finely sliced
½ cup (40 g) bean sprouts
large handful of Vietnamese mint or mint leaves
large handful of coriander leaves
lime wedges, to serve (optional)

1. Combine the stock, ginger, garlic, lemongrass, star anise, cinnamon, fish sauce, lime juice, sugar and onion in a saucepan and bring to the boil. Reduce the heat and simmer gently for about 15 minutes. Strain the broth, discarding the spices.

2. Divide the noodles among four serving bowls and top with the beef slices. Pour over the hot broth, then add the spring onion, bean sprouts and herbs. Serve with extra fish sauce and lime wedges, if you like.

Vietnamese mint has a strong peppery flavour and is widely available. If you can't find it, use regular mint instead.

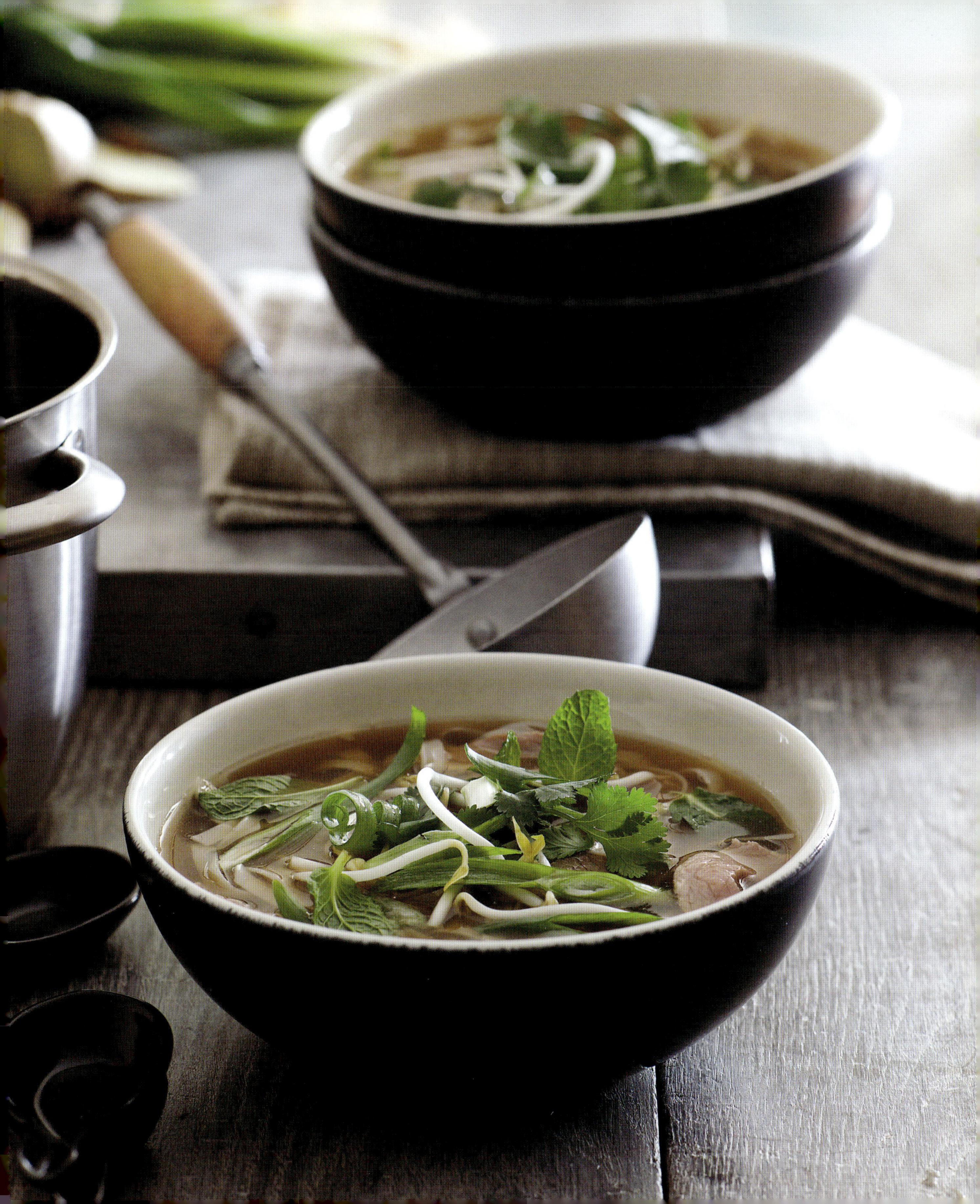

Play around with the flavour by using a variety of herbs — try rosemary or lemon thyme instead.

Slow-cooked lamb shoulder with pumpkin and feta salad

This is the perfect meal for the weekend, when you have time to potter about in the kitchen. After long, slow baking, the lamb is meltingly tender.

Serves 4

Prep time
20 minutes

Cooking time
3 hours 40 minutes

1 serve =
2 units protein
½ unit dairy
1½ units vegetables
1½ units fats

2 cloves garlic, crushed
grated zest and juice of 1 lemon
4 sprigs oregano, chopped
1 tablespoon extra virgin olive oil
800 g piece boned lamb shoulder, trimmed of fat (or use a shoulder with bone but allow for the weight of the bone)
½ cup (125 ml) salt-reduced chicken stock

Salad
300 g pumpkin (squash), cut into 2 cm dice
olive oil spray
250 g cherry or small tomatoes, halved
100 g baby spinach leaves
1 tablespoon balsamic vinegar
2 teaspoons extra virgin olive oil
100 g reduced-fat feta, crumbled

1. Preheat the oven to 160°C.
2. Combine the garlic, lemon zest and juice, oregano and olive oil in a bowl. Add the lamb and coat well. Season with salt and pepper.
3. Place the lamb and marinade in a baking dish, add the stock and cover tightly with foil or a tight-fitting lid. Bake for 3 hours.
4. Meanwhile, to prepare the salad, line a baking tray with baking paper. Place the pumpkin on the tray, spray lightly with olive oil and season.
5. Remove the foil or lid from the lamb and increase the oven temperature to 240°C. Place the pumpkin in the oven. Pour almost all of the liquid out of the baking dish and return the lamb to the oven for 10–15 minutes, or until the lamb is crisp on the outside.
6. Remove the lamb from the oven, cover loosely with foil and rest for 15–20 minutes. Reduce the temperature to 180°C, add the tomatoes to the pumpkin and bake for a further 15–20 minutes or until cooked.
7. Combine the pumpkin, tomatoes, spinach, vinegar and olive oil, then sprinkle with the feta. Serve with the lamb, drizzled with the baking juices.

* If you like, marinate the lamb for several hours or overnight for even more flavour.
* Bring the lamb to room temperature before placing in the oven to ensure the meat is evenly cooked.
* It is important to rest the meat after cooking – it will be more tender and easier to cut.

Moroccan lamb with chickpeas and spinach

This versatile lamb recipe may be served in a couple of different ways, so it's perfect for leftovers. The quantities can easily be doubled.

Serves 4

Prep time
15 minutes

Cooking time
15 minutes

1 serve =
2 units protein
1½ units bread
¼ unit dairy
½ unit vegetables
1 unit fats

1 tablespoon olive oil
1 onion, finely chopped
2 cloves garlic, crushed
700 g minced lamb
1 tablespoon Moroccan spice mix
3 tomatoes, diced
½ cup (125 ml) salt-reduced beef stock
130 g tinned chickpeas, rinsed and drained
½ cup (25 g) chopped mint
100 g baby spinach leaves
4 wholemeal pita breads
200 g reduced-fat natural yoghurt, mixed with 1 tablespoon lemon juice

1. Heat the olive oil in a non-stick frying pan over medium heat, add the onion and garlic and cook for 5 minutes or until softened. Increase the heat and add the mince, breaking up any lumps with the back of a wooden spoon. Cook until the mince is browned. Stir in the spice mix and cook for 1 minute, then add the tomato, stock and chickpeas. Cook until most of the liquid has evaporated, then stir in the mint.

2. Serve with the spinach leaves, pita bread and lemon yoghurt. Either use the pita bread as a wrap, or rip it into chip-sized pieces, toast under a grill or in the oven, and serve with the other ingredients, as you would with nachos.

Pan-fried lamb steaks with minted pea puree

This is a great example of how a few pantry staples can transform a straightforward meal into something special. If you can, marinate the steaks overnight to intensify the flavours.

Serves 4

Prep time
15 minutes, plus marinating time

Cooking time
20 minutes

1 serve =
2 units protein
½ unit vegetables*
1 unit fats

* or 1½ units with serving suggestion

1 tablespoon olive oil
1 tablespoon lemon juice
1 teaspoon dried mint
800 g lamb steaks, trimmed of fat

Minted pea puree
300 g frozen peas
1 clove garlic, crushed
⅔ cup (170 ml) salt-reduced chicken stock
small handful of finely chopped mint

1. Combine the olive oil, lemon juice and dried mint in a bowl. Add the lamb steaks and turn to coat. Cover and marinate in the refrigerator for 30 minutes, or longer if time permits.

2. To make the pea puree, combine the peas, garlic and stock in a medium saucepan. Bring to the boil, then reduce the heat and simmer for 15 minutes. Puree in a food processor. Season and stir in the mint.

3. Meanwhile, heat a non-stick frying pan over high heat and cook the lamb steaks for 3–4 minutes each side or until cooked to your liking. Rest for 5 minutes, then serve with the pea puree and steamed vegetables.

You might like to leave the mint out of the puree if fussy children object to it. It will still taste delicious.

Lamb skewers with lemon couscous and herbed yoghurt

Couscous is a fantastic side dish. It's ready in just a few minutes, and you can add all sorts of different flavourings to match the rest of the meal, such as grated lemon or lime zest, a touch of ground spice or a handful of finely chopped fresh herbs.

Serves 4

Prep time
15 minutes, plus marinating time

Cooking time
10 minutes

1 serve =
2 units protein
1 unit bread
¼ unit dairy
1 unit fats

* 1 unit vegetables with serving suggestion

800 g lean lamb steaks, diced
1 tablespoon olive oil
2 cloves garlic, crushed
2 tablespoons lemon juice
1 teaspoon ground coriander
½ teaspoon ground turmeric
lemon wedges, to serve

Herbed yoghurt
200 g reduced-fat natural yoghurt
1 tablespoon chopped coriander
1 tablespoon chopped mint
1 clove garlic, crushed

Lemon couscous
1 cup (200 g) couscous
1 cup (250 ml) salt-reduced chicken stock
2 teaspoons grated lemon zest
2 tablespoons chopped mixed herbs (such as coriander and mint)

1. Combine the lamb, olive oil, garlic, lemon juice, ground coriander and turmeric in a bowl. Cover and set aside for 30 minutes or marinate in the refrigerator for longer if time permits.

2. To prepare the herbed yoghurt, combine all the ingredients in a bowl.

3. Preheat a chargrill or grill to medium. Thread the lamb onto skewers and cook for 2–3 minutes each side or until cooked to your liking.

4. Meanwhile, place the couscous in a heatproof bowl. Bring the stock to the boil and pour over the couscous, then cover and set aside for 5 minutes. Fluff up the couscous with a fork and stir in the lemon zest and and herbs.

5. Serve the lamb skewers with the couscous, herbed yoghurt, lemon wedges and salad or steamed vegetables.

> Soak wooden skewers in water for 30 minutes before threading on the lamb, to prevent scorching when grilling.

If you don't want to use skewers, trimmed lamb chops or cutlets may be used in place of the steaks.

Fennel roasted pork with mustard cabbage

Pork and apple is a classic combination, enhanced here by the aniseed flavour of the fennel.

Serves 4

Prep time
15 minutes

Cooking time
2 hours

1 serve =
2 units protein
½ unit fruit
1 unit vegetables
1½ units fats

3 teaspoons ground fennel
3 cloves garlic, crushed
1 tablespoon extra virgin olive oil
800 g piece pork neck, trimmed of fat
½ cup (125 ml) salt-reduced chicken stock
2 apples, peeled, quartered and cored

Mustard cabbage
2 teaspoons extra virgin olive oil
1 small onion, thinly sliced
1 clove garlic, crushed
½ savoy cabbage, core removed and thinly sliced
1 tablespoon seeded mustard

1. Preheat the oven to 130°C.

2. Combine the fennel, garlic and olive oil to make a paste. Place the pork in a roasting tin and rub all over with the fennel paste. Season with salt and pepper. Pour in the stock, then cover tightly with foil and roast for 1½ hours.

3. Increase the oven temperature to 220°C. Remove the foil and add the apples to the roasting tin. Return to the oven for 20 minutes, then remove the pork and apples from the tin, cover them loosely with foil and set aside. Drain the juices from the roasting tin into a small saucepan.

4. To prepare the cabbage, heat the olive oil in a heavy-based frying pan, add the onion and stir until it just starts to colour. Add the garlic and cabbage and cook, stirring, for 10 minutes or until just tender. Stir in the mustard and season to taste.

5. Simmer the meat juices until reduced and slightly thickened, then serve with the sliced pork, apples and cabbage.

* Take the pork out of the refrigerator and bring it to room temperature before cooking – this will ensure even cooking.

* Resting time after cooking is important as it allows the juices to settle, making the meat more tender and easier to slice.

* Leftover pork can be used for sandwiches the next day – it's delicious with mustard and salad.

Spicy roasted cauliflower

This simple recipe makes a delicious accompaniment for grilled chicken, lamb or fish. If you don't have any Cajun spice mix in the pantry, use Moroccan spice mix or curry powder instead.

Serves 4

Prep time
5 minutes

Cooking time
30 minutes

1 serve =
1 unit vegetables
1 unit fats

1 small or ½ large cauliflower, cut into florets
1 tablespoon extra virgin olive oil
1 tablespoon Cajun spice mix
reduced-fat natural yoghurt, to serve (optional)

1. Preheat the oven to 200°C and line a baking tray with baking paper.
2. Combine the cauliflower, olive oil and spice mix in a bowl and toss to coat. Place the cauliflower on the tray in a single layer and roast for 30 minutes or until well coloured, turning once or twice.
3. Serve with a dollop of yoghurt, if desired, and protein from your daily allowance.

Stir-fried beans, mushrooms and asparagus

This is a delicious combination, but the ingredients given below are just suggestions – vary the vegetables according to what you have to hand, and where possible use a mixture of mushrooms for added interest.

Serves 4

Prep time
10 minutes

Cooking time
5 minutes

1 serve =
1½ units vegetables
1 unit fats

1 tablespoon olive oil
250 g green beans or snake beans, trimmed and cut into 5 cm lengths
150 g mushrooms, halved if large
1 bunch asparagus, trimmed and halved
2 cloves garlic, crushed
1 tablespoon grated ginger
4 spring onions, sliced
1 tablespoon oyster sauce
2 tablespoons soy sauce
3 tablespoons salt-reduced chicken stock or water
coriander leaves, to serve (optional)

1. Heat the olive oil in a wok or frying pan over high heat. Add the beans, mushrooms and asparagus and stir-fry for 3 minutes or until the vegetables are just starting to colour (you may need to do this in two batches to maintain the heat).
2. Add the garlic, ginger and spring onion and cook for 30 seconds until fragrant. Pour in the oyster sauce, soy sauce and stock or water and toss until heated through. Serve immediately, garnished with coriander leaves (if using), with protein from your daily allowance.

Kangaroo steak with white bean mash and chargrilled vegetables

White bean mash makes a great alternative to mashed potato – it is thick, creamy and comforting, and extremely good for you.

Serves 4

Prep time
15 minutes, plus marinating time

Cooking time
25 minutes

1 serve =
1½ units protein
1 unit bread
1 unit vegetables*
1 unit fats

* or 2 units with serving suggestion

1 tablespoon olive oil
1 tablespoon red wine vinegar
3 teaspoons Dijon mustard
2 cloves garlic, crushed
600 g kangaroo steaks or fillets
1 red capsicum (pepper), seeded and quartered
3 zucchini (courgettes), sliced
3 finger eggplants (aubergines), sliced
olive oil spray

White bean mash
1 × 400 g tin cannellini beans, rinsed and drained
100 ml salt-reduced chicken stock
1 clove garlic, crushed

1. Combine the olive oil, vinegar, mustard and garlic in a bowl. Add the steaks and rub the marinade all over. Cover and marinate in the refrigerator for up to 24 hours.

2. To make the mash, place the beans, stock and garlic in a small saucepan and bring to a simmer over medium heat. Cook for 10 minutes, then transfer to a food processor and puree (or mash with a potato masher).

3. Heat a chargrill or frying pan over medium–high heat. Spray the vegetables with olive oil and cook each side until golden and tender. Remove from the pan and keep warm. Spray the steaks with olive oil and chargrill or pan-fry for 3–4 minutes each side, depending on thickness – you want them to be quite rare, otherwise the meat will be dry. Serve with the vegetables and white bean mash, and a green salad to the side.

* It is very easy to buy kangaroo these days – look for it in the meat section of your local supermarket. If you prefer, you can use beef or lamb in its place.

* You can use red kidney beans or a tinned bean mix instead of the cannellini beans if you like.

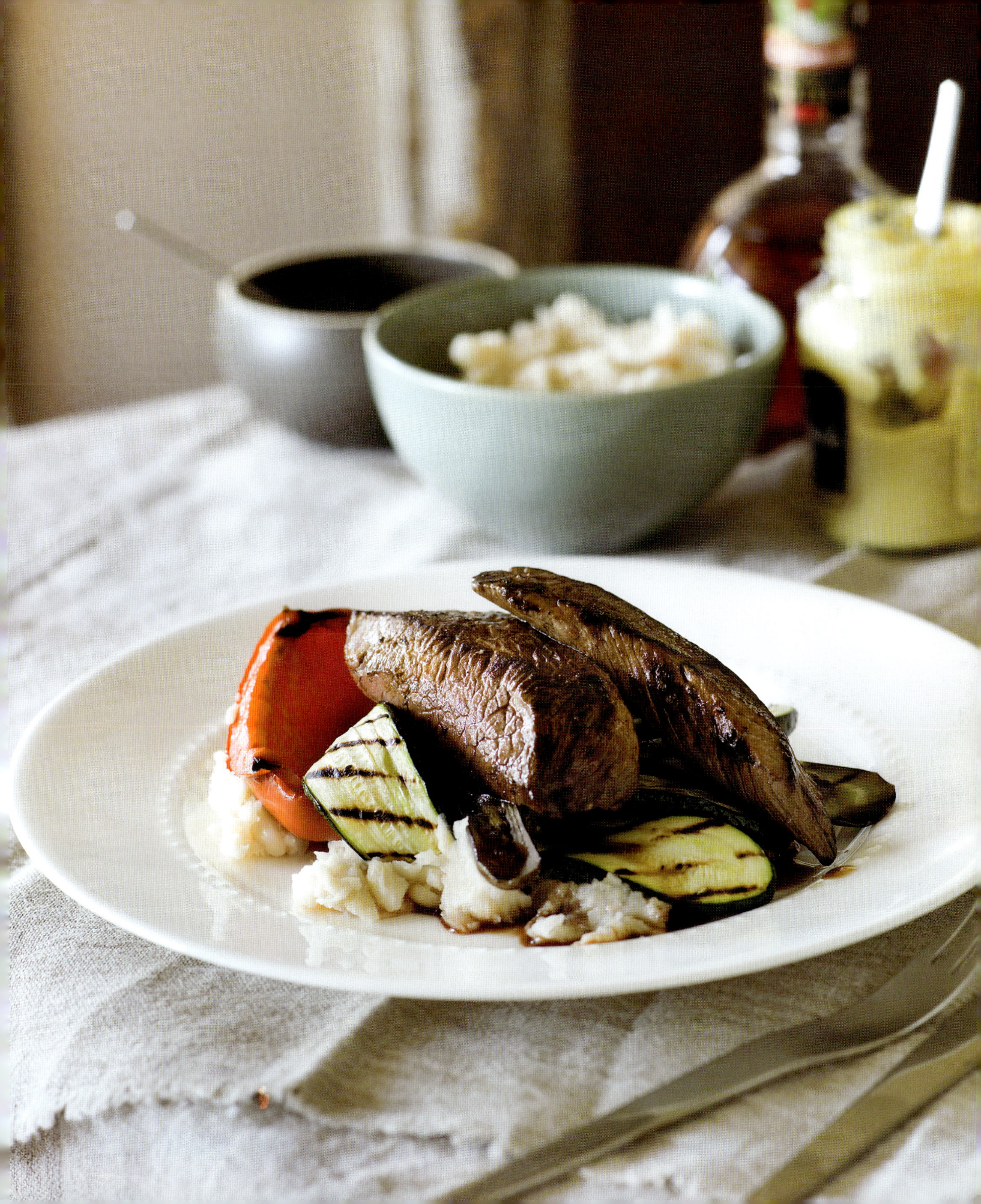

Coconut-flavoured evaporated milk is available from your local supermarket in the long-life milk section.

Chicken laksa

Laksa is traditionally made with full-fat coconut milk, which has made it off-limits for those watching their weight; this light version puts it firmly back on the menu.

Serves 4

Prep time
10 minutes

Cooking time
15 minutes

1 serve =
1 unit protein
1 unit bread
¼ unit dairy
1 unit vegetables
1 unit fats

60 g rice vermicelli noodles
1 tablespoon vegetable oil
2 tablespoons laksa paste or red curry paste (or more to taste)
2½ cups (625 ml) salt-reduced chicken stock
400 g chicken breast fillet, thinly sliced
100 g shiitake mushrooms, sliced if large
1 cup (250 ml) reduced-fat coconut-flavoured evaporated milk
100 g Chinese greens, sliced (such as pak choy or bok choy)
100 g shiitake mushrooms (or other mushrooms)
2 kaffir lime leaves, shredded (optional)
½ cup (15 g) roughly torn coriander
50 g bean sprouts
sliced cucumber, red chilli, lime wedges and fish sauce, to serve (optional)

1. Prepare the noodles according to the packet instructions.

2. Heat the oil in a large saucepan over medium heat. Add the paste and cook, stirring, for 2–3 minutes or until fragrant.

3. Pour in the stock and bring to the boil, then reduce the heat and simmer for 5 minutes. Add the chicken, mushrooms and milk and simmer for 5 minutes or until the chicken is just cooked. Add the Chinese greens, mushrooms, lime leaves and noodles.

4. Divide the laksa, coriander and bean sprouts among four bowls and finish with cucumber, chilli, lime juice and fish sauce, to taste.

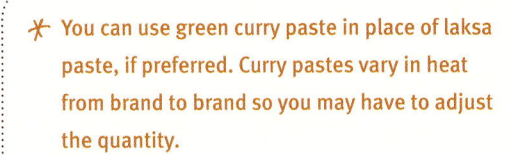

> ✶ You can use green curry paste in place of laksa paste, if preferred. Curry pastes vary in heat from brand to brand so you may have to adjust the quantity.

Chicken breasts stuffed with feta and olive tapenade

These chicken breasts taste as good as they look, and are perfect for an informal dinner with friends. Prepare them in advance, then pan-fry them when you're ready to eat.

Serves 4

Prep time
15 minutes

Cooking time
10 minutes

1 serve =
2 units protein
½ unit dairy
½ unit vegetables*

* or 1½ units with serving suggestion

- 4 × 200 g chicken breast fillets
- 100 g reduced-fat feta, crumbled
- 1 clove garlic, crushed
- 2 tablespoons olive tapenade
- 4 large basil leaves, plus extra to serve
- olive oil spray
- 200 g green beans, trimmed
- 1 tablespoon balsamic vinegar

1. Cut a deep pocket into the thickest side of the chicken breasts to create a pocket.

2. Combine the feta, tapenade and garlic in a bowl. Place a basil leaf in each pocket, then divide the feta mix among the pockets. Secure with a skewer, then lightly spray the chicken pieces with olive oil.

3. Heat a non-stick frying pan over medium heat and pan-fry the chicken for 5 minutes each side or until cooked through (the time can vary, depending on the thickness of the breasts).

4. Meanwhile, blanch the beans in boiling water for 1–2 minutes (or cook them in a microwave). Drain and toss with the balsamic vinegar.

5. Garnish the chicken with extra basil leaves and serve with the green beans and a green salad.

> To make your own olive tapenade, process 1 cup (150 g) pitted Kalamata olives, 2 chopped anchovy fillets, ½ small clove garlic, chopped, 2 tablespoons rinsed capers and 1 tablespoon olive oil to a coarse puree. Stir in 2 teaspoons sherry vinegar, to taste. Season with freshly ground black pepper. Serve any leftovers as a dip or sandwich spread.

Try sun-dried tomato paste or pesto if the kids don't like the taste of olives.

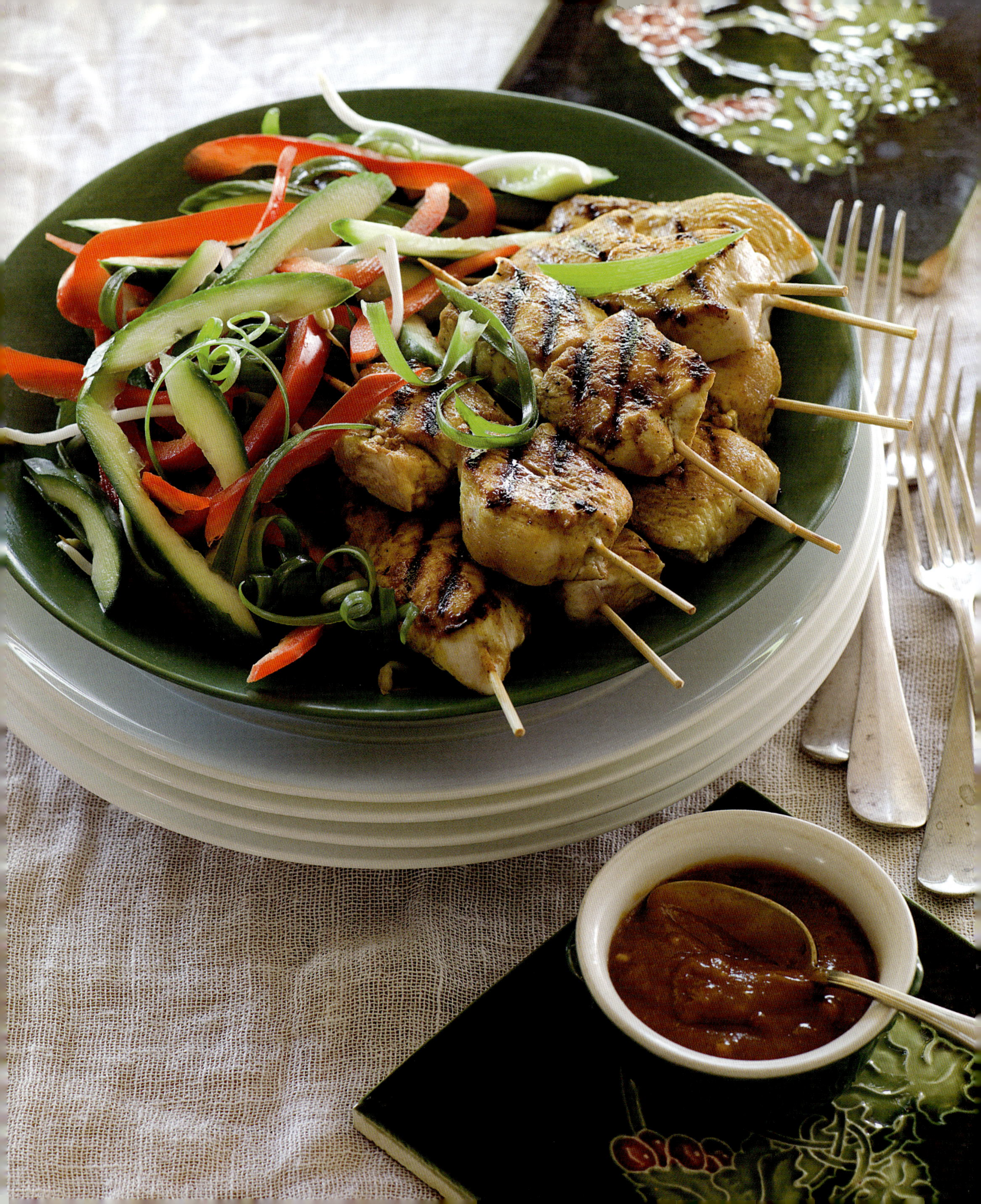

Chicken satay with peanut sauce

The peanut sauce is only mildly spicy, so the whole family can tuck into this popular dish with confidence. Any leftover satay sticks would make a great lunchbox addition.

Serves 4

Prep time
25 minutes, plus marinating time

Cooking time
10 minutes

1 serve =
2 units protein
1 unit vegetables
1 unit fats

✳ If you feel like a change, swap the chicken for diced beef or pork.

800 g chicken breast fillets, cut into 1 cm thick pieces
2 tablespoons soy sauce
2 tablespoons lime juice
2 cloves garlic, crushed
1 tablespoon vegetable oil
2 teaspoons mild curry powder
small handful of coriander leaves, to serve (optional)

Peanut sauce
1 tablespoon oyster sauce
1 tablespoon peanut butter
2 tablespoons sweet chilli sauce
1 tablespoon lime juice

Cucumber salad
1 Lebanese (small) cucumber, seeded and cut into thin strips
100 g bean sprouts
2 spring onions, thinly sliced
1 red capsicum (pepper), thinly sliced
1 tablespoon lime juice
1 teaspoon light soy sauce

1. Place the chicken, soy sauce, lime juice, garlic, oil and curry powder in a bowl and mix well. Cover and marinate in the refrigerator for at least 1 hour.

2. To make the peanut sauce, combine all the ingredients in a bowl. If you want to heat the sauce to serve, warm gently in a microwave.

3. To prepare the salad, toss all the ingredients together.

4. Heat a barbecue or chargrill to medium. Thread the chicken onto skewers and cook for 3–4 minutes each side or until cooked through. Garnish with coriander leaves (if using) and serve with the peanut sauce and cucumber salad.

✳ Many kids love peanut sauce, but for those who have a peanut allergy, the skewers are just as delicious served with sweet chilli sauce instead.

✳ If you're using bamboo skewers, soak them in water for 20 minutes or so before use to prevent scorching while grilling. You'll need 16 skewers for this recipe.

Chicken noodle soup

This classic soup is a favourite with all ages.

Serves 4

Prep time
15 minutes

Cooking time
30 minutes

1 serve =
2 units protein
1½ units bread
1½ units vegetables
1 unit fats

- 1 tablespoon olive oil
- 1 onion, chopped
- 2 carrots, diced
- 2 sticks celery, diced
- 2 potatoes, peeled and diced
- 3 cloves garlic, sliced
- 1 teaspoon dried thyme
- 2 litres salt-reduced chicken stock
- 800 g chicken breast fillets, diced
- 120 g thin noodles or spaghettini
- 1 cup (200 g) corn kernels (tinned or frozen)
- 3 tablespoons chopped flat-leaf parsley

1. Heat the olive oil in a large saucepan. Add the onion, carrot, celery and potato and cook, stirring, for 5 minutes or until the vegetables are starting to soften. Stir in the garlic and thyme. Add the stock and chicken and simmer for 15 minutes or until the vegetables are soft.

2. Add the noodles and corn and cook for 10 minutes or until cooked through. Add 1–2 cups (250–500 ml) water if the soup is too thick. Stir in the parsley and serve immediately.

> ✴ If you want to make a big batch of this soup to freeze some for later, stop at the end of step 1. The noodles and corn can be added when you are reheating the soup.
>
> ✴ Other pastas, such as macaroni or spirals, can be used in place of the spaghetti, and try adding other vegetables too.

Turkey escalopes with Asian vegetables

Escalopes are thin slices of meat. They are often served crumbed, but here they are marinated in rice wine, soy, ginger, garlic and honey and quickly stir-fried in a wok.

Serves 4

Prep time
15 minutes, plus marinating time

Cooking time
15 minutes

1 serve =
2 units protein
1 unit vegetables
1 unit fats

3 tablespoons Chinese cooking wine or sherry
4 tablespoons soy sauce
2 cloves garlic, crushed
2 teaspoons grated ginger
1 tablespoon honey
800 g turkey breast, cut into 5 mm slices
1 tablespoon vegetable oil
1 small red chilli, seeded and sliced
150 g mushrooms, sliced
1 bunch baby bok choy, quartered
4 spring onions, sliced
coriander leaves, to serve

1. Mix together the cooking wine, soy sauce, garlic, ginger and honey. Add the turkey and stir to coat, then cover and leave to marinate for 30 minutes. Remove the turkey, reserving the marinade.

2. Heat the oil in a wok or frying pan over high heat and stir-fry the turkey in batches. Remove and set aside. Add the chilli and mushrooms to the wok and stir-fry for 2 minutes, then add the bok choy, spring onion and reserved marinade. Cook until the bok choy is just wilted.

3. Serve the turkey escalopes with the stir-fried vegetables, topped with coriander leaves, and rice from your daily allowance.

* You can substitute trimmed chicken breast or thigh fillet for the turkey, if liked.

* Chinese cooking wine (also known as shaohsing rice wine) is available from Asian food stores. If you can't find it, use sherry instead.

on a shoestring 107

Salmon fishcakes with lemon yoghurt sauce

Simple but delicious, the fresh flavours in this meal should ideally be enjoyed outside on a warm evening.

Serves 4

Prep time
25 minutes, plus refrigerating time

Cooking time
10 minutes

1 serve =
1 unit protein
½ unit bread
¼ unit dairy
1 unit vegetables

1 × 800 g tin salmon, drained, bones and skin removed and mashed (this will yield approximately 400 g salmon)
2 spring onions, finely chopped
1 teaspoon finely grated lemon zest
1 tablespoon finely chopped flat-leaf parsley
½ teaspoon Worcestershire sauce
1 teaspoon Dijon mustard
2 eggs
80 g dried breadcrumbs
1 teaspoon olive oil

Lemon yoghurt sauce
200 g reduced-fat yoghurt
2 teaspoons lemon juice
1 teaspoon finely grated lemon zest

Mixed leaf and tomato salad
100 g mixed salad leaves
1 punnet (250 g) grape tomatoes, halved
1 Lebanese (small) cucumber, thinly sliced
¼ red (Spanish) onion, thinly sliced
1 teaspoon capers, rinsed and drained
1 tablespoon lemon juice

1 To make the fishcakes, combine all the ingredients, except for the breadcrumbs and olive oil, in a large bowl. Form into 12 patties with clean hands. Cover with plastic wrap and refrigerate for 1 hour.

2 To make the lemon yoghurt sauce, combine all the ingredients in a small bowl and mix well.

3 To make the mixed leaf and tomato salad, gently toss together all the ingredients.

4 Place the breadcrumbs in a small bowl and dip the fishcakes in, coating on all sides.

5 Heat the olive oil in a large frying pan over medium heat and cook the patties for 2 minutes each side, or until golden (you may need to do this in batches). Serve the fishcakes with a dollop of sauce and the salad to the side.

If preferred, the lemon yoghurt sauce can be replaced with reduced-fat mayonnaise.

Squid salad with rocket and chickpeas

The chickpeas may seem like an unusual ingredient here, but they add a mealy texture that contrasts well with the crispness of the salad.

Serves 4

Prep time
20 minutes

Cooking time
5 minutes

1 serve =
2 units protein
1 unit bread
1½ units vegetables
1 unit fats

✻ Prawns may be used in place of the squid.

800 g squid hoods, cleaned, cut into pieces and scored
2 teaspoons olive oil
½ teaspoon chilli flakes (optional)
100 g baby rocket leaves
1 × 400 g tin chickpeas, rinsed and drained
2 tomatoes, diced
½ red (Spanish) onion, thinly sliced
1 Lebanese (small) cucumber, diced
½ cup (10 g) torn flat-leaf parsley

Dressing
3 tablespoons lemon juice
2 teaspoons olive oil
1 clove garlic, crushed

1. To make the dressing, place all the ingredients in a screw-top jar and shake to combine.

2. Season the squid with salt and pepper and place in a bowl with the olive oil and chilli (if using). Gently toss to coat. Heat a non-stick frying pan over medium–high heat and cook the squid for 2 minutes each side or until just cooked (you may need to do this in batches).

3. While still hot, toss the squid in the dressing.

4. Divide the rocket among four plates, top with the chickpeas, tomato, onion, cucumber and parsley, and finish with the squid and dressing. Serve immediately.

✻ Squid can be purchased already cleaned, but if you prefer to do this yourself, simply grasp the body with one hand and the head with another and gently pull apart. Discard the quill and insides and peel off the outer skin.

✻ You can also buy squid as rings, and these are fine to use in the recipe.

Steamed mussels with spaghetti

This speedy dish is ready in the time it takes to cook the spaghetti. To reduce your prep time, buy mussels that have already been cleaned (available in cryovac packs from fishmongers and some supermarkets).

Serves 4
Prep time
15 minutes
Cooking time
20 minutes
1 serve =
1 unit protein
2 units bread
* 1 unit vegetables with serving suggestion

200 g spaghetti
750 g tomato passata
1 cup (250 ml) white wine
2 cloves garlic, crushed
2 kg mussels, cleaned and debearded
4 tablespoons roughly chopped basil, plus extra leaves to garnish
Tabasco sauce, to serve (optional)

1 Cook the spaghetti according to the packet instructions. Drain.

2 Meanwhile, place the passata, wine and garlic in a wide saucepan or deep frying pan and bring to the boil over high heat.

3 Add the mussels and cover with a tight-fitting lid. Cook for 3–4 minutes or until all the mussels have opened (discard any that do not open). Remove from the heat and stir in the basil and spaghetti. Garnish with extra basil leaves and serve hot with Tabasco, if desired, and salad.

Steamed tofu with Asian greens

This light and delicate dish works really well as a balanced meat-free option for lunch or dinner.

Serves 4
Prep time
10 minutes
Cooking time
15 minutes
1 serve =
2 units protein
1 unit vegetables
1 unit fats

800 g silken tofu, drained
2 teaspoons sesame oil
2 teaspoons vegetable oil
100 ml light soy sauce
2 teaspoons oyster sauce
1 red chilli, seeded and finely chopped
4 spring onions, finely sliced
handful of coriander leaves
8 baby bok choy or other Asian greens, steamed or blanched

1 Pour water into the base of a steamer or a wok with a steamer basket and bring to the boil. Place the tofu on a plate which will fit in the steamer and cut it into 4 cm pieces but do not break apart. Cover and steam for about 10 minutes, then drain the liquid from the steamed tofu.

2 Meanwhile, heat the oils, soy sauce and oyster sauce in a small saucepan. Stir in the chilli and spring onion, then remove from the heat.

3 Pour the sauce over the tofu and sprinkle with coriander leaves. Serve with the Asian greens and rice from your daily bread allowance.

* To save time and to increase the vegetable content of the meal, steam an assortment of chopped vegetables with the tofu.

* Passata is a tomato puree also sold as sugo or pasta sauce. Look for it in the pasta sauce section at the supermarket.

* To clean the mussels, first discard any open or broken mussels, then scrub the hairy beard from the outside.

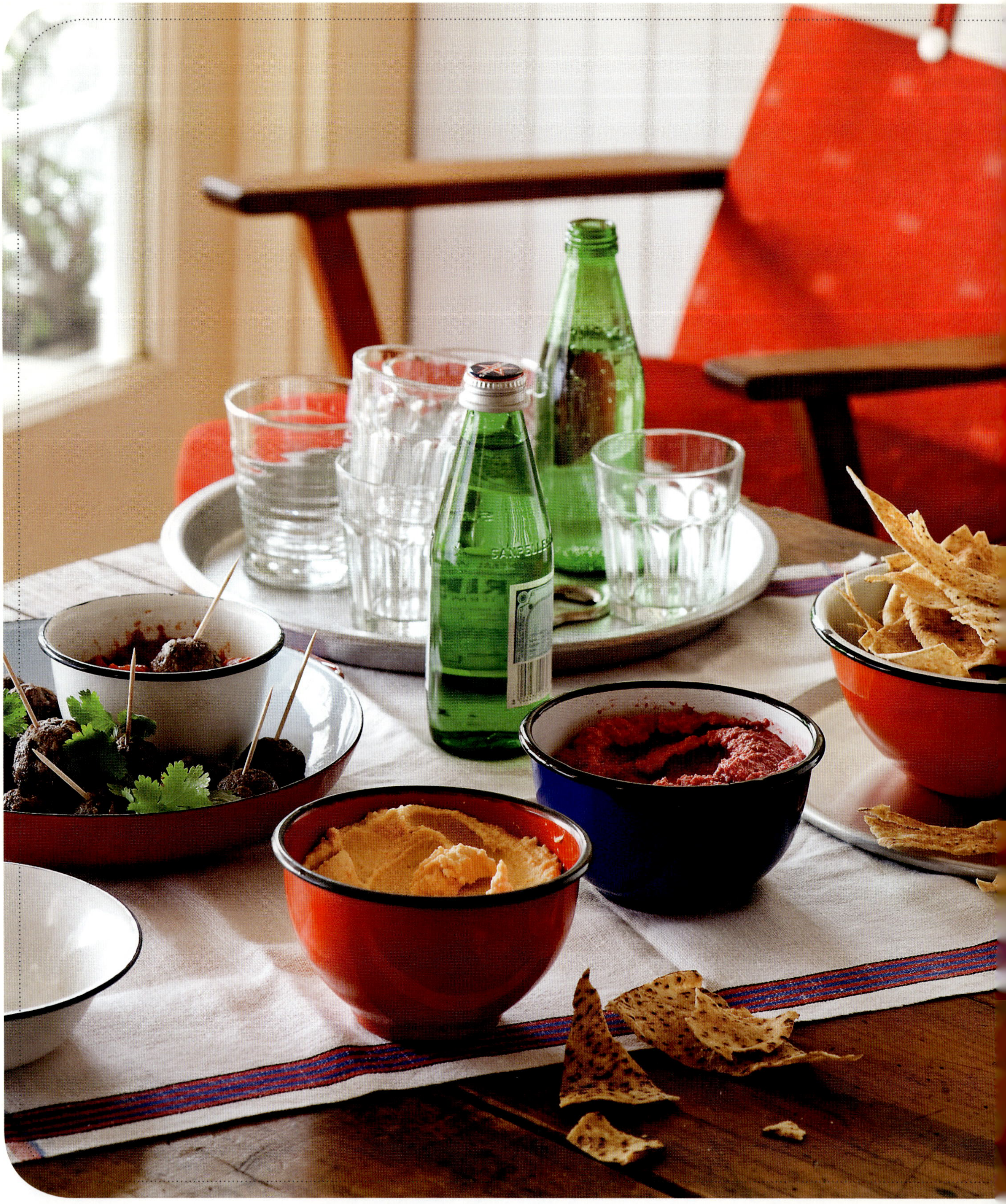

watching sport get-together

These healthy, tasty nibbles can be made ahead of time so no one misses out on the action.

Beetroot dip with pita chips

Grilled eggplant dip

Hummus

Spicy meatballs with chilli tomato sauce

Homemade pizza

Beetroot dip with pita chips

A delicious dip with a fabulous colour. And the good thing about making it yourself is that you know exactly what went into it.

Serves 4

Prep time
10 minutes

Cooking time
10 minutes

1 serve =
1 unit bread
¼ unit dairy
¼ unit vegetables

4 wholemeal pita breads
olive oil spray
1 × 450 g tin baby beetroot, drained
200 g reduced-fat natural yoghurt
1 clove garlic, crushed
2 tablespoons lemon juice
1 teaspoon ground cumin

1. Preheat the oven to 180°C. Split the pita breads in half and cut them into pieces. Spray with olive oil and place on a baking tray in a single layer. Bake for 10 minutes or until crisp.

2. Place the remaining ingredients in a food processor and process until smooth. Serve the beetroot dip with the pita chips.

Grilled eggplant dip

Roasting the eggplant until the skin is black and blistered may look alarming, but this is what gives the dip its unique smoky flavour.

Serves 4

Prep time
10 minutes

Cooking time
20 minutes

1 serve =
¼ unit vegetables
1 unit fats

1 large eggplant (aubergine)
olive oil spray
1 tablespoon extra virgin olive oil
1 onion, finely chopped
2 cloves garlic, crushed
½ teaspoon ground cumin
2 tablespoons lemon juice

1. Heat a chargrill or barbecue to medium–hot.

2. Spray the eggplant with olive oil and grill, turning, for 15 minutes or until the skin is blackened all over. Cool slightly then peel away the blackened skin. Discard the skin and mash the flesh with a fork in a bowl.

3. Heat the olive oil in a medium saucepan over medium heat and cook the onion until soft. Add the garlic and cumin and cook for a minute longer. Add the onion mixture and lemon juice to the mashed eggplant and mix well. Season to taste and serve with vegetables cut into sticks or wholemeal pita bread from your daily bread allowance.

> If you prefer, you can also cook the eggplant under a grill or roast it in a preheated 200°C oven for 50 minutes.

Hummus

Taste this as you go and add more lemon juice or chilli to suit your palate.
Include any leftover dip in a salad sandwich or wrap the next day.

Serves 4

Prep time
10 minutes

1 serve =
½ unit protein
1½ units fats

- 1 × 400 g tin chickpeas, rinsed and drained
- 2 cloves garlic, crushed
- 3 tablespoons lemon juice
- 2 tablespoons tahini
- ½ teaspoon chilli powder (optional)

1. Process all the ingredients in a food processor until smooth, adding a little water if it's too thick. Season to taste, then serve with vegetables cut into sticks or wholemeal pita bread from your daily bread allowance.

> Hailing from the Middle East, tahini is a smooth, thick paste made from hulled and ground sesame seeds. It is available from most supermarkets and health-food shops.

Spicy meatballs with chilli tomato sauce

A simplified version of the popular classic dish, the meatballs are baked in the oven then added to a homemade sauce to serve.

Serves 4

Prep time
10 minutes

Cooking time
25 minutes

1 serve =
1 unit protein
¼ unit vegetables

- 400 g lean minced beef or chicken
- 1 small onion, grated
- 1 clove garlic, crushed
- 1 teaspoon ground coriander
- 1 teaspoon ground cumin
- ¼ teaspoon ground cinnamon
- ½ teaspoon chilli powder (or to taste)
- 1 tablespoon chopped coriander

Chilli tomato sauce
- 1 × 400 g tin chopped tomatoes
- 1 tablespoon brown sugar
- 1 tablespoon white wine vinegar
- 2 small red chillies, seeded and finely chopped

1. Preheat the oven to 180°C and line a baking tray with baking paper.

2. Place the beef or chicken, onion, garlic, ground spices, chilli powder and chopped coriander in a food processor and process until well combined. Roll tablespoons of the meat mixture into balls and place on the prepared baking tray. Bake for about 20–25 minutes or until cooked through, turning from time to time.

3. Meanwhile, combine the chilli tomato sauce ingredients in a saucepan. Bring to the boil, then reduce the heat and simmer for 15 minutes or until thickened. Season to taste and serve with the meatballs.

Homemade pizza dough

There's no need to be daunted by the idea of making your own pizza dough. The recipe below is clear and straightforward, and the delectable results will make you so pleased you took the time.

Serves 4

Prep time
25 minutes, plus standing time

Cooking time
20 minutes

1 serve =
2 units bread

1½ teaspoons dried yeast
½ teaspoon sugar
1½ cups (240 g) wholemeal plain flour
½ cup (75 g) plain flour
olive oil spray

If you don't have time to make the pizza base, you can use wholemeal pita or mountain bread instead.

1. Combine the yeast and sugar with 1 cup (250 ml) warm water in a small bowl. Set aside for 10 minutes or until frothy.

2. Place the flours in a large bowl, add the yeast mixture and mix with clean hands to form a dough. Turn out onto a floured surface and knead for several minutes until the dough is smooth and elastic and springs back when pressed.

3. Spray a large, clean bowl with olive oil and add the dough. Cover with a clean tea towel and set aside for 45–60 minutes or until the dough has doubled in size.

4. Preheat the oven to 220°C. Dust a large baking tray or two pizza trays with flour.

5. Turn out the dough onto a lightly floured surface and punch it down. Roll out to a 40 cm × 30 cm rectangle, or divide the dough in half and roll to make two 25 cm round pizza bases. Transfer the dough to the prepared tray or trays and add your choice of toppings (see facing page). Bake for 15–20 minutes or until the base is crisp and cooked through.

Hawaiian

1 serve =
1 unit protein
¼ unit dairy
¼ unit fruit

Spread ⅔ cup (170 g) salt-reduced tomato passata or pasta sauce over the pizza base, then sprinkle evenly with 400 g roughly chopped reduced-fat ham, 150 g peeled, cored and diced fresh pineapple and 100 g grated reduced-fat mozzarella. Bake according to the pizza dough recipe instructions.

✻ You can use tomato paste (puree) in place of tomato passata or pasta sauce, but you will only need about half of the amount as it is a lot thicker and richer.

✻ After cooking, sprinkle with fresh herbs or rocket.

Spinach and ricotta

1 serve =
1 unit dairy
½ unit vegetables

Spread ⅔ cup (170 g) salt-reduced tomato passata or pasta sauce over the pizza base, then sprinkle evenly with 2 large handfuls baby spinach leaves, 200 g reduced-fat ricotta and 100 g pitted black olives. Bake according to the pizza dough recipe instructions.

✻ You can add smoked salmon and/or semi-dried tomatoes to this pizza, if liked.

✻ Sprinkle your cooked pizza with fresh herbs or rocket and perhaps drizzle with a little balsamic vinegar.

Margherita

1 serve =
1 unit dairy

Spread ⅔ cup (170 g) salt-reduced tomato passata or pasta sauce over the pizza base, then top with 200 g grated or sliced reduced-fat mozzarella. Bake according to the pizza dough recipe instructions. Sprinkle with a handful of basil leaves and serve.

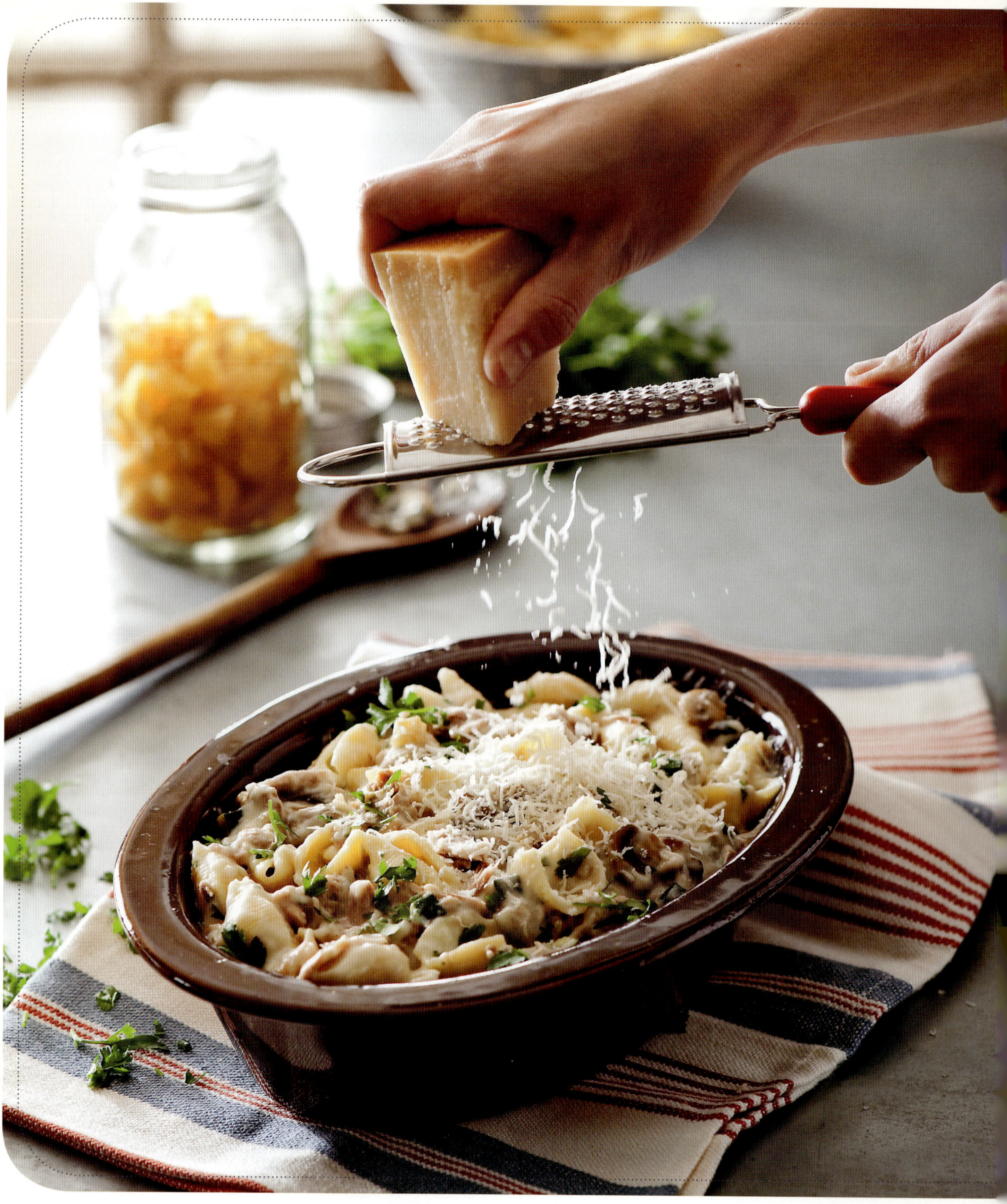

comfort classics

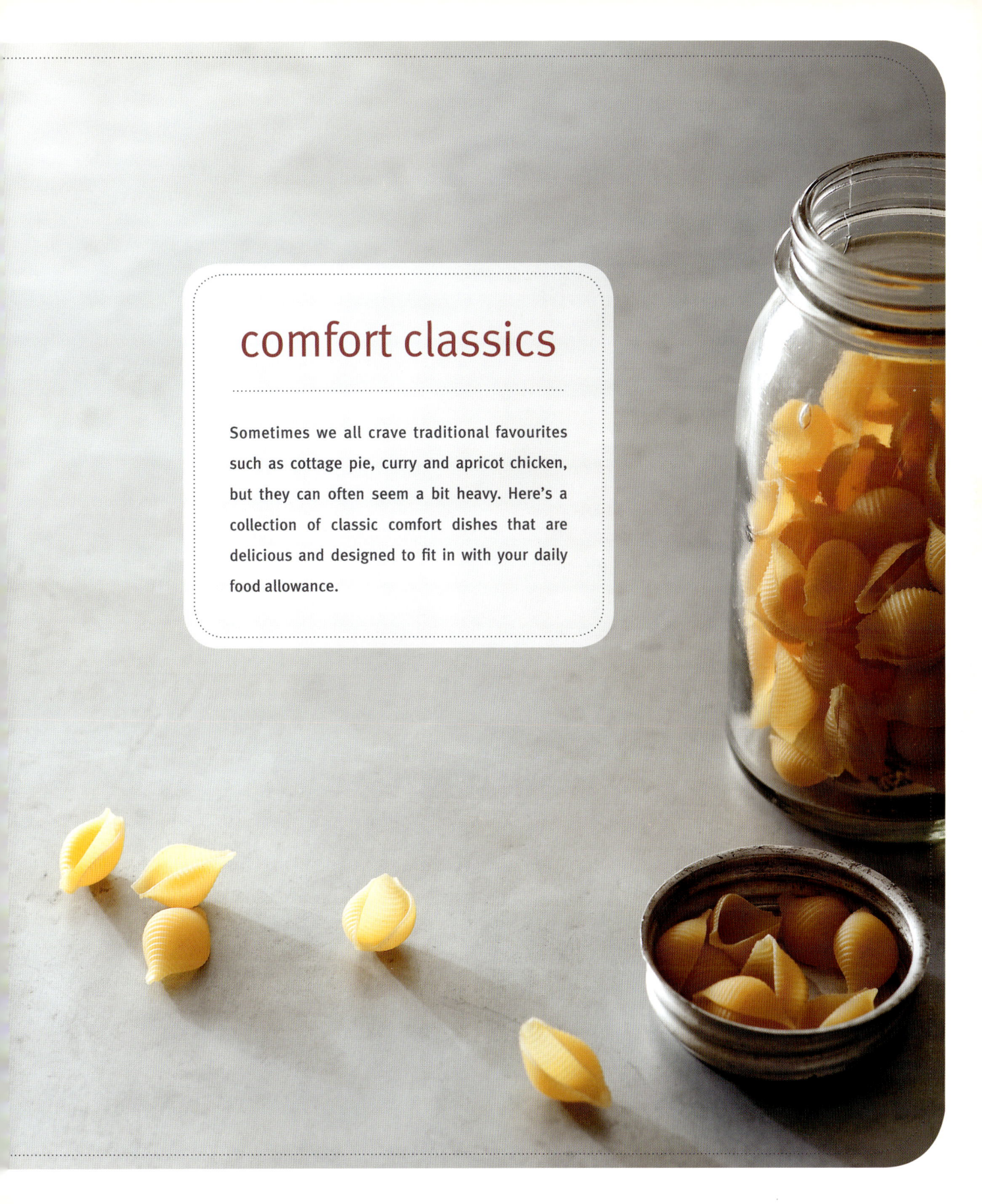

Sometimes we all crave traditional favourites such as cottage pie, curry and apricot chicken, but they can often seem a bit heavy. Here's a collection of classic comfort dishes that are delicious and designed to fit in with your daily food allowance.

Roast beef and vegetables with salsa verde

Roast beef and a generous array of roast vegetables are given a lift with the fresh, tart flavours of homemade salsa verde.

Serves 4

Prep time
20 minutes

Cooking time
1 hour

1 serve =
2 units protein
1 unit bread
1½ units vegetables
1 unit fats

✱ Eye fillet would be perfect for this recipe, but of course it can be expensive, so sirloin, scotch fillet and rump are also suitable.

800 g piece roasting beef, trimmed of fat
olive oil spray
4 potatoes, peeled and halved
4 cloves garlic, skin on
300 g pumpkin (squash), peeled and cut into 3 cm chunks
2 bulbs baby fennel, halved
4 small onions, peeled and left whole
1 tablespoon olive oil
5 small vine-ripened tomatoes, left whole

Salsa verde
handful of chopped flat-leaf parsley
½ cup (40 g) chopped basil
1 tablespoon capers, rinsed, drained and finely sliced
4 anchovy fillets, finely sliced
1 clove garlic, crushed
1 teaspoon Dijon mustard
2 tablespoons red wine vinegar
1 tablespoon extra virgin olive oil

1 Preheat the oven to 200°C.

2 Heat a medium frying pan over high heat. Season the beef with salt and pepper and spray with olive oil. Sear on all sides until well browned, then place in a large roasting tin.

3 Toss the potato, garlic, pumpkin, fennel and onions in the olive oil and arrange around the beef in the roasting tin. Roast for 40 minutes or until cooked to your liking. Remove the beef and set aside to rest, loosely covered with foil.

4 Add the tomatoes to the roasting tin and return to the oven for 10 minutes or until just cooked.

5 Meanwhile, combine all the salsa verde ingredients in a medium bowl.

6 Slice the beef and serve with the pan juices, vegetables and salsa verde.

> Add extra beef to the roasting tin (allow an additional 15 minutes per 500 g) and use it for lunch the next day – in a salad or sandwich.

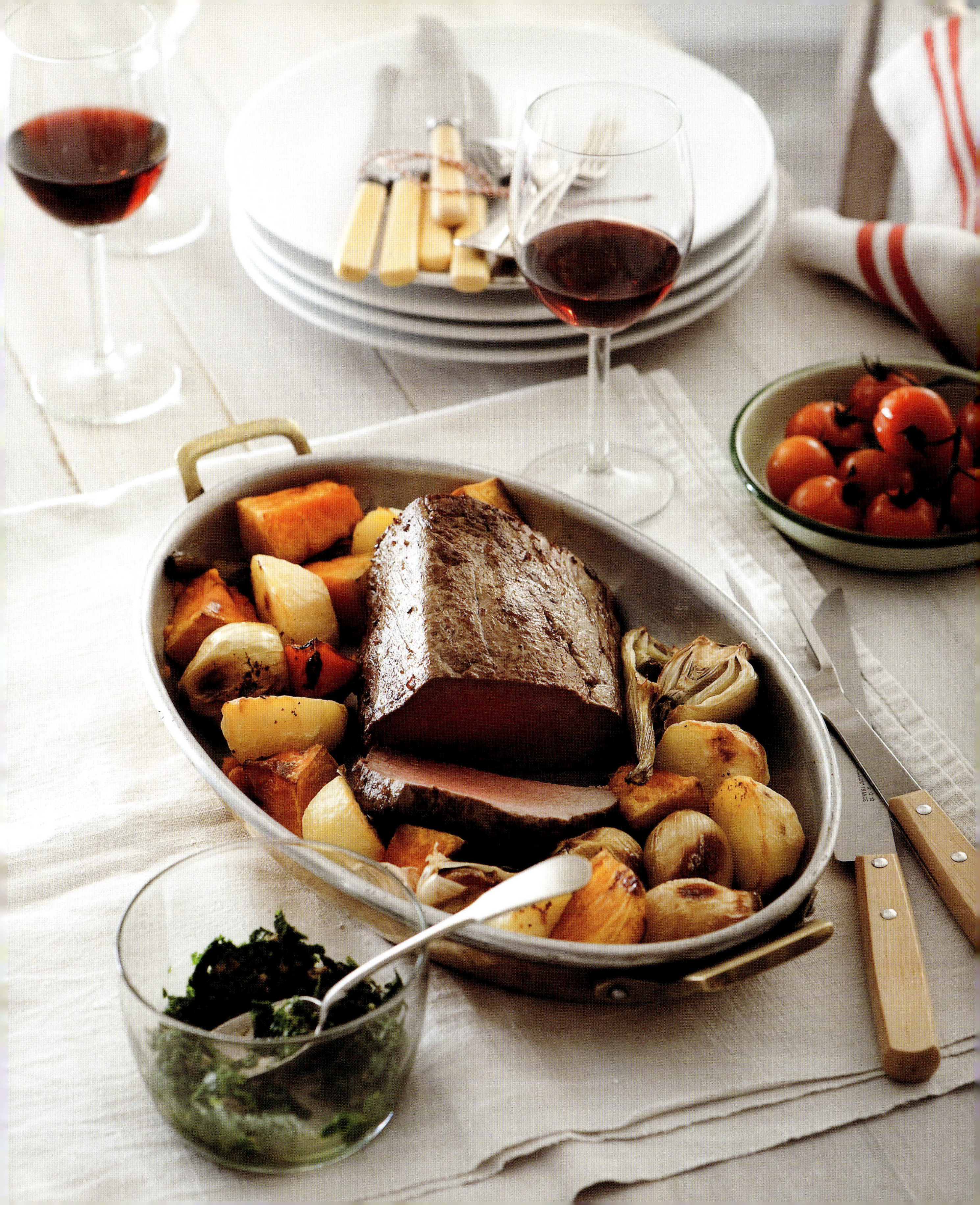

Veal parmigiana

Lightly pan-fried veal with a rich tomato sauce and golden melted cheese – what's not to like?

Serves 4

Prep time
10 minutes

Cooking time
15 minutes

1 serve =
2 units protein
½ unit dairy
½ unit vegetables*
2 units fats

* or 1½ units with serving suggestion

800 g thin veal steaks, trimmed of fat
2 tablespoons plain flour
2 tablespoons olive oil
700 ml salt-reduced tomato passata
1 teaspoon dried oregano
2 tablespoons chopped basil, plus extra leaves to serve
1 cup (100 g) grated reduced-fat mozzarella

1. Preheat the grill to high.
2. Coat the veal lightly with the flour and season with a little salt and pepper.
3. Heat the olive oil in a large non-stick frying pan over medium heat. Brown the steaks for about 2 minutes each side (it is fine if they are still pink in the middle). Place in a single layer in a shallow ovenproof dish.
4. Combine the passata, oregano and basil in a medium saucepan and warm over medium heat or in the microwave. Pour the sauce over the veal, sprinkle with the grated cheese and place under the grill until the cheese has melted.
5. Sprinkle with the extra basil leaves and serve with a salad or steamed vegetables to the side.

> If the veal steaks are too thick, cover with plastic wrap and flatten them with a rolling pin.

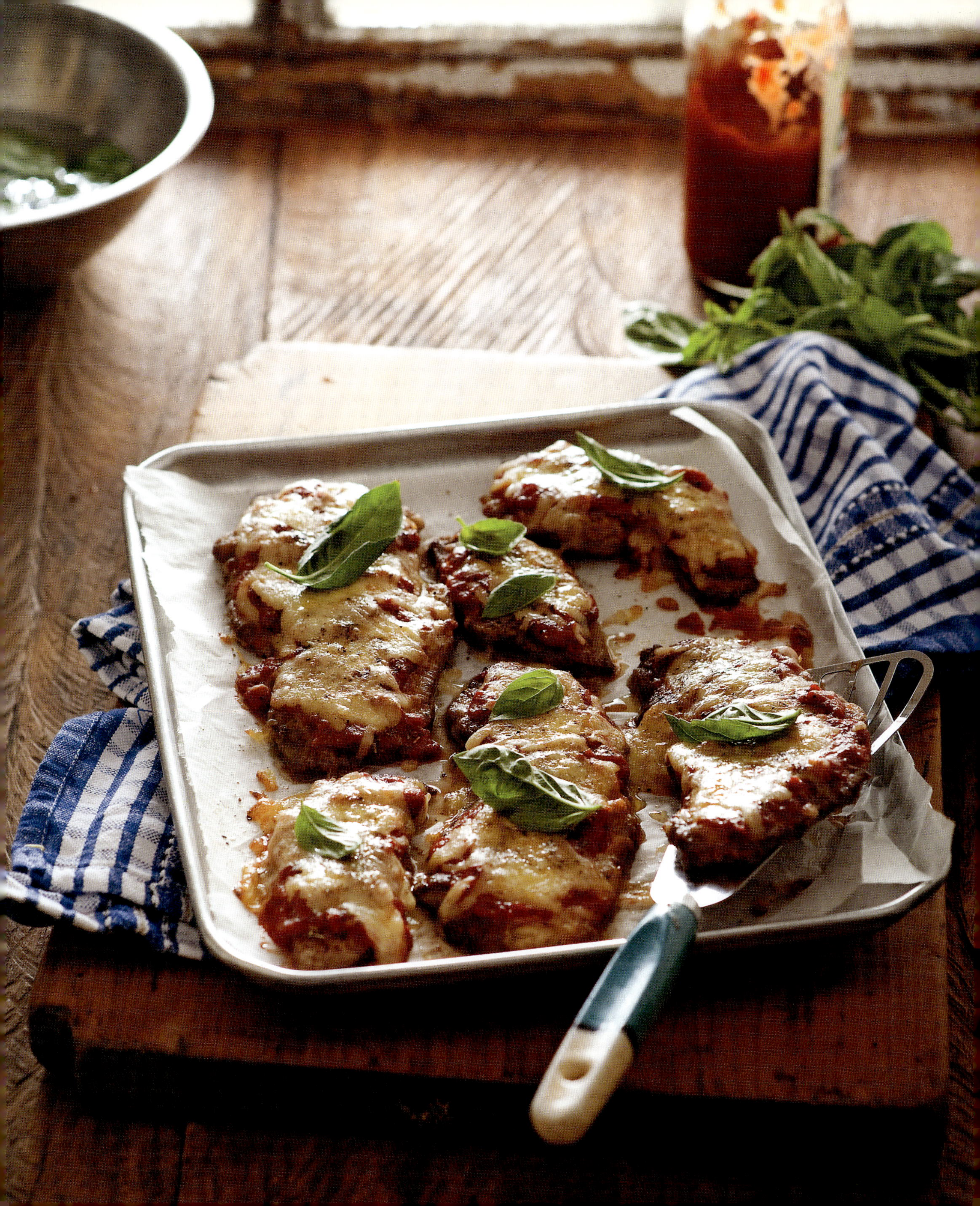

If you don't have dried oregano in your pantry, use 1 teaspoon of dried mixed herbs in its place.

Cottage pie

Just the thing for a cosy evening at home, this pie can be prepared in advance then popped in the oven when it's nearly time to eat.

Serves 4

Prep time 20 minutes

Cooking time 1¼ hours

1 serve =
2 units protein
1½ units bread
½ unit dairy
½ unit vegetables*
1 unit fats

* or 1½ units with serving suggestion

- 1 tablespoon olive oil
- 1 onion, finely diced
- 2 carrots, finely diced
- 800 g lean minced beef
- 3 tablespoons tomato paste (puree)
- 2 cloves garlic, crushed
- 2 cups (500 ml) salt-reduced beef stock
- 2 tablespoons Worcestershire sauce
- 1 teaspoon dried oregano
- 2 teaspoons cornflour
- 1 cup (120 g) frozen peas
- 800 g potatoes, peeled and cut into chunks
- 3 tablespoons reduced-fat milk
- 100 g grated reduced-fat cheddar (optional)

1. Preheat the oven to 180°C.
2. Heat the olive oil in a large saucepan over medium heat, add the onion and carrot and cook, stirring, for 5–10 minutes or until softened.
3. Increase the heat to high, add the mince and cook for 5 minutes or until browned, breaking up any lumps with the back of a wooden spoon. Add the tomato paste and garlic and cook for 1 minute, then stir in the stock, Worcestershire sauce and oregano. Simmer for 15–20 minutes or until the carrot is cooked through and the liquid has reduced.
4. Mix the cornflour with 1 tablespoon water to make a paste, then pour into the saucepan with the peas. Stir until thickened.
5. Meanwhile cook the potato in a large saucepan of boiling water for 15 minutes or until tender. Drain. Return to the saucepan and then mash with the milk. Season with a little salt and pepper.
6. Pour the beef mixture into a deep baking dish. Spread an even layer of the mashed potato on top and sprinkle with the cheddar (if using). Bake for 30–40 minutes or until golden. Serve hot, with vegetables to the side.

> If the sauce isn't thick enough at step 4, add another teaspoon of cornflour mixed with a teaspoon of water and stir through the beef mix until thickened to your liking.

comfort classics

Individual meatloaves

These mini versions are a new take on an old favourite. Of course, the mixture works just as well as a traditional meatloaf – just spoon the mixture into a loaf tin and bake for 45 minutes.

Serves 4

Prep time
20 minutes

Cooking time
35 minutes

1 serve =
2 units protein
½ unit dairy
½ unit vegetables*

* or 1½ units with serving suggestion

olive oil spray
700 g lean minced beef
2 eggs, lightly beaten
1 onion, finely chopped
3 cloves garlic, crushed
1 tablespoon tomato paste (puree)
1 small green capsicum (pepper), finely chopped
1 zucchini (courgette), grated
2 teaspoons Cajun spice mix
3 tablespoons chopped flat-leaf parsley
2 teaspoons finely grated lemon zest
50 g grated parmesan
salt-reduced tomato ketchup, to serve (optional)

1. Preheat the oven to 180°C. Spray eight ½ cup (125 ml) mini loaf tins or muffin holes with olive oil.

2. Combine all the ingredients, except the parmesan and ketchup, in a large bowl and mix thoroughly with your hands. Divide the mixture among the tins or muffin holes and sprinkle with the parmesan.

3. Bake for 35 minutes or until cooked through. Serve with tomato ketchup if you like, and a green salad to the side.

* You can replace the minced beef with lean minced lamb or a combination of lean minced veal and pork.

* Leftovers can be sliced and used to fill sandwiches or served with salad for lunch the following day.

Lamb kofta curry

The combination of spices in the kofta and sauce make this a very special dish. Double the quantities and store another meal for the family in the freezer.

Serves 4

Prep time
25 minutes

Cooking time
35 minutes

1 serve =
2 units protein
½ unit vegetables*
1 unit fats

* or 1½ units with serving suggestion

✱ Mince should always be as fresh as possible and kept refrigerated until you cook it.

700 g lean minced lamb
1 onion, finely chopped
2 cloves garlic, crushed
1 × 3 cm piece ginger, finely grated
½ teaspoon chilli powder
2 teaspoons ground coriander
4 tablespoons chopped coriander
2 eggs

Sauce
1 tablespoon olive oil
1 onion, finely chopped
1 × 2 cm piece ginger, finely grated
2 cloves garlic, crushed
1 teaspoon ground cumin
1 teaspoon ground coriander
1 teaspoon sweet paprika
½–1 teaspoon chilli powder (or to taste)
1 cinnamon stick
1 × 400 g tin chopped tomatoes
1 teaspoon garam masala
1 tablespoon lemon juice
roughly chopped coriander, to serve

1. Preheat the oven to 200°C and line a large baking tray with baking paper.

2. To prepare the koftas, place the minced lamb, onion, garlic, ginger, chilli powder, ground coriander, chopped coriander and eggs in a food processor and pulse until just combined. Form the mixture into small balls (this should make approximately 30 balls). Place on the prepared tray and bake for 15–20 minutes or until just cooked.

3. Meanwhile, to make the sauce, heat the olive oil in a large frying pan and cook the onion until browned.

4. Combine the ginger, garlic, cumin, coriander, paprika, chilli powder and 2 tablespoons water in a small bowl. Add to the pan with the cinnamon stick and cook until fragrant, then stir in the tomatoes and ½ cup (125 ml) water and simmer for 5 minutes. Add the meatballs in a single layer and simmer, covered, for 10–15 minutes or until the sauce has thickened.

5. Gently stir in the garam masala and lemon juice. Sprinkle with coriander and serve with steamed rice from your daily bread allowance and a green salad to the side.

> This dish can be frozen and stored for a later date. Either prepare the meatballs only and freeze, or complete the whole dish, without adding the coriander garnish, and freeze.

> Use any leftover roast lamb in a sandwich or serve with a salad the next day.

Roast leg of lamb with mustard and rosemary

Rosemary and lamb make a winning combination, especially if you leave the marinade on the lamb overnight.

Serves 4

Prep time
15 minutes, plus resting time

Cooking time
1 hour 10 minutes

1 serve =
2 units protein
1 unit bread
1 unit vegetables
1 unit fats

- 1 × 1.2 kg leg of lamb, trimmed of fat (should yield 800 g meat without the bone)
- 2 tablespoons seeded mustard
- 1 tablespoon olive oil
- 3 cloves garlic, crushed
- 1 teaspoon chopped rosemary
- 4 potatoes, peeled and halved
- 2 small red (Spanish) onions, peeled and quartered
- olive oil spray
- 1 bunch broccolini, trimmed
- 100 g green beans, trimmed
- 8 pattypan or button squash, halved
- 1 teaspoon seeded mustard, extra
- 1 teaspoon olive oil, extra
- ready-made fat-free gravy, to serve (optional)

1. Preheat the oven to 200°C.

2. Season the lamb with salt and pepper. Combine the mustard, olive oil, garlic and rosemary in a small bowl, then rub over the lamb. Place in a roasting tin with the potato and onion. Spray the vegetables with olive oil, then roast for 1 hour or until cooked to your liking. Remove the lamb from the tin, then cover and rest for 15 minutes before serving.

3. Meanwhile, steam the broccolini, beans and squash for 5 minutes or until just tender. Gently toss with the extra mustard and olive oil until well coated.

4. Slice the roast lamb and serve with the steamed vegetables on the side and a little gravy (if using).

> Coat the lamb with the mustard and rosemary rub up to one day ahead and refrigerate until ready to roast. This will allow the flavours to intensify.

comfort classics **129**

> Eggplant is very nutritious — especially the skin, so don't peel it off.

Moussaka stacks

All the Greek flavours are here – lamb, garlic, oregano, tomato and feta. These stacks are lighter than a traditional moussaka, but still delicious.

Serves 4

Prep time 20 minutes

Cooking time 35 minutes

1 serve =
2 units protein
½ unit dairy
1 unit vegetables*
1 unit fats

* or 2 units with serving suggestion

1 tablespoon olive oil
1 onion, finely chopped
2 cloves garlic, finely chopped
800 g lean minced lamb
½ cup (125 ml) red wine
½ cup (125 ml) salt-reduced beef stock
1 teaspoon ground cinnamon
½ teaspoon ground nutmeg
3 tablespoons tomato paste (puree)
1 tablespoon chopped oregano
1 large eggplant (aubergine), cut lengthways into 12 thin slices
4 tomatoes, sliced
olive oil spray
100 g reduced-fat feta, crumbled

1. Heat the olive oil in a medium saucepan over medium heat, add the onion and garlic and cook until softened. Add the lamb and cook for 5 minutes until browned, breaking up any lumps with the back of a wooden spoon. Add the red wine, stock, cinnamon, nutmeg, tomato paste and oregano and stir to combine. Simmer for 20 minutes or until thickened.

2. Meanwhile, heat a chargrill or large frying pan over medium heat. Spray the eggplant and tomato slices with olive oil and cook, turning once, until tender.

3. For each serve, place an eggplant slice on a plate, top with an eighth of the tomato slices, then spoon over an eighth of the lamb mixture. Repeat with a second layer of eggplant, tomato and lamb mixture. Sprinkle with the feta and serve with salad leaves dressed with lemon juice.

> As a variation, cook some extra eggplant and use to make a large moussaka in a baking dish, layering with the meat and tomatoes as above.

Pork rissoles with red grapefruit and watercress salad

The pork rissoles are enhanced by the vibrant colours and flavours in this stunning salad.

Serves 4

Prep time
25 minutes, plus refrigerating time

Cooking time
20 minutes

1 serve =
1 unit protein
½ unit fruit
1 unit vegetables
½ unit fats

400 g lean minced pork
1 small onion, grated
1 egg, lightly beaten
1 clove garlic, crushed
1 small zucchini (courgette), finely grated
2 tablespoons chopped flat-leaf parsley
1 tablespoon tomato paste (puree)
2 teaspoons Worcestershire sauce
½ teaspoon curry powder
olive oil spray

Red grapefruit and watercress salad
1 Lebanese (small) cucumber, halved and cut into 1 cm slices
½ bunch (175 g) watercress, trimmed, washed and dried
2 red grapefruit, segmented (reserve any excess juice)
½ red (Spanish) onion, thinly sliced
2 teaspoons extra virgin olive oil

1. Preheat the oven to 200°C. Line a baking tray with baking paper.

2. Combine the pork, onion, egg, garlic, zucchini, parsley, tomato paste, Worcestershire sauce and curry powder in a large bowl. Form the mixture into 12 balls, then place on the prepared tray and flatten slightly. Refrigerate for at least 30 minutes.

3. Spray the rissoles with olive oil and bake for 20 minutes or until golden and cooked through.

4. Meanwhile, to prepare the salad, combine the cucumber, watercress, grapefruit and onion in a bowl. Drizzle with the olive oil and reserved grapefruit juice and toss gently. Serve with the rissoles.

> You will find the easiest way to combine the rissole ingredients is by using your hands. Just make sure you have cleaned them thoroughly beforehand.

> Leftovers are great for lunch the next day — you could even make a double batch for work or school lunches.

Green roast chicken curry with a fresh cabbage and cucumber salad

This unusual recipe brings together the comforting familiarity of roast chicken and the unique flavours of Thailand.

Serves 4

Prep time
25 minutes

Cooking time
40 minutes

1 serve =
2 units protein
1½ units vegetables

1.5 kg whole chicken
2 tablespoons green curry paste (see page 169)
100 ml reduced-fat coconut milk
2 tablespoons fish sauce
1 clove garlic, crushed
1 tablespoon brown sugar or palm sugar
¼ teaspoon white pepper
roughly chopped mint or coriander, to serve
lime wedges, to serve
sweet chilli sauce, to serve

Cabbage and cucumber salad
100 g Chinese cabbage, finely shredded
1 Lebanese (small) cucumber, cut into ribbons
large handful of bean sprouts
1 red capsicum (pepper), thinly sliced
2 spring onions, finely sliced
2 tablespoons mint leaves
1 tablespoon lime juice
2 teaspoons fish sauce
½ teaspoon sugar or powdered sweetener

1   Preheat the oven to 190°C.

2   Remove the backbone from the chicken, then open out the chicken and flatten gently with your hands. Remove the skin and wings, and then place the chicken in a large roasting tin.

3   Combine the curry paste, coconut milk, fish sauce, garlic, brown sugar and white pepper. Pour the curry mixture evenly over the chicken and bake for about 40 minutes or until golden and cooked through.

4   Meanwhile, prepare the salad. Combine the cabbage, cucumber, sprouts, capsicum, spring onion and mint in a large bowl. Whisk together the lime juice, fish sauce and sugar and toss through the vegetables.

5   Sprinkle the chicken with mint or coriander leaves and serve with the salad, lime wedges and sweet chilli sauce.

> Any leftover chicken can be served for lunch the following day with salad or in a sandwich or wrap.

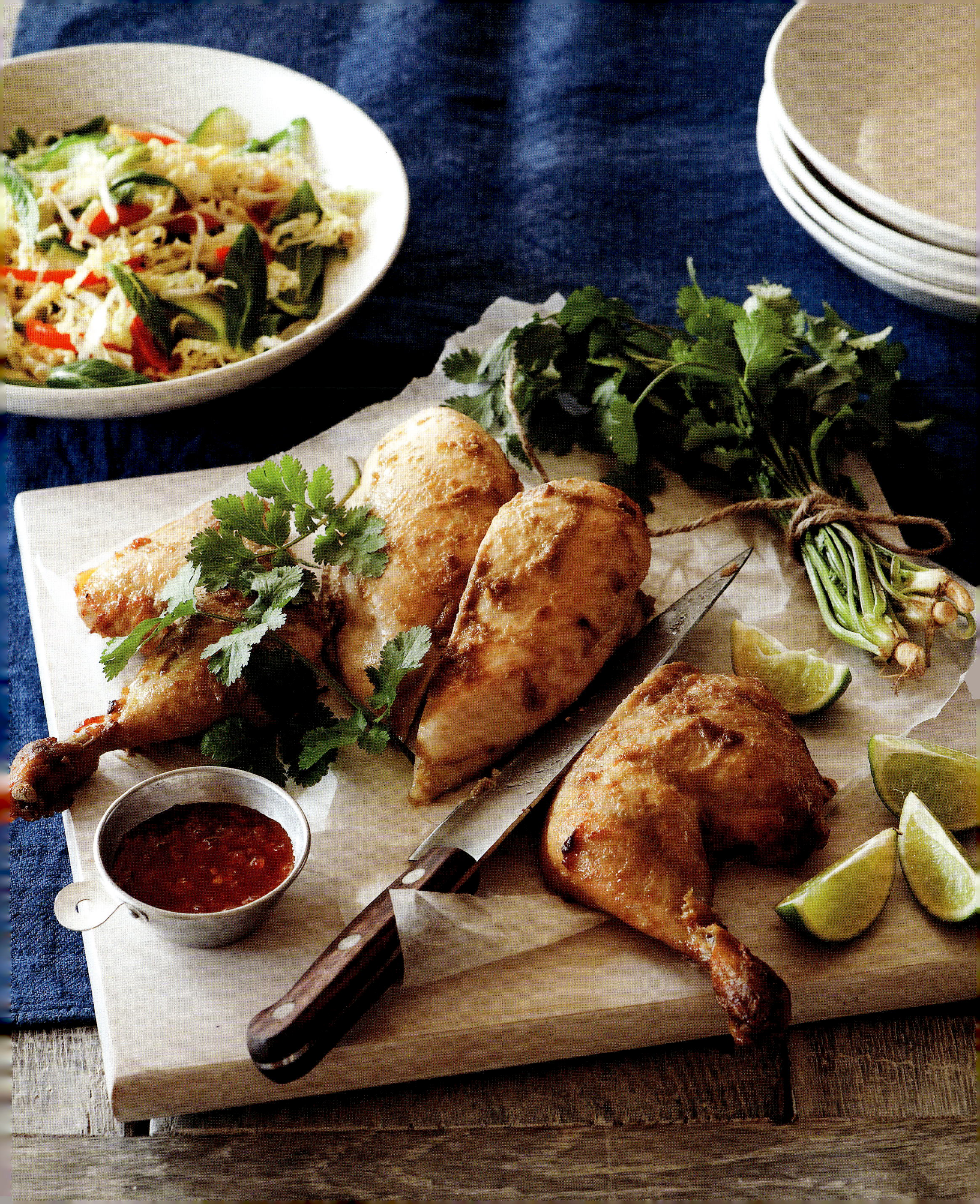

Chicken gumbo

A jewel in the crown of Cajun cuisine, a gumbo is a cross between a soup and a stew. Whatever you call it, this recipe promises a warming meal that is bursting with flavour.

Serves 4

Prep time
20 minutes

Cooking time
40 minutes

1 serve =
2 units protein
1 unit vegetables*
1 unit fats

*or 2 units with serving suggestion

✱ You could replace some of the chicken with sliced lean sausages.

- 2 teaspoons ground cumin
- 2 teaspoons smoked paprika
- 1 teaspoon chilli powder
- 1 teaspoon garlic powder
- 1 teaspoon onion powder
- 1 teaspoon dried oregano
- 800 g chicken thighs, trimmed and cut into quarters
- 1 tablespoon extra virgin olive oil
- 1 onion, chopped
- 2 cloves garlic, crushed
- 2 sticks celery, diced
- 1 green capsicum (pepper), seeded and diced
- 1 × 400 g tin chopped tomatoes
- 1 cup (250 ml) salt-reduced chicken stock
- roughly chopped flat-leaf parsley, to serve
- Tabasco sauce, to serve

1. Combine the cumin, paprika, chilli powder, garlic powder, onion powder and oregano in a large bowl. Add the chicken pieces and toss to coat well in the spice mix.

2. Heat the olive oil in a medium saucepan over medium heat. Add the chicken and cook, stirring regularly, until browned. Remove and set aside.

3. Add the onion to the pan and cook for 5 minutes or until softened, then stir in the garlic, celery and capsicum and cook for 1 minute. Add the chopped tomatoes and stock and simmer for 15 minutes. Return the chicken to the pan, then cover and simmer for 15 minutes or until the chicken is cooked through.

4. Sprinkle with parsley and a few drops of Tabasco sauce, and serve with rice from your daily bread allowance and a salad or vegetables to the side.

> If the spices start to burn when you remove the chicken from the saucepan, add a little water.

comfort classics

Apricot chicken

Moroccan cooking often includes fruit in savoury dishes, so the spice blend works perfectly here with the chicken, dried apricots and sweet apricot nectar.

Serves 4

Prep time
15 minutes

Cooking time
40 minutes

1 serve =
2 units protein
1½ units fruit
1 unit fats

* 1 unit vegetables with serving suggestion

2 tablespoons plain flour
1 tablespoon Moroccan spice mix
800 g chicken thigh cutlets, trimmed and skin removed
1 tablespoon olive oil
1 onion, chopped
3 cloves garlic, crushed
4 sprigs thyme
1 × 400 ml tin apricot nectar
90 g dried apricots
½–1 cup (125–250 ml) salt-reduced chicken stock
2 tablespoons red wine vinegar

1. Combine the flour and spice mix in a large bowl, then sprinkle over the chicken to coat lightly.

2. Heat the olive oil in a large heavy-based saucepan over medium–high heat and brown the chicken on both sides. Remove and set aside.

3. Add the onion and garlic to the pan and stir until softened. Add the thyme, apricot nectar, apricots and half the stock and bring to a simmer. Return the chicken to the pan and simmer for 20 minutes or until cooked through, adding more stock if necessary. Stir in the vinegar.

4. Serve with rice from your daily bread allowance and steamed vegetables.

> You can make your own Moroccan spice mix by combining a teaspoon each of ground cumin, ginger, coriander, cinnamon and paprika. Otherwise, look for it in the spice section at the supermarket.

comfort classics

Parmesan fish fingers with homemade wedges

The parmesan and polenta coating gives the fish fingers a wonderful crunch, and the potato wedges are equally delicious with or without the Cajun spices.

Serves 4

Prep time
25 minutes

Cooking time
40 minutes

1 serve =
2 units protein
1½ units bread
½ unit dairy
2 units fats

* 1 unit vegetables with serving suggestion

6 medium potatoes, cut into wedges
2 tablespoons olive oil
2 teaspoons Cajun spice mix (optional)
50 g grated parmesan
½ cup (85 g) polenta
2 eggs
700 g thin fish fillets, skin and bones removed, cut into 5 cm fingers
olive oil spray
lemon wedges, to serve
reduced-fat tartare sauce, to serve

1. Preheat the oven to 200°C and line two baking trays with baking paper.

2. Toss the potato wedges with the olive oil and spice mix (if using) and place on one of the trays in a single layer. Bake for 35–40 minutes, turning once or twice, until golden and crisp.

3. Meanwhile, combine the parmesan and polenta in a bowl. Place the eggs in a separate bowl and lightly beat them. Dip the fish pieces in the egg and then in the polenta mixture, shaking off any excess. Place on the other baking tray, spray with olive oil and bake for 20 minutes or until crisp.

4. Serve the fish fingers and potato wedges with lemon wedges, tartare sauce and a salad to the side.

For best results, use a thin white fish such as flathead, whiting or snapper to make the fish fingers.

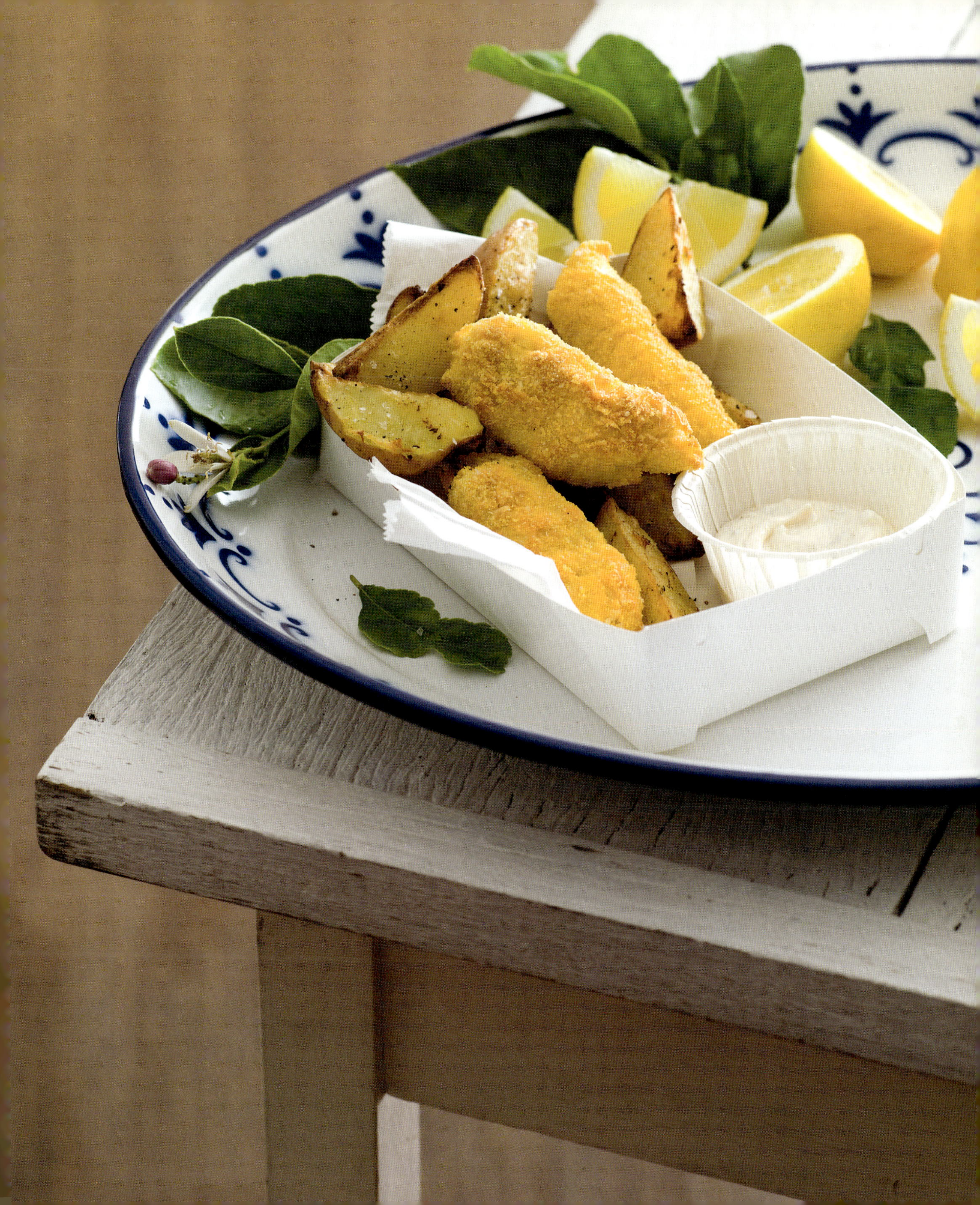

Use chunky fish, such as blue-eye cod or thick snapper, for this recipe.

Fish chowder

This soup is packed with vegetables, herbs and, of course, tempting chunks of fish. Hearty and nourishing, it needs no accompaniment.

Serves 4

Prep time
20 minutes

Cooking time
30 minutes

1 serve =
1 unit protein
½ unit bread
1 unit vegetables
1 unit fats

1 tablespoon olive oil
1 onion, finely chopped
2 cloves garlic, crushed
2 sticks celery, diced
1 carrot, diced
2 potatoes, diced
1 bay leaf
½ teaspoon dried basil
½ teaspoon dried thyme
1 × 400 g tin chopped tomatoes
2 cups (500 ml) salt-reduced chicken stock
1 zucchini (courgette), diced
400 g fish fillets, skin and bones removed, cut into large dice
roughly chopped flat-leaf parsley, to serve
Tabasco sauce, to serve (optional)

1. Heat the olive oil in a large saucepan over medium heat. Add the onion, garlic, celery and carrot and cook for 5 minutes or until the onion has softened.

2. Add the potato, bay leaf, basil, thyme, chopped tomatoes, stock, zucchini and 1 cup (250 ml) water and bring to the boil. Reduce the heat and simmer, covered, for 15 minutes or until all the vegetables are tender.

3. Add the fish pieces, then cover and simmer for a further 5–6 minutes or until just cooked through. Sprinkle with parsley and serve with a few drops of Tabasco sauce (if using).

For a bit of variety, the fish can be replaced with your choice of seafood – try prawns, scallops or a marinara mix.

comfort classics 141

Tuna conchiglie bake

A pasta bake has to come close to being the ultimate in comfort food. This clever recipe shows how you can still enjoy it without letting your diet halo slip.

Serves 4

Prep time
15 minutes

Cooking time
45 minutes

1 serve =
1 unit protein
2 units bread
1 unit dairy
1 unit vegetables*
1½ units fats

* or 2 units with serving suggestion

200 g conchiglie (shell pasta)
1 teaspoon olive oil
100 g button mushrooms, sliced
1 clove garlic, crushed
2 zucchini (courgettes), diced
1 tablespoon olive oil, extra
2 tablespoons plain flour
2½ cups (625 ml) reduced-fat milk
75 g reduced-fat cheddar, grated
1 × 425 g tin tuna in spring water, drained and flaked
3 tablespoons chopped flat-leaf parsley
50 g grated parmesan

✱ The tuna can be replaced with shredded cooked chicken or tinned salmon.

1. Preheat the oven to 180°C.

2. Cook the pasta according to the packet instructions until al dente. Drain.

3. Meanwhile, heat the olive oil in a large frying pan over medium heat. Add the mushrooms and cook for 2–3 minutes until golden. Add the garlic and zucchini and cook until the zucchini has softened. Remove from the heat and transfer to a large bowl.

4. Heat the extra olive oil in a medium saucepan. Add the flour and stir until combined and just starting to bubble. Whisk in the milk and continue whisking until the sauce has thickened. Stir in the cheddar until melted and combined.

5. Add the cheese sauce to the cooked vegetables, then stir in the tuna, parsley and drained pasta. Stir to combine, then pour into a 1.5 litre baking dish. Sprinkle with the parmesan and bake for 20–25 minutes or until golden. Serve with a salad.

Fish pie

This deceptively creamy pie can be made ahead of time, so all you have to do is be patient while it bakes. The aroma wafting through the house will ensure everyone is at the table on time, knives and forks at the ready.

Serves 4

Prep time
25 minutes

Cooking time
45 minutes

1 serve =
2 units protein
1 unit bread
½ unit dairy
½ unit vegetables*
2 units fats

* or 1½ units with serving suggestion

800 g firm white fish fillets, skin and bones removed
2 cups (500 ml) reduced-fat milk
1 onion, chopped
1 bay leaf
1 teaspoon white peppercorns
2 tablespoons olive oil
3 tablespoons plain flour
½ cup (60 g) frozen peas
3 tablespoons chopped flat-leaf parsley

Pie topping
4 potatoes, cut into chunks
200 g cauliflower, cut into large florets
3 tablespoons reduced-fat milk
olive oil spray

> Replace the fish with other types of seafood or try half smoked cod and half white fish.

1. Preheat the oven to 200°C.

2. To prepare the topping, cook the potato and cauliflower in a saucepan of boiling water for 10 minutes or until tender. Drain and return to the saucepan, then mash with the milk.

3. Meanwhile, combine the fish, milk, onion, bay leaf and peppercorns in a large saucepan over medium heat. Bring to the boil, then reduce the heat and simmer for 10 minutes. Remove the fish fillets from the pan and set aside to cool. Strain the milk and reserve, discarding the solids.

4. Heat the olive oil in a medium saucepan and stir in the flour to make a paste. Cook for 1 minute, then remove from the heat and whisk in the strained milk. Return to the heat and whisk until thickened. Stir in the peas and parsley and season to taste.

5. When the fish is cool enough to handle, break the pieces into chunks and place in a medium baking dish. Pour the sauce over the top and stir gently to combine. Top with the potato and cauliflower mash and spray lightly with olive oil.

6. Bake for 25–30 minutes or until golden. Serve with steamed vegetables.

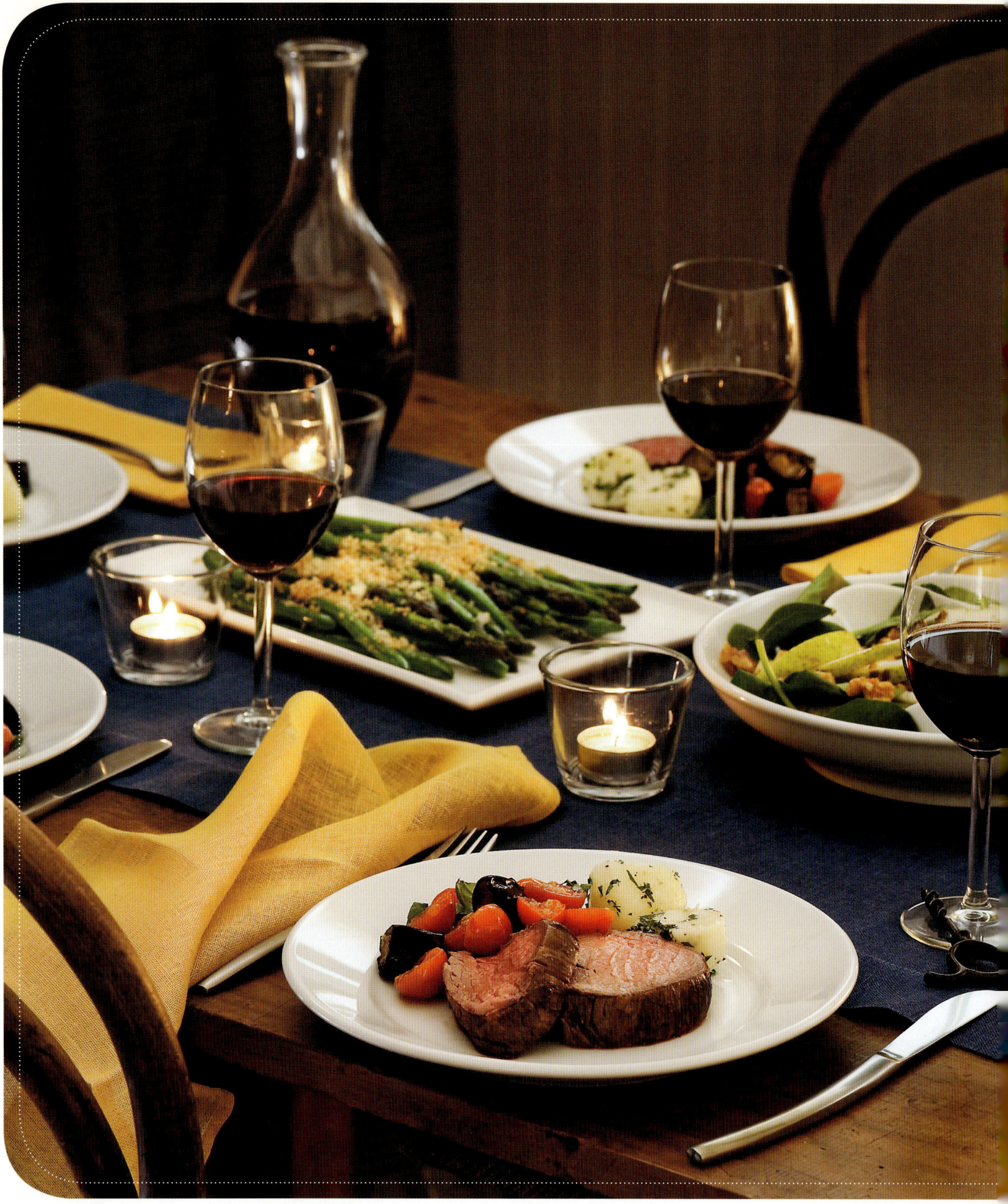

dinner party get-together

This menu proves that it's possible to combine even the most sophisticated flavours with the requirements of the CSIRO eating plan.

Cucumber bites

Scallops with prosciutto and cauliflower puree

Beef fillet with cherry tomato and eggplant compote

Green beans and asparagus with garlic breadcrumbs

Spinach, pear and walnut salad

Cinnamon oranges with spiced yoghurt

Cucumber bites

These refreshing nibblies take just minutes to prepare, and the choice of toppings is limited only by your imagination (and what you have in the pantry). Below are a few suggestions to get you started.

Serves 4

Prep time
15 minutes

1 serve =
½ unit vegetables

2 **Lebanese (small) cucumbers,** cut into 5 **mm thick slices**

1 Spread your choice of topping (see below) over the cucumber rounds and serve.

Prawn and watercress

1 serve =
¼ unit protein

Combine 200 g chopped cooked prawns, 1–2 tablespoons reduced-fat mayonnaise, 1 teaspoon lemon juice and a splash of Tabasco sauce in a bowl. Place a spoonful of the prawn mixture on each cucumber round and top with a watercress or parsley leaf. Serve with lemon wedges.

Smoked salmon and ricotta

1 serve =
¼ unit protein
¼ unit dairy

Combine 50 g reduced-fat ricotta and ½ teaspoon grated horseradish in a bowl. Spread over the cucumber rounds and top with 100 g smoked salmon, torn into pieces. Garnish with snipped chives.

Olive and egg

1 serve =
¼ unit protein

Spread 2 tablespoons olive tapenade over the cucumber rounds and top with a slice of hard-boiled egg (you will need 2 hard-boiled eggs for this). Finish with a grinding of black pepper.

Scallops with prosciutto and cauliflower puree

Scallops add a touch of luxury to any occasion. Take care not to overcook them – they only need a minute each side in a hot pan.

Serves 4

Prep time
20 minutes

Cooking time
20 minutes

1 serve =
1 unit protein
½ unit vegetables
1 unit fats

- 5 slices prosciutto
- 500 g cauliflower, cut into florets
- 2–3 tablespoons reduced-fat milk
- 1 tablespoon extra virgin olive oil
- 1 tablespoon lemon juice
- 20 scallops, roe removed
- 2 tablespoons baby herbs or snow pea sprouts
- balsamic vinegar, to serve

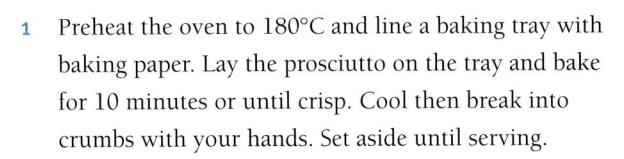

1. Preheat the oven to 180°C and line a baking tray with baking paper. Lay the prosciutto on the tray and bake for 10 minutes or until crisp. Cool then break into crumbs with your hands. Set aside until serving.

2. Meanwhile, cook the cauliflower in a saucepan of boiling water for 15 minutes or until tender. Transfer to a food processor, gradually add the milk (you may not need all of it) and puree until smooth. Season to taste.

3. Combine the olive oil, lemon juice and a pinch of salt and pepper in a bowl. Add the scallops and stir to coat. Drain. Heat a non-stick frying pan over high heat and cook the scallops for 1 minute each side.

4. Spoon the cauliflower puree onto four serving plates and top with the scallops. Crumble the prosciutto over the scallops and finish with a handful of salad leaves. Drizzle with a little balsamic vinegar, then serve immediately.

> When buying scallops, look for moist, glossy flesh with a fresh sea smell. They can be purchased either shucked or still enclosed in their shell. Store them in the fridge and use within 24 hours.

dinner party get-together

Beef fillet with cherry tomato and eggplant compote

The Mediterranean flavours in the compote are lovely with the beef, but would also go well with grilled tuna, chicken or lamb.

Serves 4

Prep time
10 minutes

Cooking time
35 minutes

1 serve =
2 units protein
1 unit bread
1 unit vegetables
1 unit fats

800 g beef fillet, trimmed of fat
olive oil spray
4 medium chat potatoes, quartered and steamed, to serve (optional)

Cherry tomato and eggplant compote
1 tablespoon extra virgin olive oil
4 baby eggplants (aubergines), thickly sliced
200 g cherry tomatoes, halved
2 cloves garlic, crushed
2 tablespoons finely shredded basil

1. Preheat the oven to 190°C. Spray the fillet with olive oil and season to taste. Heat a grill plate or non-stick frying pan over high heat, add the fillet and brown on all sides. Transfer to a roasting tin and roast for 30 minutes or until cooked to your liking. Cover and rest for 10 minutes.

2. Meanwhile, to make the compote, heat the olive oil in a non-stick frying pan and cook the eggplant for 3–4 minutes or until golden. Add the tomato and garlic and cook for a further 2 minutes or until the tomato starts to soften. Stir in the basil.

3. Serve the steaks with the compote and a side of steamed chat potatoes, if liked.

Green beans and asparagus with garlic breadcrumbs

The crunchy breadcrumbs in this dish transform the steamed greens into something special.

Serves 4

Prep time
10 minutes

Cooking time
10 minutes

1 serve =
½ unit bread
1 unit vegetables
1 unit fats

2 slices wholegrain bread
150 g green beans, trimmed
12 spears asparagus, trimmed
1 tablespoon olive oil
2 cloves garlic, crushed

1. Pulse the bread in a food processor to form fine breadcrumbs.

2. Steam or microwave the green beans and asparagus for 4–5 minutes or until tender and just cooked.

3. Heat the olive oil in a small frying pan over medium heat, add the breadcrumbs and garlic and cook, stirring, for 5 minutes or until the crumbs are golden and crunchy.

4. Serve the beans and asparagus topped with the garlic breadcrumbs.

Spinach, pear and walnut salad

Use the freshest walnuts you can find for this dish. If stored for too long, they can become rancid.

Serves 4

Prep time
10 minutes

Cooking time
10 minutes

1 serve =
1 unit vegetables
¼ unit fruit
2½ units fats

40 g walnuts
1 tablespoon extra virgin olive oil
1 tablespoon balsamic vinegar
150 g baby spinach leaves
1 pear, thinly sliced

1. Preheat the oven to 180°C and line a baking tray with baking paper. Spread out the walnuts on the prepared tray and toast them in the oven for 10 minutes or until golden brown and fragrant. Remove from the oven and allow to cool, then roughly chop.

2. Meanwhile, make a dressing by combining the olive oil and vinegar in a screw-top jar. Shake well to combine.

3. In a large bowl, gently toss together the spinach leaves, pear slices and dressing. Arrange on serving plates and scatter the walnuts over the top.

> ✻ You could serve this as a starter, side dish or, as the French do, following the main course of your dinner party. You can even serve this in place of the scallops with prosciutto and cauliflower puree (see page 147) if you want to keep your protein units down.
>
> ✻ 50 g shaved parmesan or reduced-fat goat's cheese would make a delicious addition to this salad, and would add ¼ unit dairy per serve.

✻

for the **Cinnamon oranges with spiced yoghurt** recipe, see page 182

dinner party get-together 149

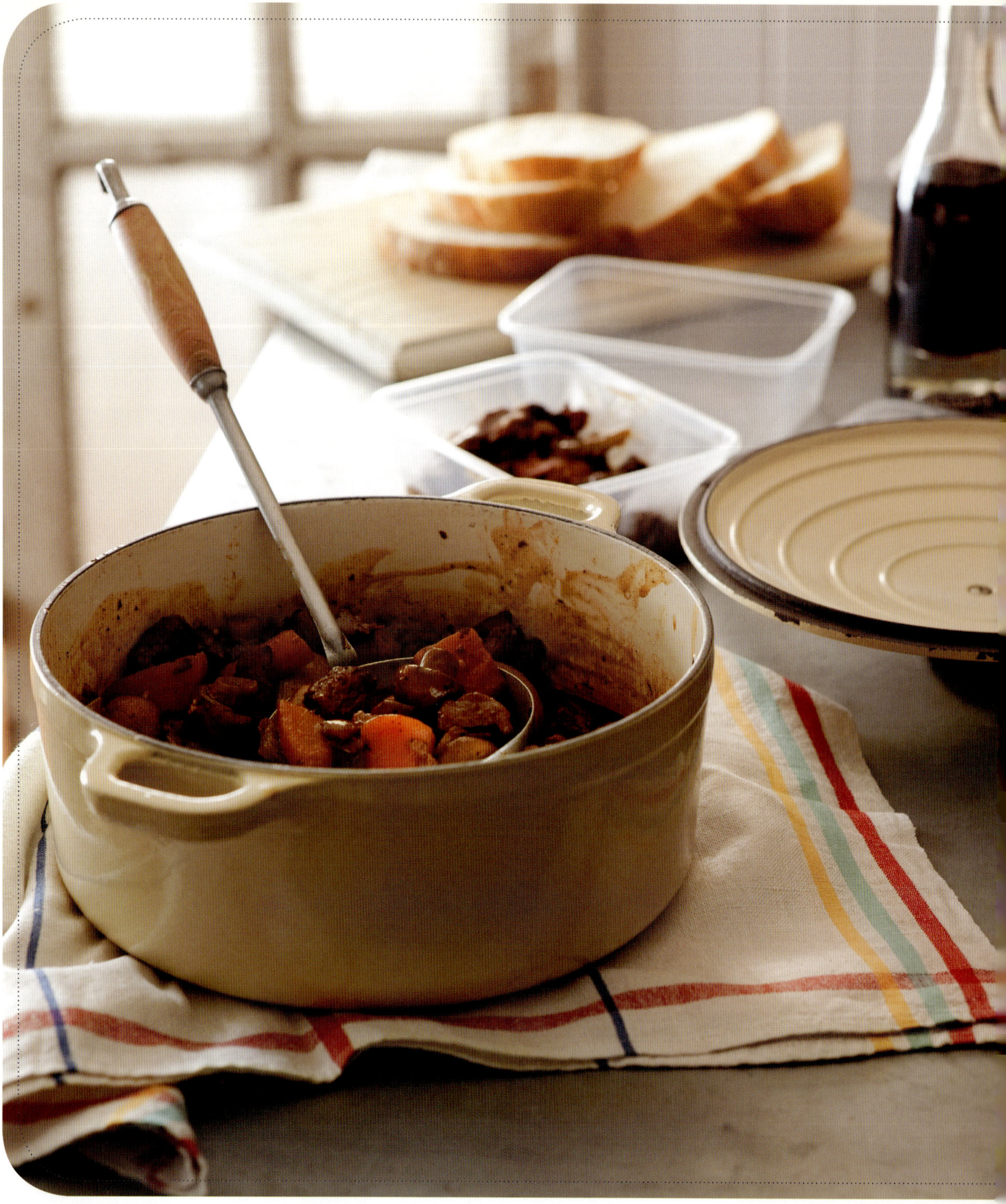

stock and store

Often it's just not realistic to cook a new meal for every dinner or lunch. Here is a collection of tasty and nutritious recipes that you can prepare when you have a bit of time and store in your refrigerator or freezer, ready to be reheated and served throughout the week.

Beef goulash

Goulash is a delicious dish originating from Eastern Europe, perfect for a cold winter's day.

Serves 4

Prep time
20 minutes

Cooking time
1¾ hours

1 serve =
2 units protein
¼ unit vegetables*
2 units fats

* or 1¼ units with serving suggestion

2 tablespoons olive oil
800 g lean stewing steak, trimmed of fat, cut into 3 cm pieces
2 onions, sliced
1 red capsicum (pepper), seeded and chopped
2 cloves garlic, crushed
1 tablespoon sweet paprika
1 teaspoon caraway seeds
2 tablespoons tomato paste (puree)
3 sprigs thyme
1 litre salt-reduced beef stock
1 tablespoon plain flour

1. Heat the olive oil in a large heavy-based saucepan over high heat and brown the beef in batches. Remove and set aside.

2. Add the onion, capsicum and garlic to the pan and cook, stirring, for 5 minutes or until softened. Stir in the paprika, caraway seeds and tomato paste and cook for 1 minute, then add the thyme and stock. Return the beef to the pan. Bring to the boil, then reduce the heat, cover and simmer for 1½ hours or until the beef is tender.

3. Blend the flour with a little water and add gradually to the pan, stirring constantly, until the sauce has thickened. Serve the goulash with rice, barley, mashed potato or pasta noodles from your daily bread allowance and steamed green vegetables.

> ✳ The goulash can be prepared the day before, stored in the refrigerator and then gently reheated. You can also divide it into meal-sized portions and freeze. It will then be ready to thaw and reheat at the end of a busy day, or to have as a nutritious lunch to take to work.
>
> ✳ You could use chuck, gravy, skirt or round cuts of beef for this dish.

Sweet paprika adds a prominent flavour to this dish that is not spicy, and therefore child-friendly.

The quantities can easily be doubled to make extra portions of Bolognese sauce, which can be frozen for a later date.

Bolognese

An old-time favourite, Bolognese sauce is wonderfully versatile and may be served in a number of different ways. For something a little different, replace the minced beef with lean minced lamb and feel free to add extra vegetables.

Serves 4

Prep time
10 minutes

Cooking time
30 minutes

1 serve =
1 unit protein
2 units vegetables
1 unit fats

- 1 tablespoon olive oil
- 1 onion, finely chopped
- 400 g lean minced beef
- 2 cloves garlic, crushed
- 1 carrot, finely diced
- 1 stick celery, finely diced
- 100 g mushrooms, finely diced
- ½ cup (125 ml) red wine
- 700 ml salt-reduced tomato passata
- 2 × 400 g tins chopped tomatoes
- 1–2 teaspoons low-fat beef stock powder
- 2 teaspoons dried oregano
- 2 bay leaves

1. Heat the olive oil in a large saucepan over medium heat and cook the onion until softened. Add the minced beef and cook until starting to brown, breaking up any lumps with the back of a wooden spoon. Add the garlic, carrot, celery and mushrooms and cook, stirring, for 5 minutes or until softened.

2. Pour in the wine and bring to the boil. Add the remaining ingredients and simmer, uncovered, for 25–30 minutes or until thickened. See below for serving suggestions.

Spaghetti Bolognese

1 serve =
2 units bread
1 unit dairy

Cook 2 cups (170 g) spaghetti or your favourite pasta according to the packet instructions. Drain. Divide among four plates, and top with Bolognese sauce. Garnish with shaved parmesan and flat-leaf parsley or oregano leaves.

Pasticcio (pasta bake)

1 serve =
2 units bread
1 unit dairy

Place 4 cups (360 g) cooked pasta, such as penne, in the base of a 4 litre baking dish and pour over the Bolognese sauce. To make a white sauce, blend 2 tablespoons cornflour with 2 cups (500 ml) reduced-fat milk. Pour into a small saucepan and cook, stirring constantly, over low heat until thickened. Pour the white sauce over the Bolognese. Top with 100 g grated reduced-fat cheese and bake in a preheated 180°C oven for 35–40 minutes or until golden.

Cannelloni

1 serve =
2 units bread
½ unit dairy

Fill 200 g cannelloni tubes with the Bolognese. Pour the remaining Bolognese into the base of a 2 litre baking dish and arrange the stuffed cannelloni on top, pushing down as you go so they are slightly submerged. Top with 100 g grated reduced-fat cheese and bake in a preheated 180°C oven for 30 minutes or until golden on top.

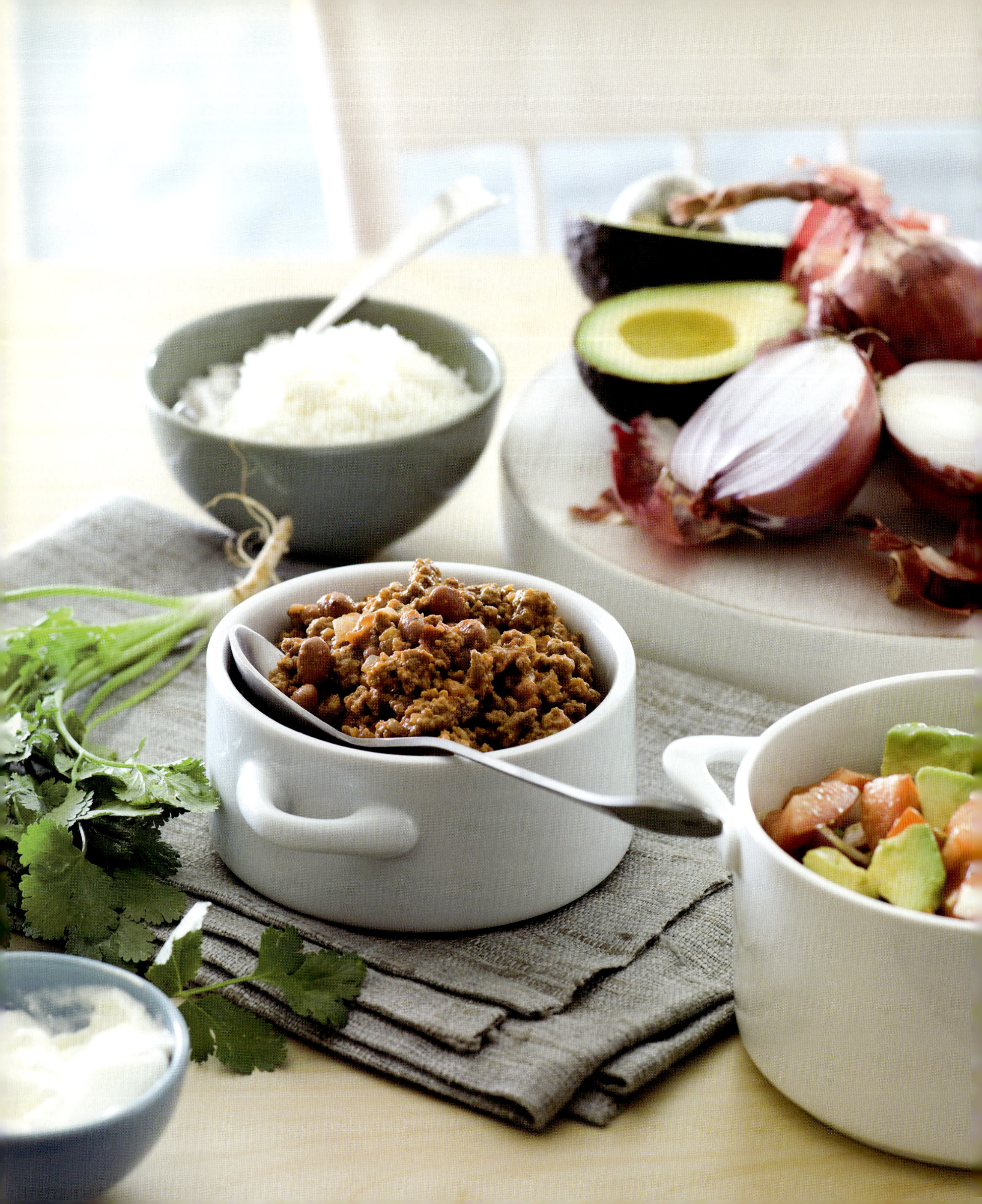

Tex-Mex chilli beef

This is another recipe that can be served in a number of different ways. These days, there are healthier versions of tortillas available at supermarkets – use these to make burritos, enchiladas and quesadillas with your Tex-Mex chilli beef.

Serves 4

Prep time
15 minutes

Cooking time
50 minutes

1 serve =
2 units protein
½ unit vegetables
2½ units fats

1 tablespoon olive oil
1 onion, finely chopped
2 cloves garlic, crushed
600 g lean minced beef
1–2 teaspoons chilli powder
2 teaspoons paprika
3 teaspoons ground cumin
1 teaspoon dried oregano
3 tablespoons tomato paste (puree)
1½ cups (375 ml) salt-reduced beef stock
1 × 400 g tin chopped tomatoes
1 × 400 g tin kidney beans, rinsed and drained
120 g diced avocado
2 tomatoes, finely diced
1 red (Spanish) onion, finely diced
4 tablespoons extra light sour cream
3 tablespoons roughly chopped coriander

1. Heat the olive oil in a large saucepan over medium heat and cook the onion for 2–3 minutes or until softened. Add the garlic and beef and cook, stirring to break up any lumps with the back of a wooden spoon, for 5 minutes or until the meat is browned. Stir in the chilli powder, paprika, cumin and oregano and cook for 1–2 minutes or until fragrant.

2. Add the tomato paste, stock, tomato and beans and bring to the boil, then reduce the heat and simmer for 40 minutes or until thickened and cooked through. Season to taste.

3. Combine the avocado, tomato and red onion in a medium bowl.

4. Divide the chilli beef among four bowls and top each portion with a little avocado salad, a tablespoon of sour cream and a sprinkling of coriander. Serve with rice from your daily bread allowance.

Enchiladas

1 serve =
2 units protein
2 units bread
½ unit dairy
1 unit vegetables

Spoon the chilli beef mixture onto 8 warm tortillas, top with 2 cups (120 g) shredded lettuce, 4 sliced or diced tomatoes and 100 g grated reduced-fat cheese and roll up.

Tex-Mex lettuce cups

1 serve =
2 units protein
½ unit dairy
1 unit vegetables

Spoon the chilli beef mixture into 8 large iceberg lettuce leaves, top with 4 sliced or diced tomatoes and 100 g grated reduced-fat cheese and serve.

Bourguignon-style beef casserole

You'll feel as if you've been whisked away to Provincial France as you indulge in this hearty meal. It is a wonderful dish for a long Sunday lunch with family and friends.

Serve 4

Prep time
15 minutes

Cooking time
1 hour 40 minutes

1 serve =
2 units protein
1½ units vegetables*
1 unit fats

* or 2½ units with serving suggestion

1 tablespoon olive oil
100 g lean rindless bacon, diced
700 g lean stewing beef, trimmed of fat and cut into 3 cm pieces
8 baby onions, peeled and left whole
2 carrots, diced
2 sticks celery, diced
4 cloves garlic, crushed
200 g button mushrooms
1 cup (250 ml) red wine
1 cup (250 ml) salt-reduced beef stock
2 tablespoons tomato paste (puree)
2 strips orange zest
3 sprigs thyme
2 teaspoons cornflour (optional)

1 Preheat the oven to 160°C.

2 Heat the olive oil in a flameproof casserole dish over medium heat and brown the bacon and beef in batches. Remove from the dish. Add the onions, carrot and celery and cook, stirring, for 5 minutes until lightly coloured, then stir in the garlic, mushrooms, wine, stock, tomato paste, orange zest and thyme.

3 Bring to the simmer, then cover and bake in the oven for 1½ hours. If a thicker sauce is desired, blend the cornflour with a little water and stir through the casserole as soon as it has been removed from the oven, until it has thickened. Serve with a large bowl of steamed vegetables.

* Make a double batch and freeze in serving sizes, for an easy weeknight meal.

* This casserole also works beautifully with the same quantity of trimmed leg of lamb in place of the beef.

stock and store

Scotch broth

With no fat units, and filled with tasty vegetables, this hearty and healthy meal is just the thing when you're trying to be extra good.

Serves 4

Prep time
20 minutes

Cooking time
2 hours

1 serve =
2 units protein
½ unit bread
1 unit vegetables*

* or 2 units with serving suggestion

- ½ cup (100 g) pearl barley
- 1 kg lamb neck chops, trimmed of fat
- 2 cups (500 ml) salt-reduced beef stock
- 1 onion, chopped
- 1 leek, white part only, finely sliced and washed
- 1 carrot, diced
- 1 parsnip, peeled and diced
- 1 swede, peeled and diced
- 1 cup (80 g) shredded cabbage
- ½ cup (60 g) frozen peas
- roughly chopped flat-leaf parsley, to serve

1. Place the barley in a large bowl, cover with cold water and set aside to soak.

2. Place the lamb in a large saucepan with 1.5 litres water. Bring to the boil, then reduce the heat and simmer, uncovered, for 45 minutes, skimming the surface as required.

3. Drain the barley and add to the lamb with the stock, onion, leek, carrot, parsnip and swede. Cover and simmer for 45 minutes.

4. Remove the lamb with a pair of tongs and add the cabbage and peas to the broth. Cook for a further 10 minutes. When the lamb has cooled slightly, remove the meat from the bones, then roughly chop it and return it to the broth (discard the bones). Stir in the parsley, season to taste and serve with extra steamed vegetables.

> This will be more than enough broth for four people and can yield eight lunch-sized servings, so freeze any leftovers in meal-sized portions for a later date.

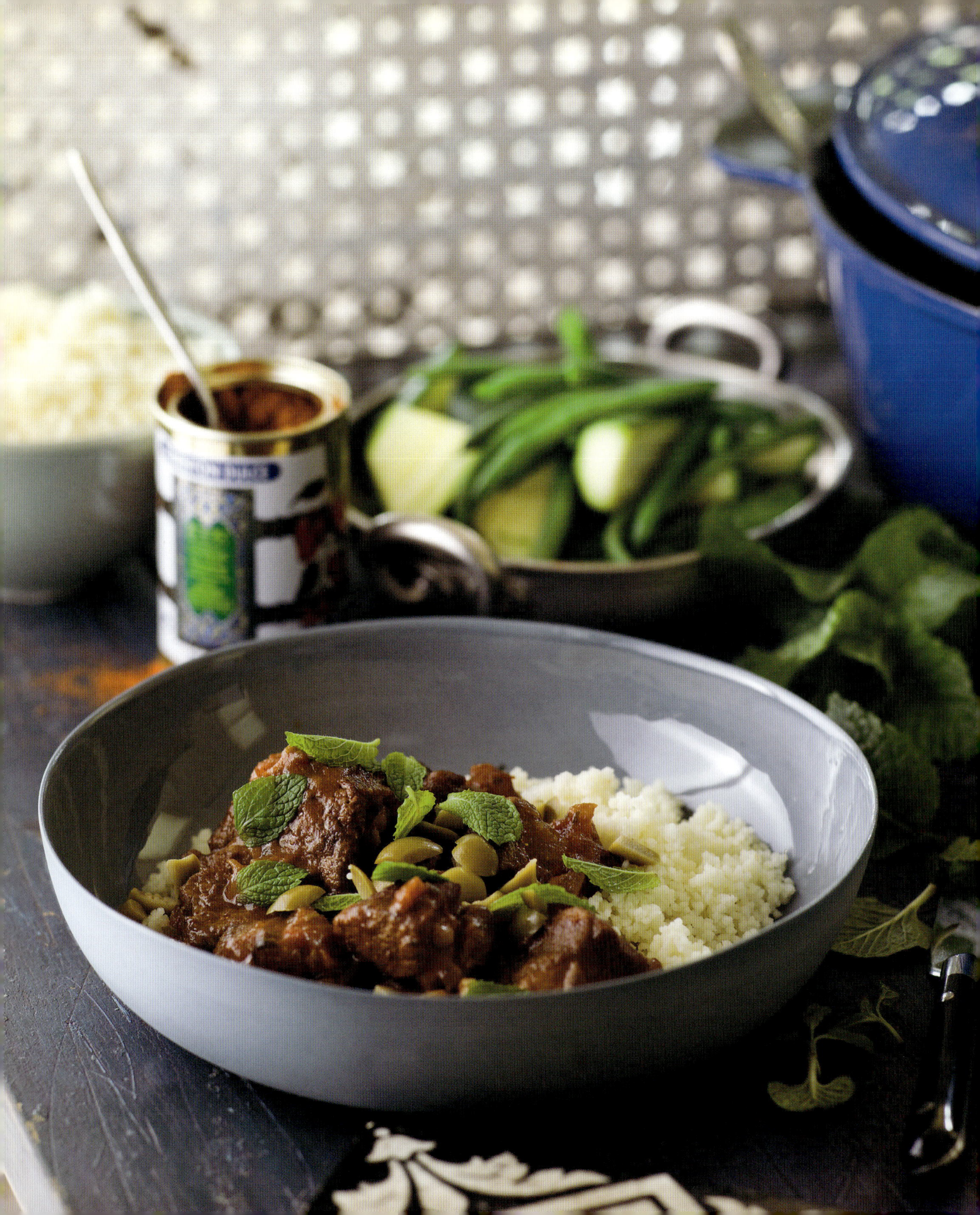

Braised Moroccan lamb

Look for bright green Sicilian olives – their buttery flavour and soft texture work wonderfully in this braise.

Serves 4

Prep time
15 minutes

Cooking time
1 hour 20 minutes

1 serve =
2 units protein
½ unit vegetables*
1 unit fats

* or 1½ units with serving suggestion

1 tablespoon olive oil
800 g lean leg of lamb, trimmed of fat and cut into 3 cm chunks
1 onion, diced
2 cloves garlic, crushed
2 teaspoons ground cumin
1 teaspoon ground ginger
2 teaspoons sweet paprika
3 tablespoons roughly chopped coriander
1 × 400 g tin chopped tomatoes
2 tablespoons tomato paste (puree)
1 cup (250 ml) salt-reduced beef stock
1 tablespoon honey
8 green olives, chopped
small mint leaves, to garnish

1. Preheat the oven to 170°C.

2. Heat the olive oil in a flameproof casserole dish over high heat. Brown the lamb in batches, then remove from the dish.

3. Add the onion and garlic to the dish and cook for 2–3 minutes or until beginning to soften, then add the cumin, ginger and paprika and stir until fragrant. Return the lamb to the dish, along with the coriander, chopped tomatoes, tomato paste and stock.

4. Bring to a simmer, then cover and bake in the oven for 1 hour or until the lamb is tender. Just before serving, stir in the honey and garnish with a scattering of olives and mint leaves. Serve with couscous from your daily bread allowance and steamed green beans.

- Lamb meat is often sold packed and diced, which can cut down on preparation time.

- If you like, the diced lamb can be replaced with 4 × 200 g frenched lamb shanks.

Mulligatawny

This flavoursome soup is traditionally served in India and Sri Lanka. Translated from Tamil, mulligatawny literally means 'pepper water', although pepper is not an essential ingredient. Make it a day ahead and refrigerate until you're ready to heat it through and serve.

Serves 4
Prep time 15 minutes
Cooking time 45 minutes

1 serve =
2 units protein
1 unit bread
½ unit vegetables
1 unit fats

1 tablespoon vegetable oil
1 onion, chopped
2 cloves garlic, crushed
1 × 3 cm piece ginger, grated
2 carrots, diced
1 stick celery, diced
1 tablespoon curry paste (or to taste)
1.5–2 litres salt-reduced beef stock
4 tablespoons red lentils
700 g lean lamb, trimmed of fat and finely diced
6 curry leaves or 2 bay leaves
2 teaspoons garam masala
4 tablespoons basmati rice
2 medium potatoes, peeled and diced
juice of 1 lemon
3 tablespoons reduced-fat coconut-flavoured evaporated milk (optional)
roughly chopped coriander, to serve (optional)

1 Heat the oil in a large saucepan over medium heat. Add the onion, garlic, ginger, carrot and celery and gently cook for 5 minutes or until softened.

2 Stir in the curry paste, then add the stock, lentils, lamb, curry or bay leaves and garam masala and stir to combine. Bring to the boil, then reduce the heat and simmer, covered, for 25 minutes. Add the rice and potato and cook for a further 15 minutes. Stir in the lemon juice and evaporated milk (if using) until heated through, then serve, sprinkled with coriander if liked.

* For a different take on this dish, use chicken instead of lamb, and chicken stock in place of the beef stock.
* There will almost certainly be leftovers, so have them for lunch the next day.

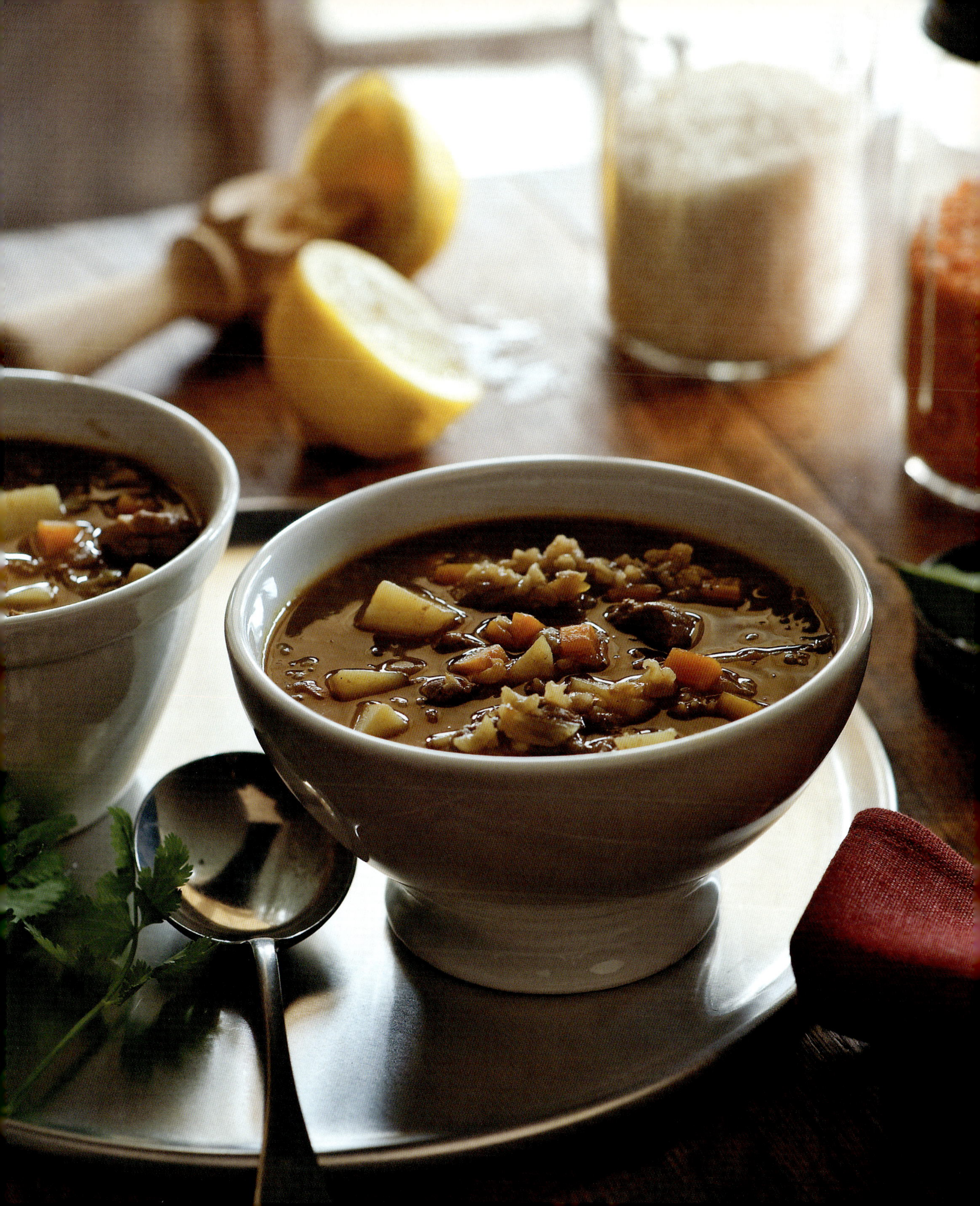

The pumpkin can easily be replaced with sweet potato, for a slightly different flavour.

Chicken tagine

A tagine is the name for a Moroccan stew and the conical-shaped terracotta dish it is traditionally cooked in. Don't worry if you don't have a tagine – the recipe works just as well in a heavy-based saucepan.

Serves 4

Prep time
15 minutes

Cooking time
40 minutes

1 serve =
2 units protein
½ unit fruit
1 unit vegetables*
1½ units fats

* or 2 units with serving suggestion

1½ tablespoons olive oil
800 g chicken thigh fillets, trimmed of fat and cut into 5 cm pieces
1 onion, finely chopped
6 cloves garlic, crushed
2 sticks celery, thinly sliced
3 teaspoons ground coriander
1 teaspoon ground ginger
1 × 400 g tin chopped tomatoes
60 g dried apricots, roughly chopped
2 teaspoons grated lemon zest
2 tablespoons lemon juice
1 cinnamon stick
2 cups (300 g) diced pumpkin (squash)
1 cup (250 ml) salt-reduced chicken stock
3 tablespoons chopped coriander, plus extra sprigs to garnish

1. Heat the olive oil in a medium saucepan over medium heat. Add the chicken in batches and cook for 5 minutes or until golden. Remove and set aside. Add the onion, garlic and celery to the pan and cook for 5 minutes or until the onion has softened.

2. Add the ground coriander and ginger and sauté for a further 1 minute, then add the chopped tomatoes, apricot, lemon zest, lemon juice, cinnamon, pumpkin and stock.

3. Return the chicken to the pan and bring the mixture to the boil, then reduce the heat and simmer for 20 minutes or until the chicken and pumpkin are cooked through. Season to taste and stir in the coriander. Garnish with extra coriander and serve with couscous from your daily bread allowance and steamed vegetables.

> Add a finely sliced red chilli at the beginning of step 2 if you like a bit of heat in your food.

stock and store

Chicken and vegetable country stew

Worcestershire sauce is the secret ingredient in this tasty and easy-to-prepare stew, which is delicious on a winter's night.

Serves 4
Prep time 15 minutes
Cooking time 40 minutes

1 serve =
2 units protein
½ unit bread
1 unit vegetables
2 units fats

2 tablespoons olive oil
800 g chicken thigh fillets, trimmed of fat and cut into 2 cm pieces
1 large onion, finely chopped
2 cloves garlic, crushed
2 sticks celery, sliced
2 carrots, finely diced
1 tablespoon tomato paste (puree)
2 medium potatoes, peeled and finely diced
2 cups (500 ml) salt-reduced chicken stock
1 teaspoon dried oregano
1 tablespoon Worcestershire sauce
1 zucchini (courgette), cut into 1 cm dice
½ cup (60 g) frozen peas
½ cup (80 g) frozen corn
1½ tablespoons cornflour
roughly chopped flat-leaf parsley, to serve

1. Heat the olive oil in a large heavy-based saucepan over medium–high heat. Add the chicken in batches and cook for 2–3 minutes or until golden. Remove and set aside. Add the onion, garlic, celery and carrot to the pan and cook for 5 minutes or until the onion has softened.

2. Stir in the tomato paste, then add the potato, stock, oregano and Worcestershire sauce and return the chicken to the pan. Bring to the boil, then reduce the heat and simmer, covered, for 15 minutes.

3. Add the zucchini, peas and corn and cook for a further 10 minutes or until all the vegetables are tender and cooked through.

4. Mix the cornflour with 3 tablespoons water and add to the pan, stirring until the sauce has thickened. Season to taste, then garnish with parsley and serve.

There will be leftovers, so freeze these in individual containers for a quick lunch to grab in a rush.

stock and store

Chinese master stock

This is a very handy base to have on hand in your freezer. It can be used repeatedly for poaching meat – just follow the instructions in step 3 to keep the stock fresh and flavoursome for each use.

Makes 2 litres
Prep time 10 minutes
Cooking time 35 minutes
1 serve = a free list item

- 1 cup (250 ml) light soy sauce
- 1 cup (250 ml) Chinese cooking wine
- 3 cloves garlic, peeled
- 1 × 4 cm piece ginger, julienne
- 3 spring onions
- 2 sticks cinnamon
- 4 star anise
- 4 tablespoons brown sugar
- 3 strips orange zest

1. Combine all the ingredients in a large saucepan with 2 litres water. Bring to the boil, then reduce the heat and simmer for 30 minutes.

2. The stock can now be used to poach a whole chicken or cuts such as chicken thigh or leg.

3. After every use bring the stock to the boil, then strain and allow to cool. Freeze in an airtight container. When you're ready to use it again, allow it to thaw then top it up to 2 litres with water. Add fresh garlic, ginger and spring onions each time you reuse the stock, and fresh spices every second time.

> To poach a whole chicken or chicken pieces, bring the stock to a simmer and gently drop the chicken into the liquid. Bring to the boil, then reduce heat to a simmer and cook for 20 minutes or until chicken is cooked through. Remove from the heat then cover and allow the chicken to cool in the stock. Strip the chicken from the bone and serve cold in a salad or hot with steamed Asian greens.

Chicken meatballs

Children often enjoy lending a helping hand to roll these meatballs and are delighted with the finished dish, knowing they helped prepare it.

Serves 4
Prep time 25 minutes
Cooking time 35 minutes

1 serve =
2 units protein
½ unit bread
1½ units vegetables*
1 unit fats

*or 2½ units with serving suggestion

✻ The meatballs can be frozen either before or after baking.

olive oil spray
2 slices wholemeal bread, crusts removed
4 tablespoons reduced-fat milk
800 g lean minced chicken
1 onion, finely chopped
2 cloves garlic, crushed
3 tablespoons chopped coriander
3 tablespoons chopped flat-leaf parsley
2 teaspoons ground cumin
2 teaspoons finely grated lemon zest

Tomato sauce
1 tablespoon extra virgin olive oil
1 onion, finely chopped
2 cloves garlic, crushed
2 teaspoons ground cumin
2 teaspoons paprika
2 × 400 g tins chopped tomatoes
2 tablespoons chopped coriander
2 tablespoons chopped flat-leaf parsley
1 tablespoon lemon juice (or to taste)

✻ Use a jar of salt-reduced ready-made pasta sauce as a short cut if you don't have time to make your own.

✻ Having wet hands while rolling the meatballs will make the task a lot easier.

1 Preheat the oven to 200°C. Spray a large baking tin with olive oil.

2 Place the bread slices in a bowl, pour over the milk and set aside to soak for a few minutes.

3 Place the minced chicken, onion, garlic, herbs, cumin and lemon zest in a large mixing bowl. Squeeze the excess milk from the soaked bread and add the bread to the bowl. Using your hands, mix all the ingredients until well combined. Roll tablespoons of the mixture into balls, then place them in the baking tin. Bake for 15 minutes or until the meatballs are cooked through and lightly golden.

4 Meanwhile, to prepare the tomato sauce, heat the olive oil in a large frying pan over medium heat and fry the onion for 4–5 minutes or until softened. Add the garlic and spices and cook for a further 30 seconds. Stir in the tomatoes and 1 cup (250 ml) water and bring to the boil, then reduce the heat and simmer for 10 minutes.

5 Add the baked meatballs to the sauce and simmer for an extra 10–15 minutes or until the sauce has thickened. Stir in the coriander, parsley and lemon juice and season to taste. Serve with rice, couscous or pasta from your daily allowance, with a crisp salad to the side.

Thai green curry paste

It's much healthier to make your own curry paste as the supermarket varieties are often laden with unnecessary amounts of fats and sugars. This homemade paste can be used in the green roast chicken curry on page 134, or in the Thai fishcakes on page 28.

Makes ½ cup (150 g)

Prep time 15 minutes

Cooking time 10 minutes

1 serve = a free list item

- 1 tablespoon shrimp paste
- 8–12 small green chillies, roughly chopped
- 1 teaspoon freshly ground black pepper
- 8 cloves garlic
- 2 teaspoons grated ginger
- 1 red (Spanish) onion, roughly chopped
- 2 tablespoons coriander roots and stems
- 2 stalks lemongrass, white part only, roughly chopped
- 2 teaspoons ground coriander
- 1 teaspoon ground cumin
- 4 kaffir lime leaves, chopped

1. Preheat the oven to 180°C.
2. Wrap the shrimp paste in foil and roast for 5–10 minutes or until warmed through.
3. Pound the roasted shrimp paste with the remaining ingredients in a mortar and pestle, or blend together in a food processor to make a thick paste.
4. Divide into portions, then place in an airtight container and freeze for a later date. It will keep for a month or so.

GREEN CURRY

Fry 2–3 tablespoons curry paste in 1 tablespoon vegetable oil until fragrant, then add 1–2 cups (250–500 ml) fish or chicken stock and ½ cup (125 ml) reduced-fat coconut milk. Add 2 cups (320 g) trimmed and diced fish or chicken and 1–2 cups (100–200 g) sliced and diced mixed vegetables and simmer for 5–10 minutes or until cooked through. Serve with lemon wedges, fresh coriander or mint and rice from your daily bread allowance.

✱ Shrimp paste (or belachan) is sold in Asian supermarkets and some mainstream supermarkets – try looking in the international food section. Don't be put off by the smell – it adds a delicious flavour to your curry. Roasting it helps mellow the flavour.

✱ Kaffir lime leaves are available from supermarkets and greengrocers. Freeze any leftovers in a zip-lock bag for future use.

stock and store

Spanish-style fish stew

This stew has quite a light texture, which allows the seafood to be the star. Pay a visit to your fishmonger and use whatever looks fresh on the day.

Serves 4

Prep time
10 minutes

Cooking time
35 minutes

1 serve =
2 units protein
1½ units vegetables
1 unit fats

- 1 tablespoon olive oil
- 1 onion, finely chopped
- 3 cloves garlic, crushed
- 2 sticks celery, finely sliced
- 1 bulb fennel, finely sliced
- ½ teaspoon chilli flakes
- 2 teaspoons mild Spanish paprika
- 1 litre salt-reduced fish or chicken stock
- 2 × 400 g tins chopped tomatoes
- 2 bay leaves
- 1 teaspoon sugar
- 800 g mixed seafood, such as white fish fillets, prawns, mussels, scallops and calamari
- 1 tablespoon lemon juice
- 3 tablespoons chopped flat-leaf parsley, plus extra leaves to garnish
- lemon wedges, to serve (optional)

1. Heat the olive oil in a large saucepan over medium heat and sauté the onion, garlic, celery and fennel until soft but not coloured. Stir in the chilli and paprika, and sauté for a further minute.

2. Add the stock, tomato, bay leaves and sugar. Bring to the boil, then reduce the heat and simmer, uncovered, for 25 minutes. You can cool the fish stew base at this stage and freeze until required. Otherwise, carry on with the recipe.

3. Add the seafood to the pan and gently submerge it in the liquid. Cover and simmer for 5 minutes until the fish is just cooked. Gently stir in the lemon juice and parsley, and season to taste. Garnish with extra parsley leaves and serve with lemon wedges, if liked.

VARIATIONS

- Pan-fried or grilled white fish fillets or prawns may be served on top of the stew with the parsley and lemon wedges, instead of adding seafood to the stew at step 3.

- Carry out steps 2 and 3 to make the stew base ahead of time. Refrigerate or freeze, depending on when you wish to use it. Instead of cooking the seafood in the saucepan at step 3, you could place your seafood in a large ovenproof dish, pour over the prepared stew base, then cover and bake in a preheated 180°C oven for 20–30 minutes or until the seafood is just cooked.

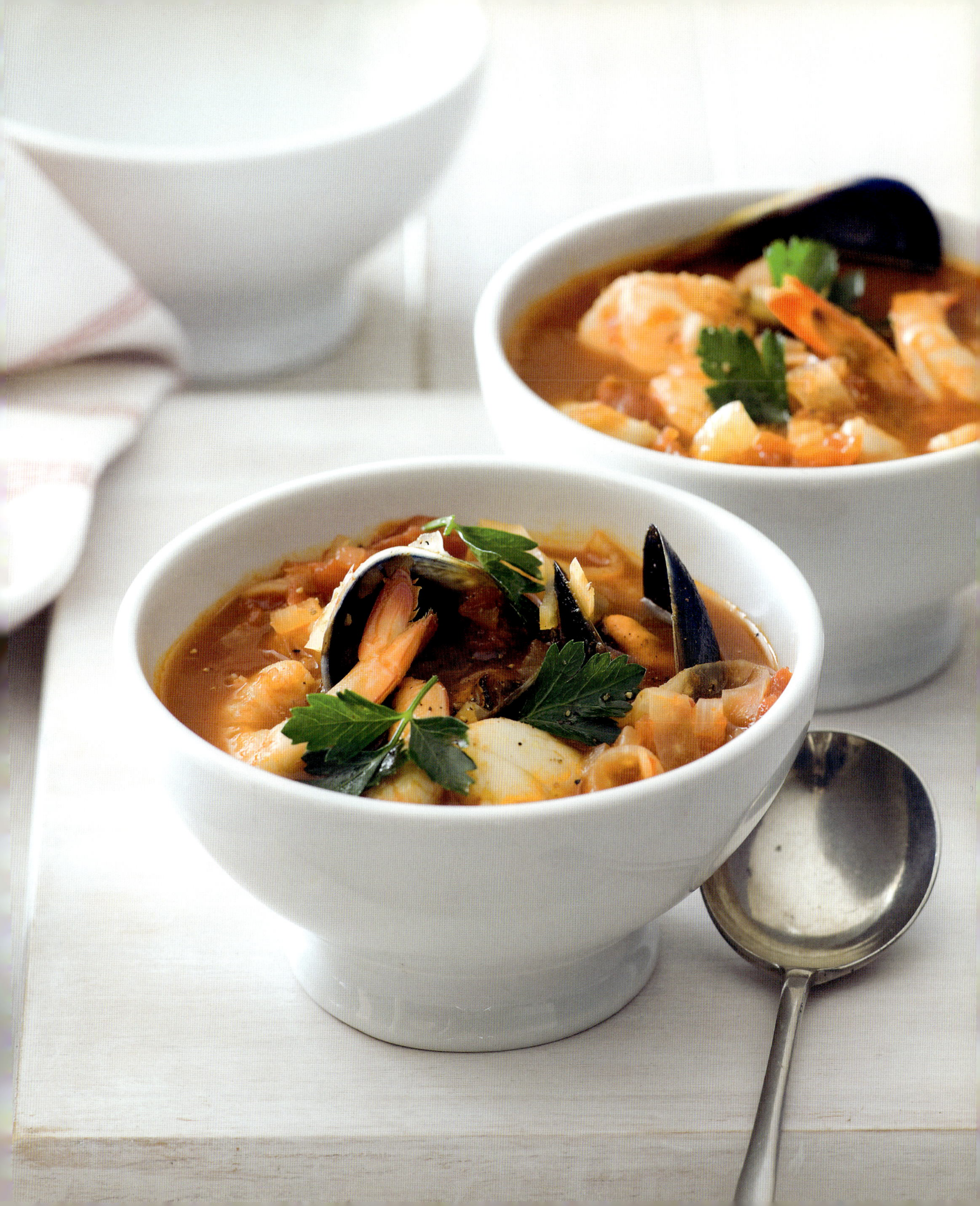

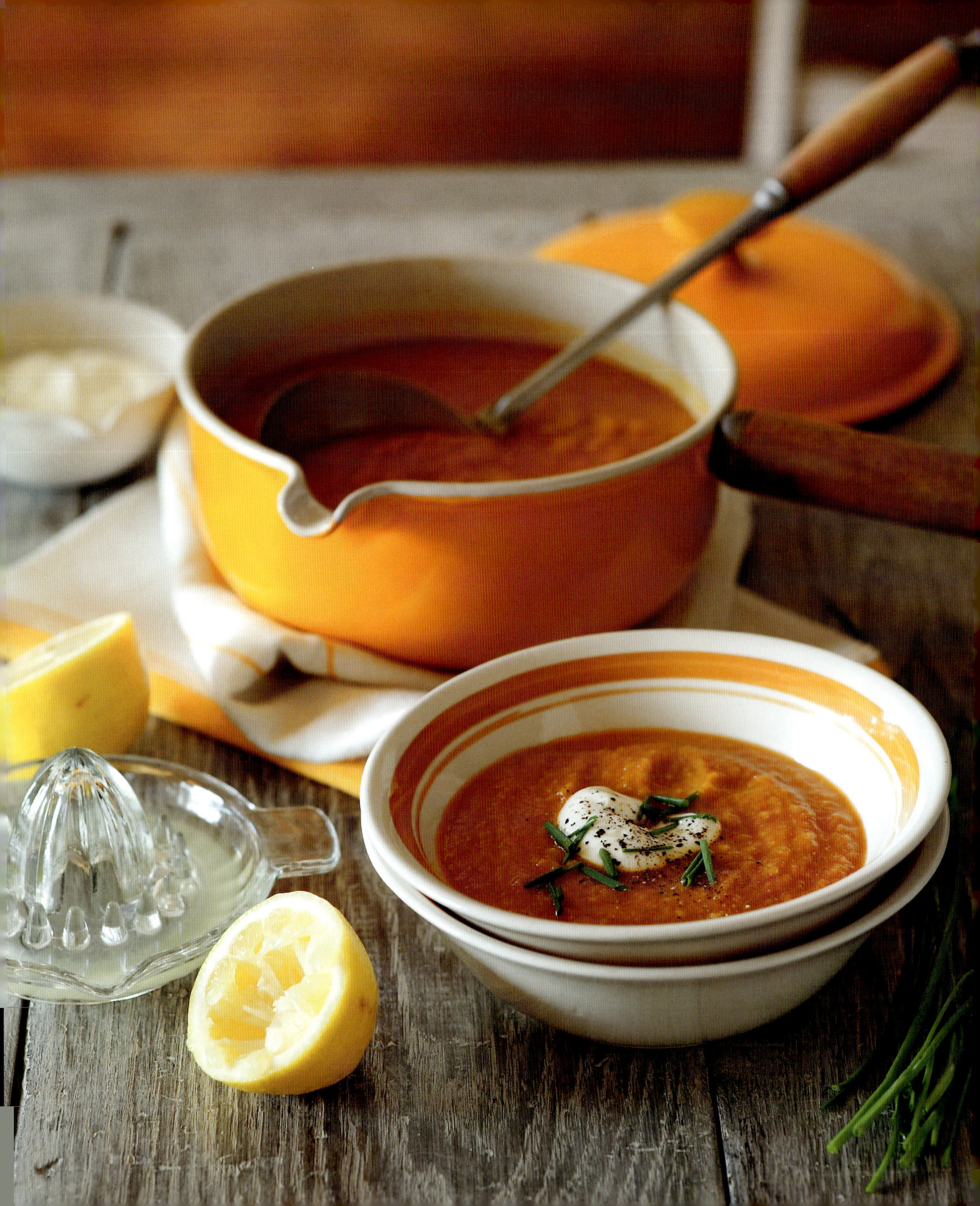

Cauliflower, lentil and tomato soup

Thick and hearty, this curried soup will warm you inside and out. The serves are generous so there will probably be leftovers, which you can enjoy the next day.

Serves 4

Prep time
15 minutes

Cooking time
30 minutes

1 serve =
¼ unit bread
2 units vegetables
1 unit fats

- 1 tablespoon extra virgin olive oil
- 1 large onion, finely chopped
- 2 carrots, diced
- 1 stick celery, diced
- 2 cloves garlic, crushed
- 1 teaspoon grated ginger
- 2 teaspoons curry powder
- 600 g cauliflower, cut into small florets
- 1.5 litres salt-reduced chicken or vegetable stock
- ½ cup (100 g) red lentils
- 1 × 400 g tin chopped tomatoes
- 2 tablespoons lemon juice
- roughly chopped chives, to serve
- reduced-fat yoghurt, to serve

1. Heat the olive oil in a large saucepan over medium heat and sauté the onion, carrot, celery, garlic and ginger for 5 minutes. Add the curry powder and cook for a further minute or until fragrant.

2. Stir in the cauliflower, stock, lentils and chopped tomatoes. Bring to the boil, then reduce the heat and simmer, covered, for 20 minutes or until the vegetables and lentils are tender.

3. Puree the soup in a blender, or in the pan with a stick blender, then return to the heat. Stir in the lemon juice and season to taste. Finish with a dollop of reduced-fat yoghurt, some chopped chives and a grinding of black pepper.

Carrot and parsnip soup

Double the quantities for this warming soup and save it for an evening when you don't have time to cook.

Serves 4

Prep time
15 minutes

Cooking time
45 minutes

1 serve =
¼ unit dairy
1½ units vegetables
1 unit fats

- 1 tablespoon extra virgin olive oil
- 1 onion, chopped
- 1 clove garlic, crushed
- 300 g carrots, sliced
- 300 g parsnips, peeled and sliced
- 150 g pumpkin, peeled and sliced
- 1 litre salt-reduced chicken or vegetable stock
- 1 cup (250 ml) reduced-fat milk
- roughly chopped flat-leaf parsley, to serve

1. Heat the olive oil in a large saucepan over medium heat and sauté the onion, stirring, for 4–5 minutes or until softened. Add the garlic, carrot, parsnip and potato and cook, stirring, for a further minute, then pour in the stock and bring to the boil.

2. Reduce the heat and simmer for 30 minutes or until the vegetables are soft. Allow to cool slightly, then puree the soup with a stick blender or in a food processor. Return to the saucepan, add the milk, season and heat through.

3. Serve sprinkled with chopped parsley and, if liked, bread from your daily allowance.

Vegetable curry

Serve this curry with grilled meat, poultry or fish from your daily protein allowance. If you opt for a vegetarian option, boost your protein intake by stirring in a 400 g tin of rinsed and drained chickpeas or 400 g diced tofu at step 4. Warm through and serve.

Serves 4
Prep time 10 minutes
Cooking time 25 minutes
1 serve =
1 unit vegetables
½ unit fats

2 teaspoons vegetable oil
1 onion, chopped
2 cloves garlic, crushed
1 × 3 cm piece ginger, finely grated
½ teaspoon chilli powder
1 teaspoon ground cumin
1 teaspoon ground coriander
1 teaspoon ground turmeric
3 cups (600 g) mixed vegetables, diced
1 × 400 g tin chopped tomatoes
1½ teaspoons garam masala
handful of baby spinach leaves (optional)
1 tablespoon lemon juice
curry leaves and roughly chopped coriander, to serve (optional)

1. Heat the oil in a medium saucepan over medium heat and sauté the onion, garlic, ginger, chilli powder, cumin, coriander and turmeric for about 3 minutes or until fragrant.

2. Add any harder vegetables you have selected to use (such as potato, carrot or pumpkin) and stir until combined with the spice mix. Stir in the chopped tomatoes and ½ cup (125 ml) water.

3. Cover and simmer for 10 minutes, then add any remaining softer vegetables (such as eggplant, capsicum, broccoli or zucchini) and cook for a further 10 minutes or until all the vegetables are tender.

4. Stir in the garam masala, spinach (if using) and lemon juice. Season to taste and serve with meat or fish from your daily protein allowance or rice from your daily bread allowance, garnished with curry leaves and coriander (if using).

> Select from the following vegetables to use in your curry: potato, cauliflower, pumpkin, beans, zucchini (courgette), eggplant (aubergine), mushrooms, capsicum (pepper), broccoli, peas and corn.

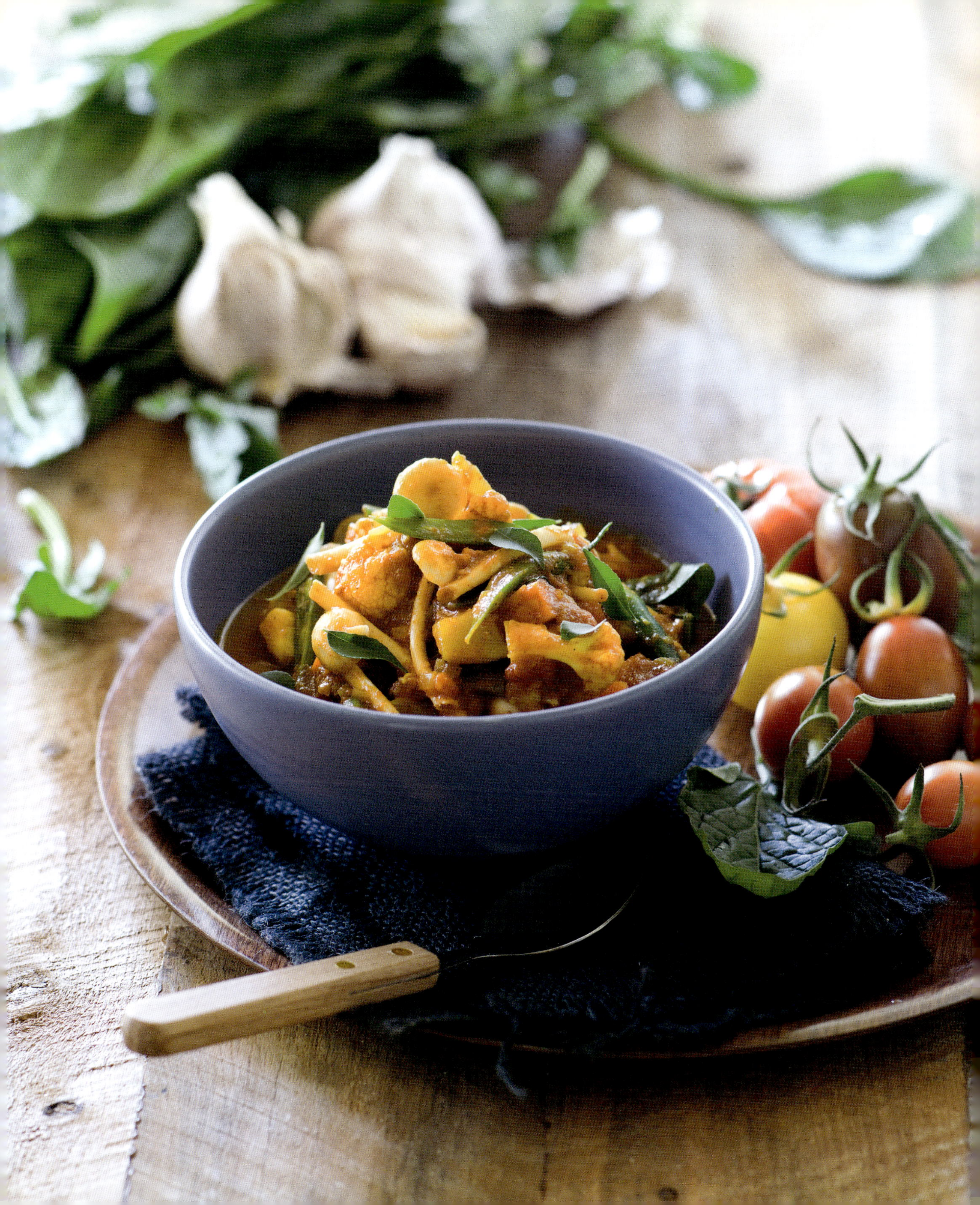

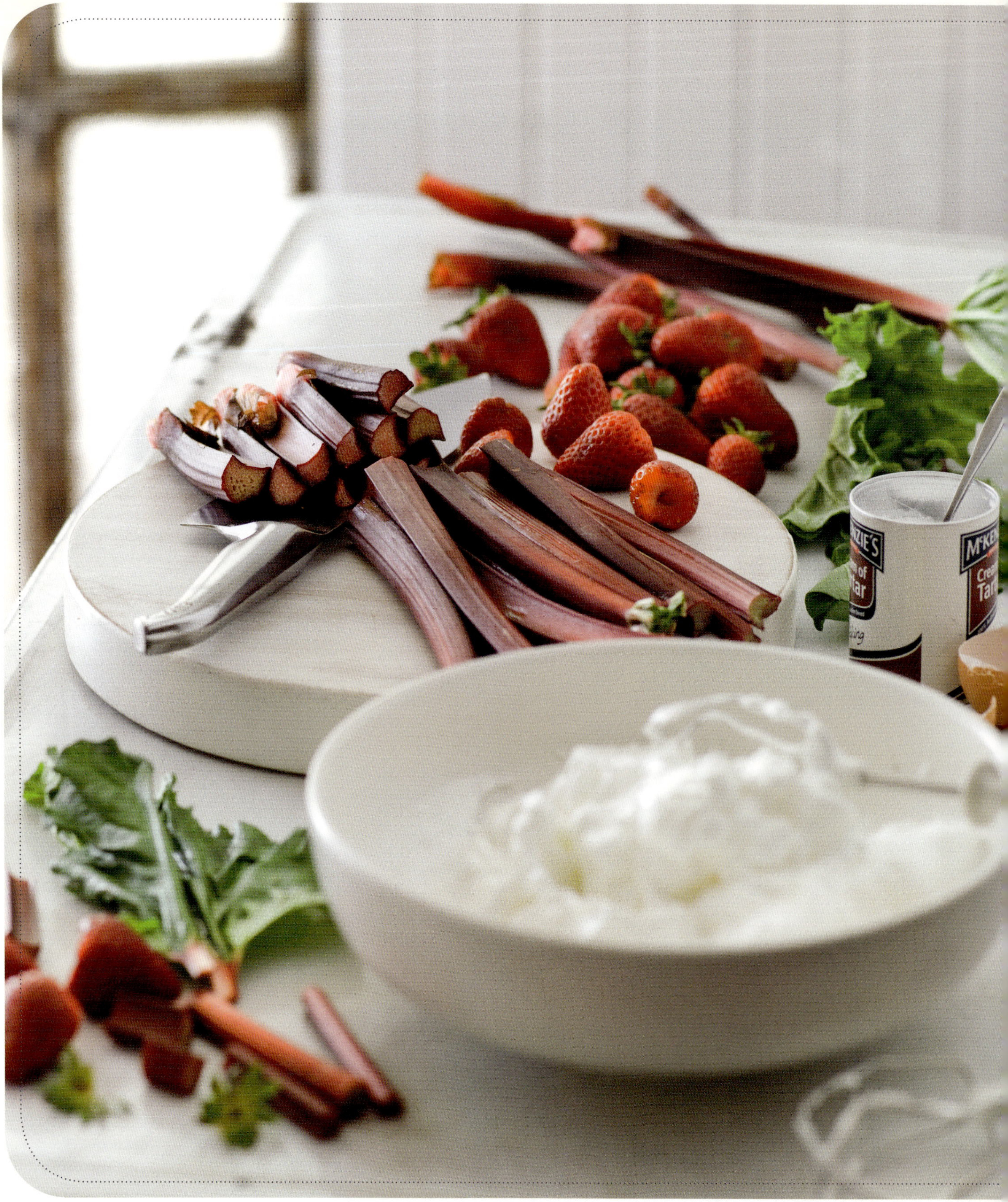

something sweet

It's true, sweet treats are still on the menu. Whether you need to cool down on a hot summer's day with a silky watermelon sorbet, or warm up in winter with a comforting apple crumble, you'll find something for everyone's tastes in this chapter. Indulge in these sweet delights guilt-free, without blowing out your daily food allowance.

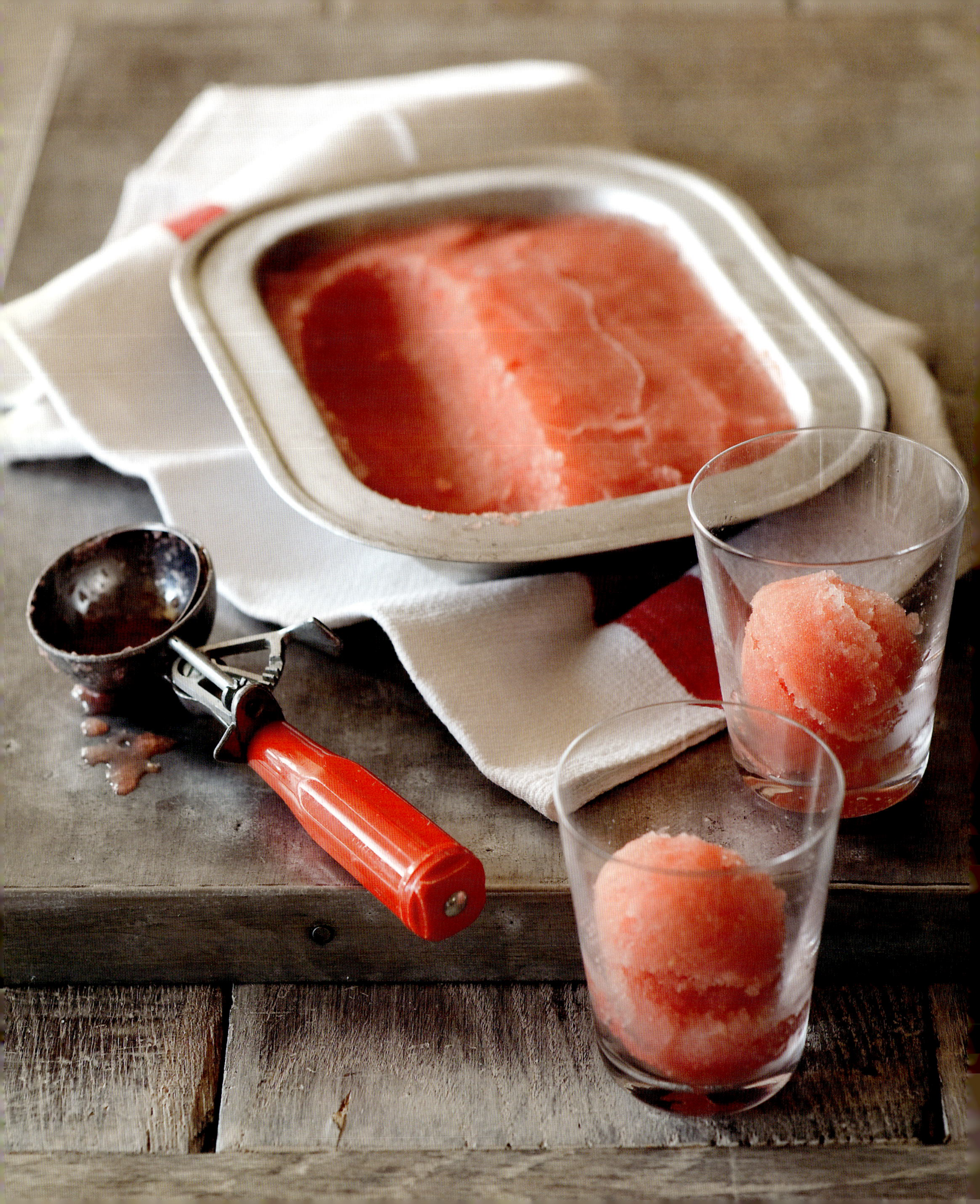

Watermelon sorbet

For a cooling treat on a hot summer's day, indulge in this lovely dessert.

Serves 4

Prep time
25 minutes

Chilling time
5 hours

1 serve =
1 unit fruit

- 700 g seedless watermelon, roughly diced and chilled
- 2 tablespoons lime juice
- 2 tablespoons sugar or powdered sweetener

1. Combine all the ingredients in a food processor and process until smooth.
2. If you have an ice-cream maker, churn the ice-cream according to the manufacturer's instructions.
3. If you don't have an ice-cream maker, freeze the watermelon mixture in a shallow container for 2–3 hours or until just set. Pulse in a food processor or blender until smooth, then return to the freezer for a further hour or until frozen. Once again, pulse in a food processor or blender until smooth, then return to the freezer and allow the sorbet to freeze until solid. Remove from the freezer 20 minutes before serving.

> Depending on what is in season, use other fruits, such as rockmelon or peach, in place of the watermelon.

Apricot and almond yoghurt pops

Kids and adults alike will enjoy cooling down with these icy pops. You can vary the fruit and nut combinations according to taste – the options are endless!

Serves 4

Prep time
10 minutes

Chilling time
overnight

1 serve =
½ unit dairy
½ unit fruit
1 unit fats

20 g flaked almonds
30 g sultanas
400 g reduced-fat apricot yoghurt
1 tablespoon sesame seeds

1. Finely chop the almonds and sultanas or pulse in a food processor. Combine with the yoghurt and sesame seeds in a large bowl, then divide among four 100 ml icy-pole moulds. Place in the freezer overnight.

2. To serve, dip the moulds in hot water to loosen.

> These can be made with other fruit-flavoured reduced-fat yoghurts: try mango, strawberry or blueberry – whatever takes your fancy.

Berry banana freeze

Another icy treat for a warm day. It takes just a few minutes to whip this up, and the results are sensational.

Serves 4

Prep time
5 minutes

Chilling time
2–3 hours

1 serve =
1 unit fruit

3 bananas
200 g frozen mixed berries

1. Peel and roughly chop the bananas and place in a freezer bag. Freeze for 2–3 hours or until solid.

2. Puree the banana and berries in a food processor until smooth. Serve immediately or scoop into an airtight container and return to the freezer until ready to serve.

> You could use this mixture to make icy poles for the kids. Just scoop into six 100 ml icy-pole moulds and return to the freezer for 1–2 hours until solid.

Mango pudding

For mango lovers everywhere, this creamy dessert is sure to be a hit.

Serves 4

Prep time
10 minutes, plus refrigerating time

1 serve =
½ unit dairy
½ unit fruit

- 2 medium mangoes, peeled and stones removed
- 200 ml reduced-fat evaporated milk
- 4 tablespoons sugar or powdered sweetener
- 1½ tablespoons powdered gelatine
- fresh berries, to serve (optional)

1. Puree the mangoes in a food processor or blender. Transfer to a bowl and mix in the milk and sugar or sweetener.

2. Stir the gelatine into 200 ml hot water until dissolved. Add to the mango mixture and stir well to combine.

3. Pour the mixture into four glasses or bowls and refrigerate for 2 hours or until set. Serve with fresh berries, if liked.

* You can use 400 g tinned or thawed frozen mango flesh if fresh mangoes aren't in season.

* This is the perfect dessert to follow a spicy Asian meal. Try serving it with a squeeze of lime juice.

something sweet

Cinnamon oranges with spiced yoghurt

This simple recipe lets the spices do the talking. The creamy spiced yoghurt brings it all together beautifully.

Serves 4

Prep time
10 minutes, plus refrigerating time

Cooking time
10 minutes

1 serve =
½ unit dairy
1 unit fruit

2 tablespoons sugar
1 cinnamon stick
2 cloves
1 star anise
4 oranges, peeled and sliced, reserving the peel from 1 orange
½ teaspoon vanilla bean paste

Spiced yoghurt
400 g reduced-fat vanilla yoghurt
1 tablespoon honey
¼ teaspoon ground cinnamon, plus extra to serve (optional)

1 Combine the sugar and 1 cup (250 ml) water in a small saucepan over medium heat and bring to the boil, stirring until the sugar has dissolved. Add the cinnamon, cloves, star anise and reserved orange peel. Simmer for 5 minutes, then remove from the heat and set aside to cool.

2 Stir the vanilla paste through the spice syrup, then strain, discarding the solids. Place the orange slices in a large bowl and pour the strained syrup evenly over the top. Cover with plastic wrap and refrigerate for at least 2 hours or overnight.

3 To make the spiced yoghurt, combine all the ingredients in a bowl.

4 Divide the orange slices among four bowls and top with a dollop of spiced yoghurt. Garnish with star anise or sprinkle with a little extra cinnamon, if desired, and serve.

> Vanilla bean paste is a convenient substitute for vanilla beans, and is available in the baking section at your local supermarket. Unlike vanilla essence or extract, it contains vanilla seeds. You can substitute vanilla extract if vanilla bean paste is not available.

This dessert looks gorgeous if you use blood oranges when in season, or a mixture of both regular and blood oranges.

Spiced strawberries with ricotta cream

The perfect ending to a friendly barbecue get-together (see page 77) or a sweet treat for any time of the week.

Serves 4

Prep time
10 minutes,
plus cooling time

Cooking time
10 minutes

1 serve =
½ unit dairy
1 unit fruit

500 g strawberries, washed and hulled
1 cup (250 ml) unsweetened orange juice
2 tablespoons sugar
1 cinnamon stick
4 star anise
2 teaspoons Grand Marnier (optional)

Ricotta cream
100 g reduced-fat ricotta
200 g reduced-fat vanilla yoghurt
1 teaspoon caster sugar or
    powdered sweetener

1. Place the strawberries in a large bowl and set aside.
2. Combine the orange juice, sugar, cinnamon and star anise in a medium saucepan over medium heat, stirring until the sugar has dissolved. Bring to the boil, then reduce the heat and simmer for 5 minutes or until slightly reduced. Stir in the Grand Marnier (if using), then cool to room temperature. Pour the syrup over the strawberries and set aside for 30 minutes to develop the flavours.
3. Meanwhile, to make the ricotta cream, combine all the ingredients in a food processor until smooth.
4. To serve, remove the cinnamon and star anise from the strawberry mix and spoon the strawberries into four bowls or serving glasses. Drizzle with a little of the syrup and serve with the ricotta cream.

> Other berries may be used in this recipe (raspberries, blackberries or mixed) or try a combination of strawberry and mango. As always, buy what's fresh and in season.

Vary the liqueur if you like — try framboise. Leave it out altogether if serving children or replace it with ½ teaspoon vanilla extract.

For a winning tropical fruit combination, serve the custard with a mix of pineapple, kiwi fruit, star fruit and lychees.

Coconut custard

This custard pudding is a summery delight, and can be served with any seasonal fruit.

Serves 4

Prep time
10 minutes

Cooking time
30 minutes

1 serve =
½ unit protein
½ unit dairy

4 eggs
1½ cups (375 ml) reduced-fat coconut-flavoured evaporated milk
½ cup (125 ml) reduced-fat milk
4 tablespoons sugar or powdered sweetener

1. Preheat the oven to 160°C.
2. Whisk together all the ingredients until well combined. Strain and pour into four 200 ml ramekins or ovenproof dishes. Place the ramekins in a roasting tin and pour enough hot water into the tin to come halfway up the sides of the ramekins.
3. Bake for 30 minutes or until just set (the centre should still be wobbly). Remove the custards from the roasting tin and allow to cool. If not eating within an hour of cooling, refrigerate until ready to serve. Serve with your choice of fruit.

> This can also be made with unflavoured evaporated milk and served with mixed berries and/or oranges.

something sweet 187

Grilled peaches with raspberry coulis

This dessert can also be made with other seasonal fruits, such as mangoes, apricots, pineapple or nectarines.

Serves 4

Prep time
5 minutes

Cooking time
5 minutes

1 serve =
1½ units fruit

4 peaches, peeled, halved and stones removed
olive oil spray

Raspberry coulis
300 g frozen raspberries, thawed
1 tablespoon sugar or powdered sweetener
3 tablespoons orange juice

1. To prepare the raspberry coulis, combine the raspberries, sugar or powdered sweetener and orange juice in a food processor and blend until smooth. Strain and set aside.

2. Heat a chargrill or heavy-based frying pan over medium heat. Spray the peaches with olive oil and grill for 2–3 minutes each side or until golden.

3. Divide the grilled peaches among four plates, drizzle with the raspberry coulis and serve with a small scoop of reduced-fat, sugar-free ice-cream or dairy dessert from your daily dairy allowance, if liked.

- The peaches can easily be grilled on the barbecue for a sweet end to a weekend get-together.
- If liked, the raspberry coulis may be heated and served as a hot syrup. It also makes an excellent topping to a scoop of reduced-fat ice-cream for a quick and easy dessert.

Apple crumble with custard

This crumble is a warming end to any meal, and can be made with many different fruit combinations so you will never tire of it.

Serves 4

Prep time
10 minutes

Cooking time
35 minutes

1 serve =
½ unit bread
½ unit dairy
1 unit fruit
1 unit fats

1 × 800 g tin apple pie fruit
4 tablespoons plain wholemeal flour
4 tablespoons rolled oats
2 tablespoons brown sugar
½ teaspoon ground cinnamon
2 tablespoons light margarine
400 g reduced-fat custard

1. Preheat the oven to 180°C.
2. Spread the apple in the base of an 18 cm × 18 cm ovenproof dish.
3. Combine the flour, oats, sugar and cinnamon in a medium bowl. Using your fingers, rub the margarine into the dry ingredients until the mixture resembles coarse breadcrumbs. Sprinkle the crumble mix over the apple.
4. Bake for 35 minutes, then serve hot with a splash of reduced-fat custard.

> ✻ Spraying the top lightly with olive oil halfway through cooking will result in a darker golden crumble topping.
>
> ✻ Using different fruit in your crumble can produce equally delicious results – try tinned pears, mangoes or apricots, or use the rhubarb and strawberry filling from page 191.

something sweet

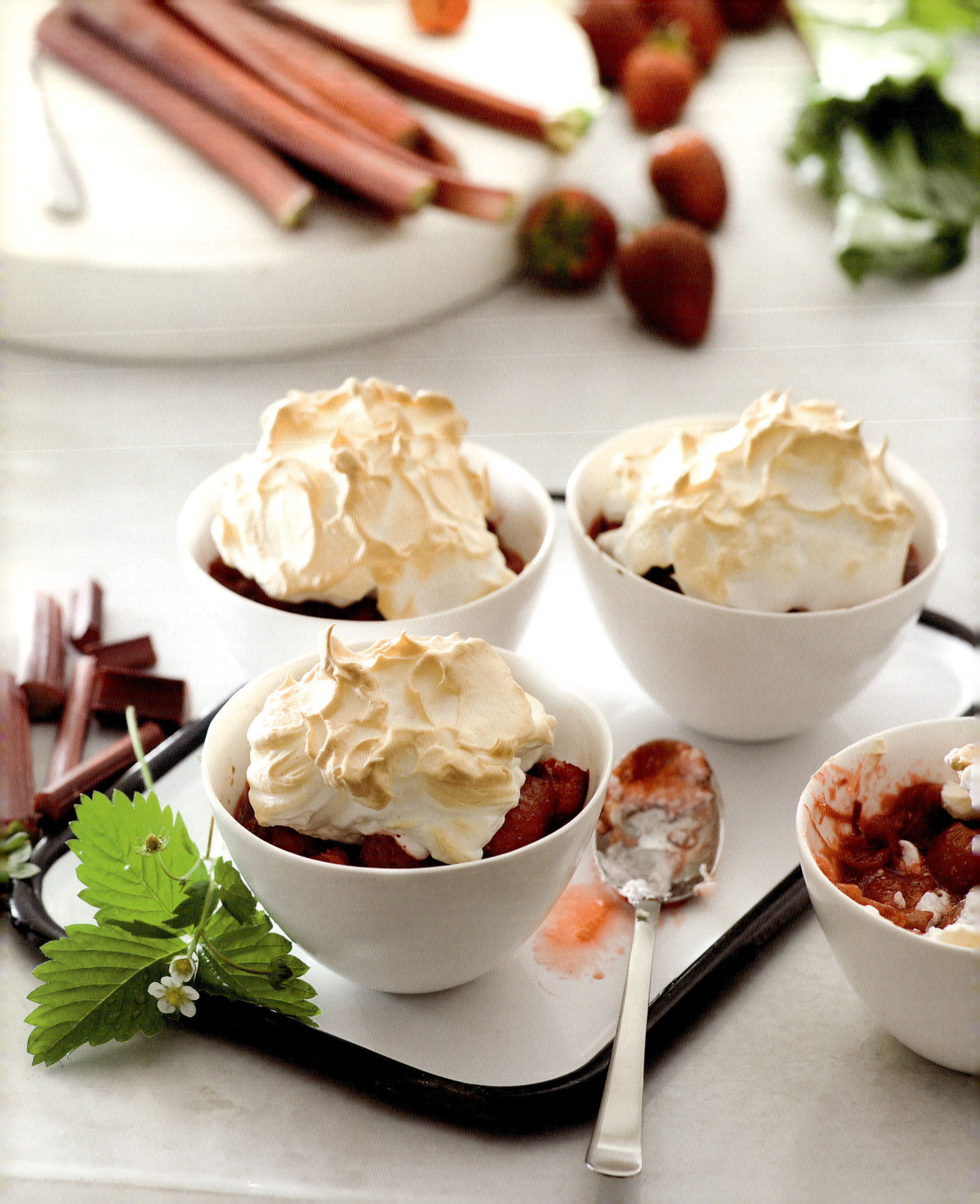

Rhubarb and strawberry meringues

This pudding looks impressive, but it's really not that tricky to throw together. Serve it at the table and enjoy the admiring praise.

Serves 4

Prep time
15 minutes

Cooking time
30 minutes

1 serve =
1 unit fruit

8 stalks (350 g) rhubarb, cut into 2 cm pieces
4 tablespoons sugar or powdered sweetener
2 teaspoons grated orange zest
250 g strawberries, washed and hulled

Meringue
3 egg whites
¼ teaspoon cream of tartar
3 tablespoons caster sugar

✴ For egg whites to beat successfully, the bowl and beaters must be spotlessly clean and clear of any grease.

✴ To make one large pudding, spoon the mixture into a 1.5 litre ovenproof dish and proceed with the recipe.

1 Preheat the oven to 180°C.

2 Place the rhubarb, sugar or sweetener, orange zest and ½ cup (125 ml) water in a medium saucepan. Bring to the boil, then reduce the heat and simmer for 10 minutes or until the rhubarb is nearly tender. Stir in the strawberries, then transfer the mixture to four 1½ cup (375 ml) ovenproof dishes.

3 To make the meringue, beat the egg whites and cream of tartar with an electric mixer until soft peaks form, then gradually add the sugar while still beating. Beat until stiff peaks form and the mixture is glossy. Spoon over the rhubarb mixture and bake for 15 minutes or until lightly golden on top. Serve with reduced-fat vanilla yoghurt or reduced-fat, sugar-free ice-cream, if liked.

Apricot strudel

Crisp pastry and a warm fruit filling make this dessert feel like a real indulgence, but the good news is you can enjoy it guilt-free.

Serves 4

Prep time
15 minutes

Cooking time
25 minutes

1 serve =
½ unit bread
½ unit fruit
½ unit fats

1 × 400 g tin apricot pie fruit or apricot halves in juice, well drained
25 g slivered almonds
4 sheets filo pastry
olive oil spray
icing sugar, for dusting

1. Preheat the oven to 200°C and line a baking tray with baking paper.

2. Roughly chop the apricots and combine with the almonds in a bowl.

3. Lay one sheet of pastry on a clean work surface and spray lightly with olive oil. Place the remaining sheets on top, spraying each with olive oil as you go. With the longest edge closest to you, spoon the apricot mixture into a log shape across the centre of the pastry (you should have about a quarter of the width of the pastry on each side of the fruit log). Fold the edge closest to you over the fruit, then bring in the sides and roll up firmly.

4. Place the strudel, seam-side down, on the prepared baking tray and spray lightly with olive oil. Bake for 20–25 minutes or until golden. Dust lightly with icing sugar and serve with reduced-fat vanilla yoghurt or a dairy dessert from your daily dairy allowance, if liked.

For a different filling, replace the apricots with tinned apple pie fruit or cherries, or a combination of the two.

Berry cheesecake

Cheesecake is an old-time favourite, but almost always a big 'no-no' when you're watching your nutritional intake. But thanks to this clever recipe, you can have your cheesecake and eat it too, while staying within the guidelines of your daily food allowance.

Serves 8

Prep time
10 minutes, plus cooling time

Cooking time
35 minutes

1 serve =
1 unit dairy
¼ unit fruit

olive oil spray
400 g reduced-fat ricotta
1 tablespoon plain flour
3 tablespoons sugar or powdered sweetener
2 eggs
finely grated zest of 1 lime
1 teaspoon vanilla extract
150 g berries, lightly crushed and very well drained if frozen, plus extra berries to garnish (optional)
icing sugar, for dusting (optional)

1. Preheat the oven to 160°C. Spray an 18 cm springform tin with olive oil and line the base with baking paper.

2. Combine all the ingredients, except the berries, in a food processor and process until smooth. Spoon half the mixture into the prepared tin, then sprinkle the berries over the top and lightly swirl through. Finish with the remaining ricotta mixture and smooth the top of the cake.

3. Bake for 30–35 minutes or until just set. Turn the oven off and allow the cake to cool in the oven for 1 hour. Remove and cool completely before serving. If you're not eating the cake as soon as it has cooled, refrigerate until ready to serve. Garnish with extra berries and lightly dust with icing sugar if you like.

> You can use fresh or frozen berries for this cake. The best fresh berries to use are raspberries, blueberries or blackberries. Packets of frozen mixed berries from the supermarket are also a good option. If you choose to use frozen berries, make sure you give them time to thaw before incorporating them into the mix, and drain them well.

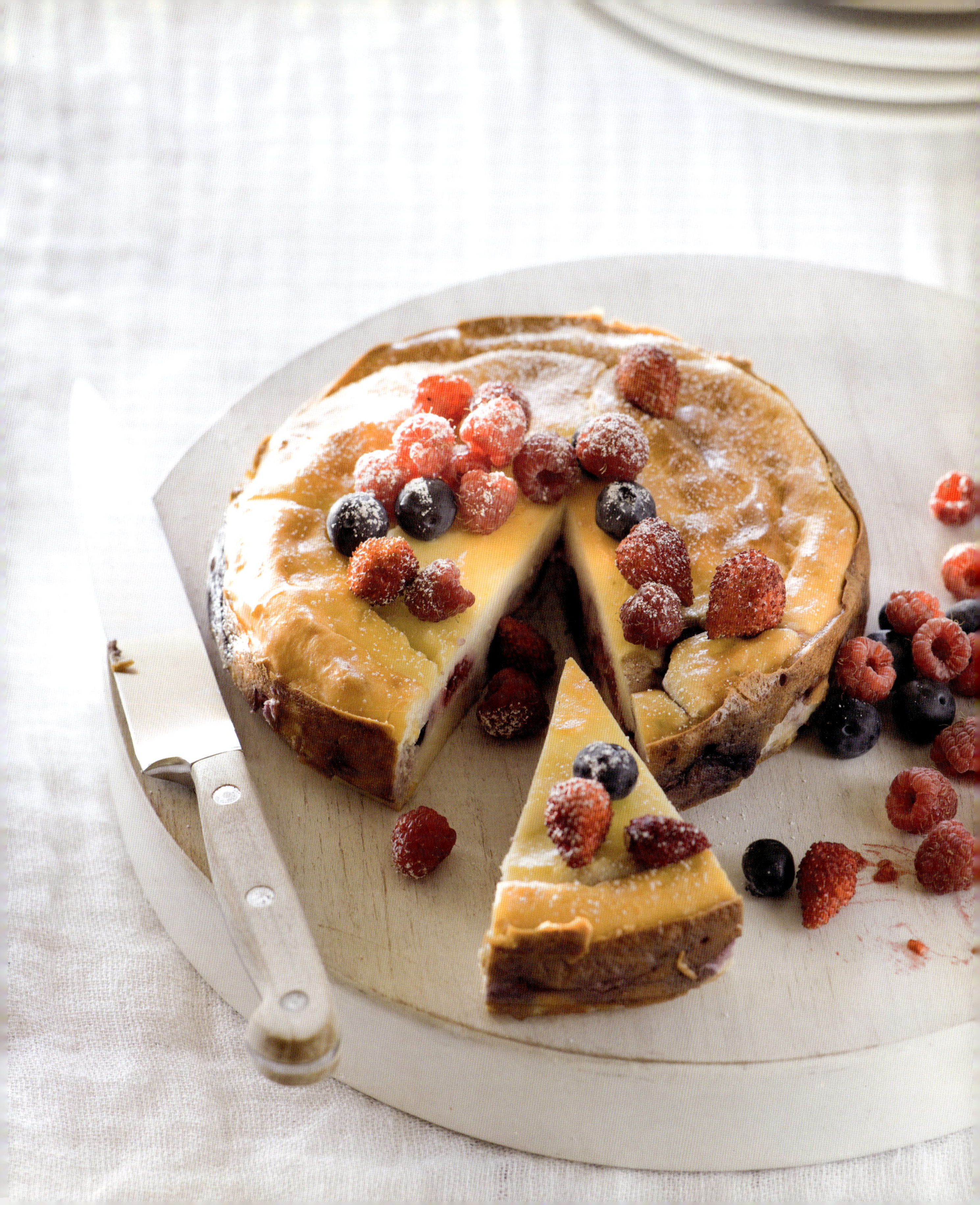

Eve's pudding

This is a lighter version of a traditional British pudding made with apples and a sponge cake topping.

Serves 4

Prep time
10 minutes

Cooking time
40 minutes

1 serve =
½ unit bread
2 units fruit

500 g tinned apple pie fruit, drained
500 g fresh or tinned berries

Sponge topping
2 eggs
4 tablespoons caster sugar or powdered sweetener
2 tablespoons plain flour
2 tablespoons self-raising flour
2 tablespoons cornflour
icing sugar, for dusting

1. Preheat the oven to 180°C.
2. Place the fruit in an 18 cm round baking dish.
3. To make the sponge topping, place the eggs and sugar or sweetener in a medium bowl and beat until thick and creamy. Sift the flours together in a separate bowl, then fold into the egg mixture.
4. Spoon the sponge mix over the fruit and bake for 30–40 minutes or until golden and firm. Dust lightly with icing sugar and serve with reduced-fat yoghurt or dairy dessert from your daily dairy allowance, if liked.

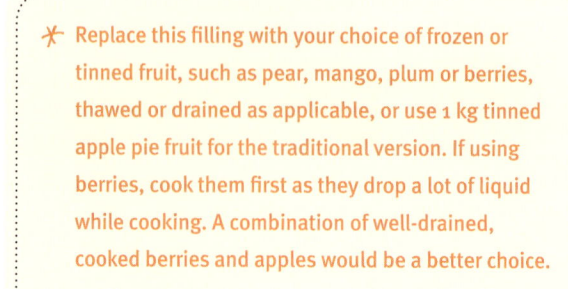

---

* Replace this filling with your choice of frozen or tinned fruit, such as pear, mango, plum or berries, thawed or drained as applicable, or use 1 kg tinned apple pie fruit for the traditional version. If using berries, cook them first as they drop a lot of liquid while cooking. A combination of well-drained, cooked berries and apples would be a better choice.

* Fresh stewed fruit can also be used in place of tinned or frozen fruit.

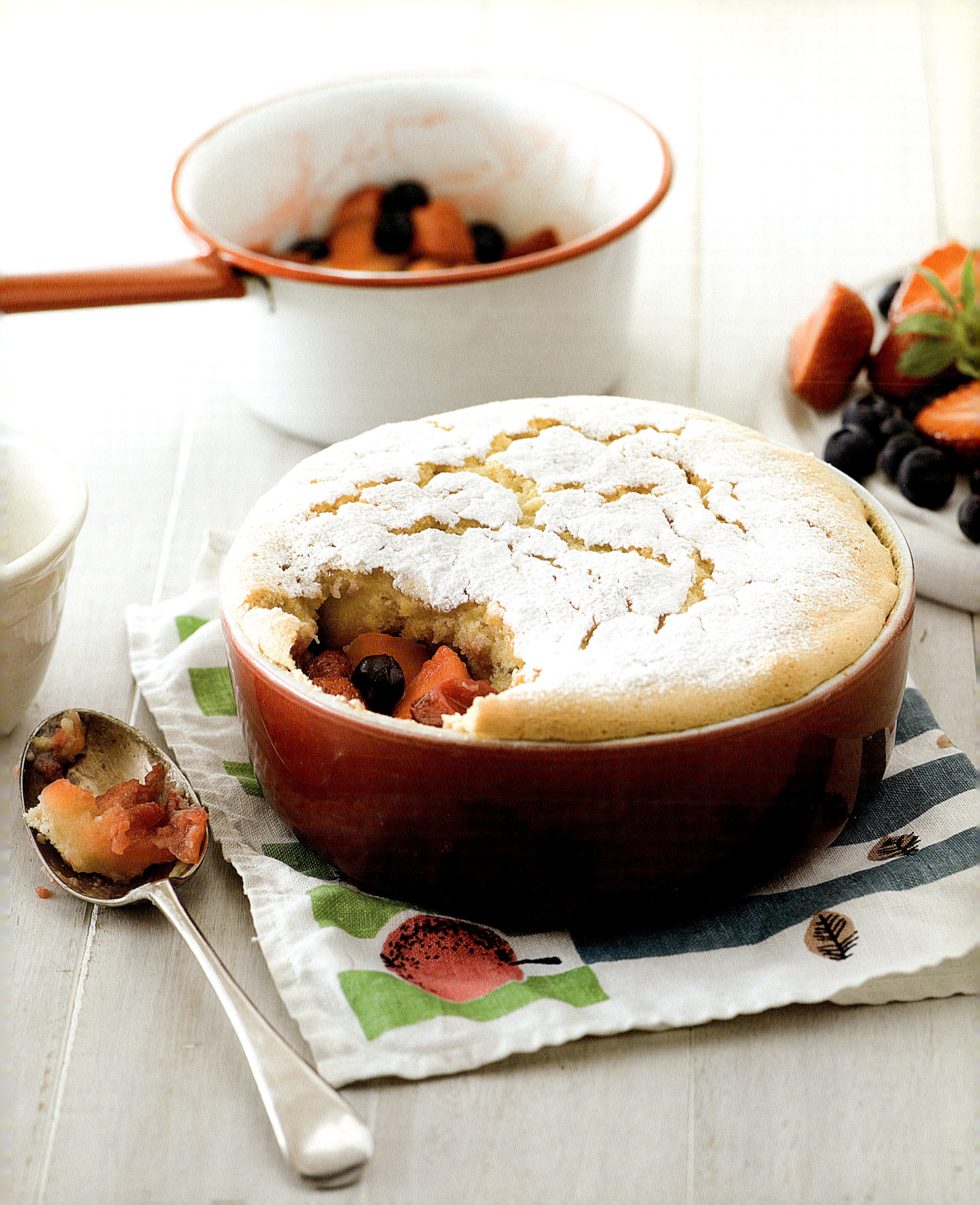

index

Antipasto salad 36
APPLES
   Apple crumble with custard 189
   Eve's pudding 196
APRICOTS
   Apricot and almond yoghurt pops 180
   Apricot chicken 137
   Apricot strudel 192
ARTICHOKES
   Bruschetta with artichoke and rocket 18
ASIAN GREENS
   Chicken laksa 101
   Japanese-style grilled fish with Asian greens 73
   Steamed tofu with Asian greens 110
   Turkey escalopes with Asian vegetables 107
ASPARAGUS
   Green beans and asparagus with garlic breadcrumbs 148
   Smoked salmon and asparagus frittata 26
   Stir-fried beans, mushrooms and asparagus 97
AVOCADO
   Avocado salad 157
   Prawn and avocado salad 44
BACON
   Pancetta and semi-dried tomato tarts 20
Baked ricotta with chilli and olives 25
BANANAS
   Berry banana freeze 180
Barbecued lamb cutlets with minty yoghurt sauce 79
BASIL
   Bruschetta with tomato and basil 18
   Grilled vegetable salad with basil and black olives 80
   Salsa 50
   Salsa verde 120
   Veal parmigiana 122
   Vinaigrette 80
BEANS
   Green beans and asparagus with garlic breadcrumbs 148
   Stir-fried beans, mushrooms and asparagus 97
   Thai-style beef and bean stir-fry 53
   White bean mash 98

BEEF
   Beef burgers with salsa 50
   Beef fajitas 85
   Beef fillet with cherry tomato and eggplant compote 148
   Beef goulash 152
   Beef rogan josh 87
   Bolognese 155
   Bourguignon-style beef casserole 158
   Chimichurri steak with cos salad 60
   Cottage pie 125
   Individual meatloaves 126
   Roast beef and vegetables with salsa verde 120
   Spicy meatballs with chilli tomato sauce 115
   Stir-fried beef and broccolini in oyster sauce 56
   Teriyaki beef with egg noodles 56
   Tex–Mex chilli beef 157
   Thai-style beef and bean stir-fry 53
   Vietnamese beef broth (beef pho) 88
Beetroot dip with pita chips 114
BERRIES
   Berry banana freeze 180
   Berry cheesecake 194
   Eve's pudding 196
   Mixed berry smoothie 12
   Raspberry coulis 188
   Rhubarb and strawberry meringues 191
   Spiced strawberries with ricotta cream 184
Bolognese 155
Bourguignon-style beef casserole 158
Braised Moroccan lamb 161
BREADCRUMBS 67
   Garlic breadcrumbs 148
BROCCOLINI
   Stir-fried beef and broccolini in oyster sauce 56
bruschetta toppings 18
BRUSSELS SPROUTS
   Shaved cabbage and brussels sprout salad 33
CABBAGE
   Cabbage and cucumber salad 134
   Mustard cabbage 96
   Shaved cabbage and brussels sprout salad 33

   Spicy chicken noodle salad 38
   Warm cabbage salad 63
Cajun turkey skewers with orange and red onion salad 68
Cannelloni 155
CAPERS
   Mediterranean-style chicken with olives and capers 68
   Salsa verde 120
Carrot and parsnip soup 173
CASSEROLES see stews and casseroles
CAULIFLOWER
   Cauliflower, lentil and tomato soup 173
   Fish pie 143
   Scallops with prosciutto and cauliflower puree 147
   Spicy roasted cauliflower 97
CEREAL
   Cinnamon and sultana porridge 13
   Muesli 12
Chargrilled balsamic chicken 80
Chargrilled vegetable pinwheel sandwiches 22
CHEESE
   Cheese sauce 142
   Chicken breasts stuffed with feta and olive tapenade 102
   Enchiladas 157
   Greek salad 46
   Ham and cheese pinwheel sandwiches 22
   Parmesan fish fingers with homemade wedges 138
   Pumpkin and feta salad 91
   Smoked salmon and cream cheese cucumber bites 146
   Tex-Mex lettuce cups 157
   Tomato and cheese mini frittatas 14
   Veal parmigiana 122
   see also ricotta
CHEESECAKE
   Berry cheesecake 194
CHERRY TOMATO
   Cherry tomato and cucumber salad 64
   Cherry tomato and eggplant compote 148

CHICKEN
　Apricot chicken 137
　Chargrilled balsamic chicken 80
　Chicken breasts stuffed with feta and
　　olive tapenade 102
　Chicken cakes 25
　Chicken gumbo 136
　Chicken laksa 101
　Chicken and mango salad 41
　Chicken meatballs 168
　Chicken noodle soup 106
　Chicken nuggets with potato wedges 67
　Chicken satay with peanut sauce 105
　Chicken tagine 165
　Chicken tikka with cherry tomato and
　　cucumber salad 64
　Chicken and vegetable country stew 166
　Chicken and vegetable pasta salad 31
　Green roast chicken curry with a fresh
　　cabbage and cucumber salad 134
　Mediterranean-style chicken with olives
　　and capers 68
　poached in Chinese master stock 167
　Spicy chicken noodle salad 38
CHICKPEAS
　Hummus 115
　Moroccan lamb with chickpeas and spinach 92
　Rocket, sweet potato and chickpea salad 35
　Squid salad with rocket and chickpeas 109
CHILLI
　Baked ricotta with chilli and olives 25
　Chilli tomato sauce 115
　Lime and chilli sauce 28
　Mexican eggs 15
　Tex–Mex chilli beef 157
　Thai green curry paste 169
　Thai-style beef and bean stir-fry 53
Chimichurri steak with cos salad 60
Chinese master stock 167
Chinese mushroom omelette 75
Cinnamon oranges with spiced yoghurt 182
Cinnamon and sultana porridge 13
Coconut custard 187

COMPOTE
　Cherry tomato and eggplant compote 148
　Dried fruit compote 13
coriander, roots and stems 53
CORN
　Chicken noodle soup 106
　Chicken and vegetable country stew 166
　Spiced corn and tomato 69
Cos salad 60
Cottage pie 125
COUSCOUS
　Lemon couscous 94
　Roast vegetable and couscous salad 47
Creamy tomato sauce 78
CRUMBLE
　Apple crumble with custard 189
　fruit for 195
CUCUMBER
　Cabbage and cucumber salad 134
　Cherry tomato and cucumber salad 64
　Cucumber bites 146
　Cucumber salad 105
　Greek salad 46
CURRY
　Beef rogan josh 87
　Chicken laksa 101
　Chicken tikka with cherry tomato and
　　cucumber salad 64
　Green curry 169
　Green roast chicken curry with a fresh cabbage
　　and cucumber salad 134
　Lamb kofta curry 127
　Mulligatawny soup 162
　Vegetable curry 174
CURRY PASTE 101
　Thai green curry paste 169
CUSTARD
　Coconut custard 187
daily food allowance 4–5
DIPS
　Beetroot dip with pita chips 114
　Grilled eggplant dip 114
　Hummus 115

　Salsa 50
　Tuna, ricotta and red onion spread 23
DRESSINGS
　Mustard dressing 44
　Vinaigrette 78, 80
　Yoghurt dressing 41
Dried fruit compote 13
EGGPLANT
　Cherry tomato and eggplant compote 148
　Grilled eggplant dip 114
　Moussaka stacks 131
　Warm eggplant salad 81
EGGS
　Mexican eggs 15
　Olive and egg cucumber bites 146
　Salad Niçoise 32
Enchiladas 157
Eve's pudding 196
Fennel and red onion salad 33
Fennel roasted pork with mustard cabbage 96
FISH
　Fish chowder 141
　Fish kebabs with spiced corn and tomato 69
　Fish pie 143
　Japanese-style grilled fish with Asian greens 73
　Parmesan fish fingers with homemade
　　wedges 138
　Salad Niçoise 32
　Spanish-style fish stew 170
　Thai fishcakes with lime and chilli sauce 28
　see also salmon; tuna
free list 5
FRITTATA
　Smoked salmon and asparagus frittata 26
　Tomato and cheese mini frittatas 14
Garlic breadcrumbs 148
Garlic and herb butterflied leg of lamb 45
GRAPEFRUIT
　Red grapefruit and watercress salad 132
Greek salad 46
Green beans and asparagus with
　garlic breadcrumbs 148
Green curry 169

index **199**

Green roast chicken curry with a fresh
    cabbage and cucumber salad 134
Grilled eggplant dip 114
Grilled peaches with raspberry coulis 188
Grilled vegetable salad with basil and
    black olives 80
Ham and cheese pinwheel sandwiches 22
Hawaiian pizza 117
HERBS
    Garlic and herb butterflied leg of lamb 45
    Herbed yoghurt 94
    Roast leg of lamb with mustard
        and rosemary 129
    Salsa verde 120
    Spicy chicken noodle salad 38
Homemade pizza dough 116
Honey-mustard pork with warm cabbage salad 63
Hummus 115
Individual meatloaves 126
Japanese-style grilled fish with Asian greens 73
Kangaroo steak with white bean mash
    and chargrilled vegetables 98
kitchen, stocking 8–9
LAMB
    Barbecued lamb cutlets with minty
        yoghurt sauce 79
    Braised Moroccan lamb 161
    Garlic and herb butterflied leg of lamb 45
    Lamb kofta curry 127
    Lamb skewers with lemon couscous
        and herbed yoghurt 94
    Mongolian lamb 61
    Moroccan lamb with chickpeas and spinach 92
    Moussaka stacks 131
    Mulligatawny soup 162
    Pan-fried lamb steaks with minted pea puree 92
    Roast leg of lamb with mustard
        and rosemary 129
    Scotch broth 159
    Slow-cooked lamb shoulder with pumpkin
        and feta salad 91
    Warm lamb salad with yoghurt dressing 41
Layered sushi 23
Lemon couscous 94
Lemon yoghurt sauce 108
LENTILS
    Cauliflower, lentil and tomato soup 173
    Lime and chilli sauce 28
MANGO
    Chicken and mango salad 41
    Mango pudding 181
    Mango and watercress salad 74
Margherita pizza 117

MEATBALLS
    Chicken meatballs 168
    Pork rissoles with red grapefruit
        and watercress salad 132
    Spicy meatballs with chilli tomato sauce 115
MEATLOAF
    Individual meatloaves 126
    Mediterranean baked salmon with
        rocket salad 70
    Mediterranean-style chicken with olives
        and capers 68
MERINGUES
    Rhubarb and strawberry meringues 191
Mexican eggs 15
Minted pea puree 92
Minty yoghurt sauce 79
Mixed berry smoothie 12
Mongolian lamb 61
Moroccan lamb with chickpeas and spinach 92
Moussaka stacks 131
Muesli 12
Mulligatawny soup 162
MUSHROOMS
    Chinese mushroom omelette 75
    Stir-fried beans, mushrooms and asparagus 97
    Warm mushroom salad on toast 15
MUSTARD
    Honey-mustard pork with
        warm cabbage salad 63
    Mustard cabbage 96
    Mustard dressing 44
    Roast leg of lamb with mustard
        and rosemary 129
NOODLES
    Chicken laksa 101
    Chicken noodle soup 106
    Spicy chicken noodle salad 38
    Teriyaki beef with egg noodles 56
    Vietnamese beef broth (beef pho) 88
OLIVES
    Baked ricotta with chilli and olives 25
    Braised Moroccan lamb 161
    Bruschetta with tuna and olive 18
    Chicken breasts stuffed with feta
        and olive tapenade 102
    Greek salad 46
    Grilled vegetable salad with basil
        and black olives 80
    Mediterranean-style chicken with
        olives and capers 68
    Olive and egg cucumber bites 146
    Salad Niçoise 32
    Tapenade 102

OMELETTE
    Chinese mushroom omelette 75
ONIONS see red onions
ORANGES
    Cinnamon oranges with spiced yoghurt 182
    Orange and red onion salad 68
Pancetta and semi-dried tomato tarts 20
Pan-fried lamb steaks with minted pea puree 92
Parmesan fish fingers with homemade wedges 138
PARSNIPS
    Carrot and parsnip soup 173
passata 111
PASTA
    Cannelloni 155
    Chicken and vegetable pasta salad 31
    Pasticcio (pasta bake) 155
    Spaghetti Bolognese 155
    Steamed mussels with spaghetti 110
    Tuna conchiglie bake 142
Pasticcio (pasta bake) 155
PEACHES
    Grilled peaches with raspberry coulis 188
Peanut sauce 105
PEARL BARLEY
    Scotch broth 159
PEARS
    Spinach, pear and walnut salad 149
PEAS
    Minted pea puree 92
PEPPERS see red capsicum
PIES (POTATO-TOPPED)
    Cottage pie 125
    Fish pie 143
Pinwheel sandwiches 22
PIZZA
    Hawaiian pizza 117
    Homemade pizza dough 116
    Margherita pizza 117
    Spinach and ricotta pizza 117
PORK
    Fennel roasted pork with mustard
        cabbage 96
    Honey-mustard pork with
        warm cabbage salad 63
    Pork rissoles with red grapefruit
        and watercress salad 132
PORRIDGE
    Cinnamon and sultana porridge 13
POTATOES
    Cottage pie 125
    Fish pie 143
    Homemade wedges 138
    Potato wedges 67

Prawn and avocado salad 44
Prawn and watercress cucumber bites 146
PROSCIUTTO
    Scallops with prosciutto and cauliflower puree 147
PUMPKIN
    Chicken tagine 165
    Pumpkin and feta salad 91
Raspberry coulis 188
RED CAPSICUM
    Beef fajitas 85
    Salsa 50
    Warm lamb salad with yoghurt dressing 41
Red grapefruit and watercress salad 132
RED ONIONS
    Avocado salad 157
    Chimichurri sauce 60
    Fennel and red onion salad 33
    Greek salad 46
    Orange and red onion salad 68
    Salsa 50
    Tuna, ricotta and red onion spread 23
Rhubarb and strawberry meringues 191
RICE
    Layered sushi 23
    Tomato risotto 58
RICOTTA
    Baked ricotta with chilli and olives 25
    Ricotta cream 184
    Ricotta hotcakes 14
    Salmon and ricotta pinwheel sandwiches 22
    Spinach and ricotta pizza 117
    Tuna, ricotta and red onion spread 23
Roast beef and vegetables with salsa verde 120
Roast leg of lamb with mustard and rosemary 129
Roast vegetable and couscous salad 47
ROCKET
    Bruschetta with artichoke and rocket 18
    Rocket salad 70
    Rocket, sweet potato and chickpea salad 35
    Squid salad with rocket and chickpeas 109
    Warm lamb salad with yoghurt dressing 41
SALADS
    Antipasto salad 36
    Avocado salad 157
    Cabbage and cucumber salad 134
    Cherry tomato and cucumber salad 64
    Chicken and mango salad 41
    Chicken and vegetable pasta salad 31
    Cos salad 60
    Cucumber salad 105
    Fennel and red onion salad 33
    Greek salad 46
    Grilled vegetable salad with basil and black olives 80
    Mango and watercress salad 74
    Mixed leaf and tomato salad 108
    Orange and red onion salad 68
    Prawn and avocado salad 44
    Pumpkin and feta salad 91
    Red grapefruit and watercress salad 132
    Roast vegetable and couscous salad 47
    Rocket salad 70
    Rocket, sweet potato and chickpea salad 35
    Salad Niçoise 32
    Shaved cabbage and brussels sprout salad 33
    Spicy chicken noodle salad 38
    Spinach, pear and walnut salad 149
    Squid salad with rocket and chickpeas 109
    Warm cabbage salad 63
    Warm eggplant salad 81
    Warm lamb salad with yoghurt dressing 41
    Warm mushroom salad on toast 15
SALMON
    Mediterranean baked salmon with rocket salad 70
    Salmon fishcakes with lemon yoghurt sauce 108
    Salmon and ricotta pinwheel sandwiches 22
    Smoked salmon and asparagus frittata 26
    Smoked salmon and cream cheese cucumber bites 146
Salsa 50
Salsa verde 120
Salt and pepper calamari with mango and watercress salad 74
sample eating styles 6–7
SANDWICHES
    Chargrilled vegetable pinwheel sandwiches 22
    Ham and cheese pinwheel sandwiches 22
    Salmon and ricotta pinwheel sandwiches 22
SAUCES
    Bolognese 155
    Cheese sauce 142
    Chilli tomato sauce 115
    Chimichurri sauce 60
    Creamy tomato sauce 78
    Lemon yoghurt sauce 108
    Lime and chilli sauce 28
    Minty yoghurt sauce 79
    Peanut sauce 105
    Salsa verde 120
    Tomato sauce 168
    White sauce 155
Scallops with prosciutto and cauliflower puree 147
Scotch broth 159
SEAFOOD
    Prawn and avocado salad 44
    Prawn and watercress cucumber bites 146
    Salt and pepper calamari with mango and watercress salad 74
    Scallops with prosciutto and cauliflower puree 147
    Seafood platter 78
    Spanish-style fish stew 170
    Squid salad with rocket and chickpeas 109
    Steamed mussels with spaghetti 110
    see also fish
Shaved cabbage and brussels sprout salad 33
SKEWERS
    Cajun turkey skewers with orange and red onion salad 68
    Chicken satay with peanut sauce 105
    Fish kebabs with spiced corn and tomato 69
    Lamb skewers with lemon couscous and herbed yoghurt 94
Slow-cooked lamb shoulder with pumpkin and feta salad 91
Smoked salmon and asparagus frittata 26
Smoked salmon and cream cheese cucumber bites 146
SMOOTHIES
    Mixed berry smoothie 12
SORBET
    Watermelon sorbet 179
SOUPS
    Cauliflower, lentil and tomato soup 173
    Carrot and parsnip soup 173
    Chicken gumbo 136
    Chicken laksa 101
    Chicken noodle soup 106
    Fish chowder 141
    Mulligatawny 162
    Scotch broth 159
    Vietnamese beef broth (beef pho) 88
Spaghetti Bolognese 155
Spanish-style fish stew 170
Spiced corn and tomato 69
Spiced strawberries with ricotta cream 184
Spiced yoghurt 182
Spicy chicken noodle salad 38
Spicy meatballs with chilli tomato sauce 115
Spicy roasted cauliflower 97
SPINACH
    Moroccan lamb with chickpeas and spinach 92
    Spinach, pear and walnut salad 149
    Spinach and ricotta pizza 117

SPREADS
    Tuna, ricotta and red onion spread 23
Squid salad with rocket and chickpeas 109
Steamed mussels with spaghetti 110
Steamed tofu with Asian greens 110
STEWS AND CASSEROLES
    Beef goulash 152
    Bourguignon-style beef casserole 158
    Chicken gumbo 136
    Chicken tagine 165
    Chicken and vegetable country stew 166
    Spanish-style fish stew 170
STIR-FRY
    Stir-fried beans, mushrooms
        and asparagus 97
    Stir-fried beef and broccolini in
        oyster sauce 56
    Thai-style beef and bean stir-fry 53
STOCK
    Chinese master stock 167
stocking your kitchen 8–9
STRAWBERRIES
    Rhubarb and strawberry meringues 191
    Spiced strawberries with ricotta cream 184
STRUDEL
    Apricot strudel 192
SUSHI
    Layered sushi 23
SWEET POTATO
    Rocket, sweet potato and chickpea
        salad 35
TAGINE
    Chicken tagine 165
TARTS (NO PASTRY)
    Pancetta and semi-dried tomato tarts 20
Teriyaki beef with egg noodles 56
Tex–Mex chilli beef 157
Tex-Mex lettuce cups 157
Thai fishcakes with lime and chilli sauce 28
Thai green curry paste 169
Thai-style beef and bean stir-fry 53
TOFU
    Steamed tofu with Asian greens 110

TOMATOES
    Avocado salad 157
    Bruschetta with tomato and basil 18
    Cauliflower, lentil and tomato soup 173
    Cherry tomato and cucumber salad 64
    Cherry tomato and eggplant compote 148
    Chilli tomato sauce 115
    Creamy tomato sauce 78
    Enchiladas 157
    Greek salad 46
    Hawaiian pizza 117
    Margherita pizza 117
    Mediterranean-style chicken with olives
        and capers 68
    Mexican eggs 15
    Mixed leaf and tomato salad 108
    Moussaka stacks 131
    Pancetta and semi-dried tomato tarts 20
    passata 111
    Salad Niçoise 32
    Salsa 50
    Spiced corn and tomato 69
    Tex-Mex lettuce cups 157
    Tomato and cheese mini frittatas 14
    Tomato risotto 58
    Tomato sauce 168
    Veal parmigiana 122
    Veal saltimbocca with tomatoes
        and zucchini 54
    see also cherry tomatoes
TUNA
    Bruschetta with tuna and olive 18
    Salad Niçoise 32
    Tuna conchiglie bake 142
    Tuna, ricotta and red onion spread 23
TURKEY
    Cajun turkey skewers with orange
        and red onion salad 68
    Turkey escalopes with Asian vegetables 107
Veal cutlets with tomato risotto 58
Veal parmigiana 122
Veal saltimbocca with tomatoes
    and zucchini 54

VEGETABLES
    Chargrilled vegetable pinwheel sandwiches 22
    Chicken and vegetable country stew 166
    Chicken and vegetable pasta salad 31
    free list 5
    Grilled vegetable salad with basil
        and black olives 80
    Kangaroo steak with white bean mash
        and chargrilled vegetables 98
    Roast beef and vegetables with salsa verde 120
    Roast vegetable and couscous salad 47
    Scotch broth 159
    Vegetable curry 174
    see also particular vegetables
Vietnamese beef broth (beef pho) 88
Vietnamese mint 88
Vinaigrette 78, 80
WALNUTS
    Spinach, pear and walnut salad 149
Warm cabbage salad 63
Warm eggplant salad 81
Warm lamb salad with yoghurt dressing 41
Warm mushroom salad on toast 15
WATERCRESS
    Mango and watercress salad 74
    Prawn and watercress cucumber bites 146
    Red grapefruit and watercress salad 132
Watermelon sorbet 179
White bean mash 98
White sauce 155
YOGHURT
    Apricot and almond yoghurt pops 180
    Dried fruit compote 13
    Herbed yoghurt 94
    Lemon yoghurt sauce 108
    Minty yoghurt sauce 79
    Mixed berry smoothie 12
    Ricotta cream 184
    Spiced yoghurt 182
    Yoghurt dressing 41
ZUCCHINI
    Veal saltimbocca with tomatoes
        and zucchini 54